Oct. 14, 2001

To Louise ——
    Great meeting you
today Louise —— Hope
you enjoy seeing California
with me.
            All my Best!

                    Seal Beach

C HILLINGER'S ALIFORNIA

CHILLINGER'S CALIFORNIA

Stories from All 58 Counties

With a foreword by Bob Hope

CHARLES HILLINGER

CAPRA PRESS
SANTA BARBARA

Dedicated to my wife, Arliene; son, Brad; and daughter, Tori Lindman.

Cover design, book design, typography and image scanning
by Frank Goad, Santa Barbara

Front cover photo: Robert Lachman

LIBRARY OF CONGRESS CATALOGING-IN-PUBLICATION DATA

Hillinger, Charles.
Hillinger's California : stories from all 58 counties /
Charles Hillinger.
p. cm.
ISBN 0-88496-425-6 (paper : alk.paper)
1. California—History, Local—Anecdotes. 2. California—
Description and travel—Anecdotes. 3. California—Biography—
Anecdotes. I. Title.
F861.6.H55 1997   97-4359
979.4—dc21   CIP

Capra Press
Post Office Box 2068
Santa Barbara, CA 93120

CONTENTS

ACKNOWLEDGMENTS

FIRST TO ARLIENE, my wife of 50 years, who has been the love of my life and tolerated prolonged absences when I was away gathering information and covering out-of-town stories and put up with my workaholic habits when I was at home. No one could ask for a prettier, more affectionate, more understanding and fun-to-be-with wife than Arliene. And what a cook!

My thanks to a special friend throughout my career, Otis Chandler, publisher of the *Los Angeles Times,* who made the *Times* one of America's great newspapers and made my travels possible, and to Bill Thomas, editor of the *Times,* who encouraged me to do the human and general interest stories. Over the years I worked for many great editors at that newspaper, the likes of Smokey Hale, Gil Fletcher, Jack Goulding, Glen Binford, Frank Haven, Frank McCullough, John Brownell, Art Berman, and John Foley.

My thanks to Con Keyes for his excellent photo on the back cover, and to John Malmin, Art Rogers, Cal Montney, Fitzgerald Whitney, whose photos appear in the book and with whom I worked all those years at the *Times.* I spent half my life on the road with them and all the other outstanding photogs at the *Times,* like Frank Q. Brown, Bruce Cox, and Steve Fontanini, to name but a few. My thanks to Skip Sahlin, Curt Kraft, Karl Rosenquist, Linda Plummer, Janmeja Singh Johl and the other photographers who also provided illustrations for this book, and to Dana Farrington for his sketch of Inskip Inn.

And to the thousands of men, women, and children I encountered and wrote about from one end of California to the other, in the hamlets, the small and mid-sized towns, the big cities, in the mountains, on the islands, along the seashore, in the valleys, on the desert, who each in his or her own way gave me their time and friendship and made it possible for me to have one of the best jobs anyone could ever dream of—I thank you.

i

Thanks, too, to Noel Young, founder-publisher of Capra Press, who made this book possible, and to David Dahl, who did the editing. Terrific job, and thanks so much for hanging in there with me, David. My thanks to Frank Goad, Capra's art director, who designed the book and its cover. I am grateful to Marshall Roe, a close personal friend for 45 years, who originally printed most of the photographs.

To have Bob Hope, one of California, America, and the world's greatest personalities of the 20th-century, do the foreword to my California book, well, how can I ever thank him enough. And my sincere appreciation to each and every one who takes time to travel with me to all of California's 58 counties.

FOREWORD

by

BOB HOPE

I may have been born in England, reared in Cleveland and raised in vaudeville, but California is my home…has been since 1937. And Thomas Wolfe was wrong—you can go home again…and again, and again.

My publicist, when he had nothing else better to do, added up the air miles I've travelled in my lifetime. It's something like 12 million miles—regretfully most of which were before frequent flyer credits.

I've made no secret how enjoyable it's been going places…but it's always been just as enjoyable coming home. North, south; east, west; high, low; diagonally or criss-cross—when the plane approached the great state of California I was home. I had a bird's-eye view of California and thought I knew it from every angle. Then, after reading the galleys of *Hillinger's California,* I realized how little I did know about California and how much there was to enjoy at ground level.

Charles takes you to Alameda County on the Oakland waterfront to the Last Chance Saloon. It looks the same today as it did when Jack London first began writing down his stories while sitting at the bar. Did you know that there is a "Little Switzerland" in Alpine County?

Then there's Indian Grinding Rock in Amador County—an enormous boulder where thousands of women since prehistoric times smashed acorns for dinner. (Talk about roughage!) In Calaveras County, for more than 135 years, people have been looking for the treasure of gold buried by miner Dan Buster. In the same county there is a "moaning" cave (not named after one of my audiences, I hasten to add) in which French miners found 300 human bodies perfectly preserved, but an earthquake later sealed the cave, and the bodies have never been seen again.

Did you know that Martinez in Contra Costa county is the birth-place of the martini and is also the bocce ball capital of America? That the most low down people in America live in Imperial County and that Kern County is the home of the Tubatalabuls, Indians with a happy language and built-in smiles? (I didn't either until I read Chuck Hillinger's book.)

There is a man called "Sweet Potato Joe" who swears his smiles and good thoughts make for healthy and huge sweet potatoes for Califor-nia's sweet potato country in Merced County. In Mono County, trans-planted seals from the Pacific Ocean and chickens wearing sunglasses live on top of California's third highest peak, 14,246-foot White Mountain. (This I've got to see for myself.)

How about being serenaded by the singing sand dunes in San Bernardi-no County or visiting the world's only expert on flat-footed flies or seeing a 5,000 pound sea monster come ashore in San Mateo County?

The book is filled with surprises that make California different from every other state. Chuck has left no California stone unturned—save a few golf courses which are worthy of note—but, that's anoth-er book—mine!

ONE

ALAMEDA COUNTY

JACK LONDON AND THE FIRST & LAST CHANCE

THEY COME to the old Oakland saloon from all over the world—
France, Germany, Spain, Italy, Russia, Poland, Japan, Australia,
from across America. Heinold's First and Last Chance Saloon is a
California institution, one of the most famous taverns in the West—a
weather-beaten old shack built in 1862 from the remains of a sunken
whaling ship. And it was here at Johnny Heinold's place down on the
Oakland waterfront that Jack London first began jotting down his stories.

London was a boy of 12 when he started coming to the saloon,
where he would sit for hours listening to the wild palaver of seafarers. He'd carry a pocket dictionary that he would take out and use
whenever he heard a word he didn't understand. Heinold admired
the lad's curiosity and intelligence, and gave Jack a large Webster's
dictionary and, because London's family was poor, bought the boy his

high school books. Later, he also loaned London money to attend the University of California. Heinold and London were lifelong friends.

It was at the First and Last Chance that London negotiated the purchase of the sloop "Razzle Dazzle" from oysterman French Frank, an event duly recorded in London's *John Barleycorn,* a story set in Heinold's saloon. The author mentioned the waterfront "dive", filled with interesting characters and atmosphere, in several of his books. The First and Last Chance was also a favorite of Russians and other visitors from Communist countries because London, a socialist, was the most widely read American author in the Communist world. Before the breakup of the USSR, when the Bolshoi dancers performed in San Francisco, the entire troupe spent an evening there.

Heinold had come to Oakland as a deckhand on a windjammer from Philadelphia and wound up running the saloon for 50 years, until his death in 1933. His place became a hangout for not only Jack London, but Robert Louis Stevenson, Joaquin Miller and Robert W. Service, to name a few of the literary figures who frequented the saloon over the years. When the old saloon-keeper died, his ashes were scattered over the The First and Last Chance from an airplane. Heinold's only son, George, then ran the saloon until his death in 1970. George's widow, Marge, kept it going until 1984 when Carol Brookman, the first person to own it outside the Heinold family, purchased the establishment.

The First and Last Chance has changed little since 1883 when Heinold paid $100 for the remains of a sunken whaling ship, which had become an oysterman's bunkhouse, that Heinold then converted into his saloon. The same potbellied stove is still here, the same gas lights. Same three tables and 6 stools Heinold installed before the turn of the century. The saloon seats 27, at most. Built on pilings that have collapsed over the years, the saloon slants aft with the front end of the bar a foot higher than the back. Photos of London in the First and Last Chance at various stages of his life hang on a wall. As a matter of fact, the walls and ceilings are filled with Jack London and Johnny Heinold memorabilia. London, Stevenson, Joaquin Miller and Robert Service wouldn't recognize the big city of Oakland today, but they'd still feel at right home at Heinold's First and Last Chance Saloon.

LONDON'S DAUGHTER RECALLS HER FATHER

B ECKY LONDON FLEMING, Jack London's daughter was 80-years-old when I interviewed her. At the time she had lived her entire life in Oakland.

For 30 years Fleming and her husband operated a small neighborhood stationery store in Oakland. Few knew of her relationship to one of the world's best read writers, the author of *The Call of the Wild*, *The Sea Wolf*, *The Valley of the Moon*, *Martin Eden*, *The People of the Abyss* and 46 other novels and hundreds of short stories. "I always made up my mind never to take advantage of Daddy's name," she insisted. "After I married in 1928 and became Mrs. Fleming nobody except close friends knew who I was."

Jack London had two daughters, both by his first wife, math and English teacher Bessie Maddern—Joan, who died in 1971 at the age of 71, and Bess, named after her mother, but who always went by the nickname, Becky. The author's first marriage lasted only four years. In 1904, London and Bessie Maddern were divorced. The day after the divorce the writer married Charmian Kittredge.

Bessie was given sole custody of the two girls, who were 2 and 4 at the time of the divorce. They never lived with their father. "Oh, Joan and I saw Daddy many, many times," recalled the silver-haired woman. "When Daddy wasn't sailing the Pacific on the Snark or off covering major stories like the Russo-Japanese War or the Mexican Revolution, he spent his time writing on his ranch at Glen Ellen, 50 miles north of Oakland in California's Valley of the Moon.

"Daddy would often come to Oakland to visit his mother and to spend a full day with Joan and me. He would take the two of us to Idora Amusement Park in Oakland and to his favorite restaurant, Saddle Rock. When we were older, we spent the day taking the ferry to San Francisco. Daddy loved to ride the cable cars. We would eat at the Cliff House and go to the theater." She remembered the excitement of being the daughter of the most popular writer of his time. "It seemed like everybody knew Daddy. He was the center of attention wherever he went. Motormen would clang the bells on cable cars when they spotted him and shout: 'There's Jack London. Hey, Jack!'"

Becky London Fleming recalled, "It wasn't easy in school for his daughters. If we did well, teachers would say: 'Why not. Look who your father is.' If we didn't do too well, we would hear: 'Jack London's daughter should do better than this...'" She told how her mother was jealous of Charmian "and jealous of Daddy. Every year Daddy would invite Joan and me to spend the summer at the ranch. Mother would not let us go. I'll never forgive her for that." Becky London was 14, a sophomore in high school, when her father died.

London encouraged his daughters to read from early on. He sent them boxes of books regularly—history books, biographies, science and travel books. Wherever he traveled, he never failed to write to his daughters. And, they wrote to him. "He encouraged us to be writers, to go to college," said Fleming. "We both graduated from UC Berkeley. Joan in 1921. I did in 1923. My sister wrote a successful book *Jack London and His Times*. I'm an avid reader, but not a writer."

Under terms of the divorce granted Bessie Maddern London, the author built a home in Oakland for his ex-wife and two daughters. The daughters each received an allowance of $75 a month from their father until they were 21. But the author's first wife and only children were not provided for in Jack London's will. The ranch and literary estate went to Charmian. When Charmian died at the age of 84 in 1955, the ranch and literary estate went to Irving Shepherd, son of Jack London's stepsister Eliza London Shepherd.

Becky London Fleming and her husband were of modest means all of their lives. Percy (Per) Fleming, Becky's husband, died in 1982, after 54 years of marriage. She never shared in royalties from her father's books, which sold in the millions throughout the world, from movies made from his novels or in the ownership of the ranch at Glen Ellen. Jack London continues to be one of the most popular writers in the history of the printed word.

But his daughter was not bitter. "I never felt shortchanged. I accept things as they are. I have never envied anyone. I'm an optimist," she said. "Accepting one's lot in life makes for a happier existence. I have been blessed in a thousand ways being the daughter of Jack London. Daddy was the most wonderful, the most fascinating human being I ever met. I am so proud to be his daughter..."

TWO

ALPINE COUNTY

CALIFORNIA'S LITTLE SWITZERLAND

A LPINE is California's "Little Switzerland," the highest county in the state with its lowest point over a mile up, and a dozen mountains reaching to the heavens towering over two miles. It has year-round, snow-capped mountains, spectacular granite cliffs and crags, dense stands of quaking aspen, birch and pine, rushing streams and glacial lakes.

In winter the county is one of the most isolated areas of the state. The whole county is often snowed in with the only link to the outside world, Highway 88, running from Markleeville, the county seat, to Gardnerville and Minden, Nevada. On the eastern crest of the Sierra Nevada, Alpine is 50 miles south of Reno. In winter Alpine County belongs to Nevada. The other four roads leading into the county from California are buried under snow six months of the year.

It's the only county without a high school. There are no movie theaters here or resident doctors or dentists. No traffic signals. And, very few people. Only 1,113 at last count. A third of the residents of the county are Washoe Indians. Most of the others are descendants of silver miners who came to make their fortunes in the 1840s, 50s and 60s. That was when the county had a population of 11,620, when nearly 3,000 people lived in Markleeville. But the demonetization of silver in the late 1860s ended the mining and nearly everyone left to try their luck somewhere else. Today, Markleeville, with less than 200 people, is the largest of 11 hamlets in the county. The biggest employer hereabouts is the county itself, in some cases entire families work exclusively for Alpine County.

Being without a high school, students in Alpine County must be bused across the state line to Douglas High School in Minden, Nevada. All but four of Alpine's students go to Douglas. The other four, who live in Bear Valley on the other side of the mountain, go to Bret Harte High School at Arnold in California's Calaveras County. "We would send our kids to the South Lake Tahoe High School— about the same distance as Minden—but we can't get to Tahoe in winter. The road over 7,740-foot Luther Pass is closed by snow," noted James Parsons, superintendent of the Alpine Unified School District.

Not only is Luther Pass closed much of the year by snow but so are three of the four other roads leading into the county. Those roads cross 8,314-foot Monitor Pass, 8,573-foot Carson Pass and 8,730-foot Ebbetts Pass. Only California 88, dropping down the mountain to Nevada, is open year round.

There are also three elementary schools in Alpine. Many of the students who live in remote places in the mountains are picked up at home. "Sometimes they oversleep and we have to wake them," said bus driver John Jackson. "Lloyd Lingelbach holds the record for chaining (the tires on) his bus more than 100 days in one school year," said Jackson. Lingelbach drives one school bus 23 miles each day from Kirkwood to Woodfords where they transfer to the regular Alpine County High School bus for the remaining 23 miles to Douglas High. Both Lingelbach's and Jackson's buses have slipped off icy roads and been stuck in snowbanks on a few occasions over the years. "It goes with the territory," said Jackson. "Every winter it gets so bad at times the kids get snowed in and stuck on the mountain unable to get to school." But that's how it is in remote Alpine, California's "Little Switzerland."

THREE

AMADOR COUNTY

CHAW'SE INDIAN GRINDING ROCK

A T CHAW'SE Indian Grinding Rock State Park in Amador County Margaret Dalton stood on the huge limestone out-cropping pitted with 1,185 large holes.

"I often come out here on the rock, close my eyes and dream. I see hundreds of Indian women sitting all over the rock," Dalton, a Miwok Indian, said. "In my dream I see them grinding acorns in the mortar holes that my people call chaw'ses. They grind the acorns into a fine meal with stone pestles and the meal is used to make soup, cakes and bread. As the women grind acorns, I can hear them gossiping. All around the rock in the surrounding meadow there is a great stir of activity by the huge gathering of Indians..."

Dalton, curator of the Indian cultural center here, dreamed of what life was like for her ancestors in this historic wintering grounds of the

Miwok Indians in the foothills of the High Sierra 50 miles southeast of Sacramento. Chaw'se is California's only state park devoted exclusively to the Indian culture.

"This amazing chaw'se rock is the pride of Indians throughout the West," said Miwok tribal leader Bill Franklin, adding: "There isn't another grinding rock anywhere approaching the size of this one." The pitted rock is 173 feet long, 82 feet wide. "These mortar holes were last used by my people more than a century ago," noted Franklin. "How many hundreds of years the rock was used prior to that no one knows. Stories handed down by the Miwoks say there were at least 3,200 holes on the rock in the old days."

On the giant rock are a series of barely visible petroglyphs telling a story about the Miwoks migrating from the northeast to come here to hunt deer and rabbits, to harvest acorns from the spreading oaks in the meadows and to grind the acorns on the limestone outcropping.

The chaw'se grinding rock was on a privately-owned ranch until 1962, when the state acquired the property to set aside the historic Indian encampment area. Now there are a number of Indian dwellings on the grounds of the 135-acre park, including several u'muh chahs (cedar bark tepees). Also located here is what is believed to be the largest existing hung'e—Indian ceremonial roundhouse—in the country, a 60-foot diameter structure that serves as a meeting house, religious temple, a place to cure the sick.

Franklin supervised construction of the hung'e, the u'muh chahs, the pois' koi ah' we ah (Indian football field) and the large cultural center. All of the replicas of traditional Miwok structures were designed by Franklin and built by Miwok elders, whose average age has been 70. Miwoks harvested cedar bark in the mountains to cover the exterior of the cultural center. "Indians feel at home here," said Franklin.

Chaw'se is also a special place for non-Indian visitors. "We encourage people to come here to learn first hand what life was like for the California Indians, to clear up stereotype notions, to clear up misconceptions" noted Margaret Dalton. "Indian women still gather acorns from the oak trees and grind the acorns with stone pestles," she explained. "But today when Indian women grind acorns with stone pestles, instead of a chaw'se rock, they use small stone mortars in their kitchens. Whenever Indians have minor illnesses, they dose themselves with acorn soup. And, when friends or relatives are in the hospital, Indians bring them acorn soup to build up strength. "In these modern times," she continued, "many of the old Indian ways still persist."

CHEW KEE HERB SHOP

FOR NEARLY 150 YEARS, the people of Fiddletown in Amador County have stood watch over the old Chew Kee Herb Shop, a sort of time capsule representing life in a Gold Rush-era Chinese community.

You Fong (Jimmy) Chow was the caretaker and protector of the rammed-earth adobe shop and its dust-covered contents for 61 of those years. Chow fulfilled a promise he made to his friend Fung Jong Yee on Yee's deathbed in 1904. Yee erected the shop in Fiddletown in 1851 and operated it for 53 years.

Before the old herb doctor died, Chow promised him he would guard the shop the rest of his life, keep it intact, never disturb or sell anything in the store. When Chow died in 1965 at the age of 80, the responsibility passed to the people of Fiddletown, population 112, and to Amador County. The county assumed ownership of the shop.

But rain, snow, wind, frost and decay steadily weakened the structure. Its two foot thick walls crumbled and cracked and gradually opened like a flower in bloom, leaning outward more and more. Mice and rats nibbled away at the herbs in the 146-year-old storage drawers and munched on the dust-covered 19th-Century newspapers, magazines, ledgers, records and artifacts in the shop. The roof leaked. Wallpaper made of 1880s and 1890s newspapers peeled off in places.

However, through the efforts of the Fiddletown Preservation Society led by its president, Marie Scofield, and Sacramento dentist Dr. Herbert Yee, great grandson of the herb shop's founder, Fung Jong Yee, $100,000 was spent to shore up, restore and preserve the Chew Kee Herb Shop. Scofield and Dr. Yee obtained a grant from the state Parks and Recreation Department's Office of Historic Preservation. Dr. Yee contributed $10,000 and the people of Fiddletown gave $2,500 to the restoration project. A new steep-gabled pine shingle roof identical to the original was set in place.

Concrete collars were erected around the foundation to ensure long life. The thick walls were strengthened and reinforced.

Fiddletown was first settled by gold seekers from Missouri in 1849. They called the gold camp Fiddletown because the miners were "always fiddling around."

Chow was born in a house next to the herb shop. When Yee died, Chow moved into the tiny, one-room shack behind the store, where he remained throughout his vigil.

He was a jack-of-all trades in Fiddletown.

At the time of the Gold Rush in the 1850s, an estimated 5,000 to 10,000 Chinese miners lived in Fiddletown, the second-largest Chinese settlement in America at that time. Only San Francisco had more Chinese. By the turn of the century, however, only a handful of Chinese were left in Fiddletown. Soon, they too, were gone—all except Jimmy Chow. He told everybody that he could never leave. He had to guard the herb shop.

Chew Kee Herb Shop's shelves are filled with bottles used by Fung Jong Yee. Clay cremation burial pots line the floor. A 160-year-old, 11-bar abacus sits on a dusty counter. Record books filled with vital statistics about the early-day Chinese miners line the cupboards. Fung Jong Yee's bedroom is the way it was the day he died in 1904, his clothing still tacked to the wall.

"There's nothing like this anywhere in America," Dr. Yee noted. "Everything was left intact in the shop all these years since my great-grandfather died. This has so much meaning for Chinese people. It is a visible reminder of their heritage. It really does turn back the clock."

From time to time groups of Chinese from Los Angeles, San Francisco and other Chinese communities charter buses to Fiddletown just to see the old shop. "The town is absolutely ecstatic that this remarkable treasure has been saved," said Isa Lawless, 85, longtime resident and former owner of Fiddletown's 1852 general store, who added, "Jimmy Chow would really be pleased. So would Fung Jong Yee."

FOUR

BUTTE COUNTY

INSKIP, POP. 2 (ALIVE)—AND THEN THERE'S CHARLEY

W HICH of the three residents of Inskip is mayor? That's what we asked when we were in mile-high Inskip, at the end of a winding mountain road, 35 miles northwest of Chico in Butte County.

"Look I just work here," said Bob Duffey, a lively 86-year-old in 1997, as he fired up the wood-burning stove in the lobby of the Inskip Inn erected in 1868. "Talk to my wife," said Duffey. "She's the boss. I'm the chief of police, head of search and rescue, and operator of Inskip Ski Rope Tow."

However, Kathy Duffey, 83, speculated, "Maybe Charley's the mayor. This may sound crazy," she added, "but Inskip Inn has a resident ghost—Charley. Bob and I hear him walking up and down the creaky staircase late at night outside the guest rooms. He opens and shuts doors. It's kind of spooky. We're the last people I thought would ever fall for a ghost story, but we sure believe in Charley...." That's Inskip. Population 3. Kathy and Bob Duffey—and Charley the Ghost.

The Duffeys are holed up in what's left of a booming gold mining town of the 1850s, 1860s and 1870s. Inskip during its prime had a population of 1,000. All that's left is the old inn. The Duffey's nearest neighbor is 6½ miles down the mountain.

"We average 10 to 12 feet of snow a year. We've had winter weekends when as many as 500 people bought tickets for our ski tow," Duffey noted. Duffey runs the 1,000-foot-long tow that begins across the street from the inn. Where there is enough snow and no customers Duffey has the ski runs all to himself. A reserve deputy sheriff, Duffey is the local chief of police. "We've had a few prison escapees I've had to shake out of the woods over the years. Cars have gone off the road coming up here and people are forever getting lost," Duffey said. Both Kathy and Bob are excellent trackers and rescued a number of people lost in the back country since they they purchased the Inskip Inn in 1967.

Mrs. Duffey worked for the Los Angeles Police Department's record bureau for several years when she lived in the city. Duffey was a retired Los Angeles Department of Water and Power electrical engineer. "I didn't retire until 1971. So, the first four years we owned the inn, Kathy lived here alone except for weekends, when I came up from L.A.," explained Duffey.

Since buying the isolated inn, Duffey had learned to fly and bought himself a Cessna 182 he kept at the airport at Paradise down the mountain. For years there was no telephone at Inskip, and the Duffeys had to rely on a CB. Now the inn has its own phone.

There had been two Inskip Inns. The first was built by an Irishman named Pat Kelly in 1857. It burned down in 1868 and was rebuilt the same year. Some of the inn's furniture dates back to the 1850s and includes old kerosene lamps, roll-top desks, two century-old pipe organs, and spool beds in the 10 guest rooms. One of the newest fixtures is a 1915 player piano.

Although they are the only two Inskip residents, the Duffeys are seldom alone. During the week loggers, miners, foresters and road repairmen stay at the inn. Kathy cooks three meals a day for her guests and tends bar. "My wife didn't know the difference between a martini and a bottle of beer before she came up here. Kathy's a teetotaler," Duffey said.

The Duffeys are a hardy couple. In her free time Kathy prospects for gold. Behind the bar hangs her mule skinner's license. For years Duffey manned a fire lookout tower for the U.S. Forest Service at the top of a nearby mountain. He stayed in the tower 72 hours at a stretch. "No way can we ever get bored," muses Kathy. "There isn't time. And anyway, there's always Charley."

FIVE

CALAVERAS COUNTY

DAN BUSTER'S GOLD

PEOPLE HAVE LOOKED for Dan Buster's gold since the day he died in 1863. Green rolling hills and steep gulches stretching from Fourth Crossing to Sheep Ranch to Murphys—tiny Mother Lode hamlets—have been punched full of holes by hundreds of men, women and children in 135 years of digging for Buster's buried gold.

Buster was a runaway slave who came to California to seek his fortune as a Forty-Niner and struck it rich. He paid a white attorney a big sum to buy his mother and father's freedom from slavery. The attorney stole the money. But Buster was uncanny. He hit paydirt time and time again. Sadly, his elderly parents died before he was able to buy their freedom.

One day Buster led a string of burros down a steep hill leading into Camp San Antone. Strapped to his animals' backs were sacks stuffed with gold. "My granddad weighed Dan Buster's gold that day," said Ray Cuneo, who was 61 when I interviewed him in 1971.

All that was left of the ghost town of the 1850s and 60s that was Camp San Antone was located on Cuneo's 300-acre Calaveras County ranch. "That old Black miner had $40,000 in gold in those pouches. He also had $10,000 in gold coins," Cuneo continued. "He lived his last years alone in a cabin right up there on that level spot on the hill where my sheep shed stands. My granddad told old Dan Buster. 'Why don't you leave me your gold. You got no kin.' He told granddad. 'You don't need my gold. You got the store. You got money. I buried that gold. Ain't nobody ever gonna find it.'"

Histories report that Buster never got over his disappointment that money to free his parents was stolen by a white attorney. He was quoted as having said time and time again: "I took that gold out of the ground with these old black hands. I put it back in the ground with the same hands. There it's gonna stay. No, sir, that gold will never do no white man no good."

While Buster was still alive, he was badly beaten by desperados who tried to get him to tell where he buried his gold, but the tough old Black miner refused to talk. One of the desperadoes was caught and hanged for the assault. A widow in the camp called Old Lady Kelly prepared dinner for Buster nearly every night during his last years. "Granddad said Old Lady Kelly tried to get Buster to tell her where it was buried, but he never did," Cuneo said. There were several Black miners in the area who knew Buster and knew about his gold, but he wouldn't tell them either. When Buster died in February, 1863, townspeople tore down his cabin and dug deep beneath the dwelling looking for his fortune.

Frank Cuneo, Ray Cuneo's grandfather, homesteaded the entire Camp San Antone townsite after miners pulled out in the late 1860s. He spent the rest of his lfe looking for Buster's gold whenever he had a chance. So did his son. Frank's grandson and his great grandson and now his great-great grandchildren dig for the gold from time to time.

Buster's gold is legendary in Calaveras County but Buster himself was no legend. He lived in the mining camp for 13 years, and after his death, his bones were buried in an unmarked graveyard on Ray

Cuneo's ranch.

Treasure hunters with metal detectors have systematically gone over every inch of Cuneo's land. Even spiritualists have tried to communicate with the dead miner—a group of Filipinos came carrying a strange three-legged table. They covered the table with candy, fruit and other food and left it overnight for Buster. They placed a pencil and tacked a note to the table that read: "Mr. Dan Buster. Please tell us where it's buried."

For 135 years Dan Buster has fooled them all. For 135 years the old black miner's words have been as good as gold: "Ain't nobody ever gonna find it."

MOANING CAVE

IN 1853 the *San Francisco Daily Alta Californian* and other California newspapers carried stories of a party of French miners descending deep into a cave in Calaveras County and "coming upon a collection of 300 human bodies perfectly petrified." The French miners described the cave near the hamlet of Vallecito 130 miles east of San Francisco as most peculiar in many ways. "It moaned," they reported. Now, nearly 150 years later, Moaning Cave is a popular tourist attraction. But the 300 human bodies "perfectly petrified" have never been found.

The late Addison Carley opened the cave to the public in 1922 after installing a spiral staircase with 144 steps leading down into the huge hole in the ground. The staircase was an engineering fete at the time requiring 6 months for a large crew of men to erect.

Carley, who was born in 1898, grew up in the tiny Mother Lode community of Vallecito in the Sierra Nevada foothills 15 miles north of Sonora in Calaveras County. He had known of the existence of the cave since childhood and first lowered himself into it with rope and windlass in 1921. He found a miner's pick and whiskey bottle at the bottom of the main chamber 210 feet beneath the surface. He checked the records, found the cave was on federal land and filed and obtained ownership.

Carley researched old references to the cave back to its discovery by the French miners in 1853. The miners reported at the time that "the strange cavern contains many stalactites, some of which rested on or were incorporated in the petrified bodies. The skulls indicate a race distinct from Indians."

Newspaper accounts told of the miners bringing several broken and complete petrified human heads to San Francisco where they were exhibited.

In a 1971 interview with Carley in Moaning Cave, he said ever since opening the cavern to the public he had been searching for the petrified bodies without success. "I'm convinced they're somewhere in here," he insisted. Carley believed a severe earthquake in 1863 sealed the room with the petrified people.

"I've been trying for years to find out what happened to those petrified skulls taken to San Francisco," said Carley. "My best guess is they were destroyed in the 1906 earthquake. The skulls were said to be much larger than Indian skulls found in California."

J.C.Merriam, director of the University of California's department of paleontology, reported in 1909 that human bones covered with stalactite growth in Mother Lode caves were "of considerable antiquity."

Anthropologist Phil C. Orr of the Santa Barbara Museum of Natural History led the Truman Speleological Expedition in a survey of Moaning Cave in 1952. In a scientific paper describing his findings, Orr reported: "Early-day newspapers carry many accounts of finding petrified human remains. Miwok Indians of the area believed Moaning Cave was occupied by a 'stone giant' who came out at night in search of human victims. "The thought of Miwoks burying their own people in the cave was abhorrent to them."

Orr recovered and examined "numerous human bones embedded in stone" in the floor of the main chamber of Carley's cave. The anthropologist dated human bones on the cave by measuring the coating of speleothem (cave deposits) on nails and iron fragments left in the bottom of the big room following construction of the spiral steel staircase. These fragments were coated to a thickness of 1 millimeter in 30 years. Bones were taken from the bottom of layers of solid travertine 420 mm. thick (16.5 inches). Projecting the thickness of the coating of 1 mm. for every 30 years, Orr estimates the age of the bones at 12,600 years old.

Orr discovered partial skull and skeletal remains of six to 10 individuals "although only a limited section of the cave floor had been carefully excavated." The anthropologist wrote: "By the way the bones were scattered, there was no indication of a mass burial. It would seem to indicate the remains were those of individuals who accidentally fell through the cave opening on rare intervals." Carley believed the petrified bodies in the missing chamber may date back to a much earlier period than the bones excavated by Orr.

He said the cave moaned every 1½ minutes like a person in pain until he built the spiral staircase. "I think the steel changed the way the air currents came up out of the hole," explained Carley. "It stopped moaning except only on rare occasions when we put the staircase in."

There are six known rooms in the 410-foot deep cavern. Strange shapes and figures adorning walls, and formed by the seepage include: A huge outcropping of snow-white flow stone that resembles an igloo; elephant ears dangling 12 feet from the roof. A giant eagle; a little girl's face; eagle's wings 17 feet in length, a mushroom patch.

Carley and his family led tours through the cave for a half century. Present owners of Moaning Cave are Stephen Fairchild and his family. Visitors still descend into the cave on the spiral staircase erected by Carley in 1922. Three-hour rappelling tours are conducted for anyone over age 12 by the cave operators, that includes crawling and climbing through the labyrinth of chambers.

"Visitors get a real thrill when the cave occasionally moans," said John Lamb, cave manager. "There are holes in the cave shaped like bottles. As water drips into these holes and pushes the air out, the moaning sound is heard. It's akin to blowing on a bottle top and hearing the resulting noise."

SIX

COLUSA COUNTY

THE SOUTHERN CONNECTION

URING THE 1940s through the 1970s numerous movies with Southern themes were filmed in California's Colusa County. To viewers, the movies were obviously shot on location in a typical Southern town.

"Tick...Tick...Tick," starring Jim Brown, George Kennedy and Fredric March; Sidney Poitier in "Kane;" Gregory Peck in "I Walk the Line;" Julie Harris in "Member of the Wedding;" Charlton Heston in "Warlord;" and Alfred Hitchcock's "The Birds" were a few of the films made in Colusa.

In "Tick...Tick...Tick," for example, townspeople are shown gathered outside the Southern courthouse to watch their new sheriff, a Black man, enter his office for the first time. Jim Brown portrayed the new sheriff, George Kennedy played the man he replaced and Fredric

March played a crotchety old mayor.

The courthouse in "Tick...Tick...Tick," is authentic, a historical structure with a fascinating history. Federal troops occupied it during the Civil War. Movie goers believed it was located in Mississippi , or in Alabama, Georgia, Louisiana or one of the other Southern states. Not so. It's the Colusa County Courthouse in the town of Colusa, California's second oldest county courthouse.

Completed in 1861 and in continuous use ever since, the courthouse is a stately white stucco-over-brick structure with four large columns guarding the main entrance. It's typical of many public buildings of Greek-inspired architecture erected throughout the Mississippi Valley during the mid-1800s and reflects the deep-rooted Southern heritage of the Northern California county. Southern theme films fit in quite nicely with the ambiance of Colusa County. The county seat, also called Colusa, 65 miles north of Sacramento, was settled largely by Southerners from Kentucky, Mississippi, Missouri and Georgia during the 1840s, 50s and 60s.

Colusa was widely known throughout the state during the Civil War as "California's Secessionist County." Hours after Lincoln's assassination, federal troops from San Francisco's Presidio were dispatched to Colusa. Soldiers pitched tents on the courthouse lawn. Martial law was declared. Troops patrolled the county for three months to prevent possible insurrection. Dud Shepardson, Colusa's district attorney at the time, and several leading local citizens were arrested and transported to Fort Alcatraz in San Francisco Bay for their outspoken Southern sympathies. To this day, many in the county trace their ancestry to the original Southern settlers, including most members of the small Black community.

"Because of the Deep South heritage of the first settlers," said Wilmer G. Brill, long-time editor and publisher of the Colusa Sun-Herald, a pro-South newspaper during the Civil War, "our county has been the location for several films with Southern themes." Brill noted, however, that the name of the county has no Southern significance. "That comes from an Indian tribe here in the early days of the county," he explained. "Colu was supposed to mean scratch—the tribe's peculiar marriage custom in which the bride passionately scratched the groom's face."

Population of the county according to the 1990 census was 16,275 and the county seat, 4,500. And Colusa is one of the richest agricultural counties per capita in the nation, producing rice, apricots, prunes, stock, corn and row crops.

It was the late Leo Yates, a local rancher, in his role as film production assistant and locations man, who was responsible for attracting movie companies here. MGM, Universal Studios, Columbia, Screen Gems, and Paramount were among the top studios filming on location.

"Whenever studios plan a film with a Southern locale they send me a copy of the script," said Yates during a 1972 interview. "I line up the old Southern buildings for sets. The courthouse appeared as a major location throughout Sidney Poitier's film 'Kane.' This part of Northern California is so much like the South in so many ways, the buildings, the people," related Yates. "It's much cheaper for a film company to come up here on location , less than 500 miles from Los Angeles, than to travel three to four times as far to a Southern site."

Marjorie Yates, 76 in 1995, told us that it was about the time of her husband Leo's death in 1973 that movie companies stopped coming to Colusa to make films. "It's too bad. They should still be coming here. It brought a lot of business and great exposure for our community. I'll tell you what happened: One day when the main street in downtown was blocked off to film a sequence, a woman complained she was unable to park in front of the newspaper office because the cameras and actors were in her way. She told the mayor her objections to film companies using Colusa locations. At the next city council meeting an ordinance was passed declaring henceforth no movies were ever to be made here. And that's why films with Southern themes are no longer being shot in Colusa County, California's 'Dixie,'" noted Mrs. Yates.

SEVEN

CONTRA COSTA COUNTY

BOCCE BALL CAPITAL OF AMERICA

MARTINEZ, the historic Contra Costa County town on the Carquinez Strait, 32 miles northeast of San Francisco, is where John Muir hung his hat the last 24 years of his life. It's the birthplace of the martini and of Joe DiMaggio. And it is also the bocce ball capital of America. But more on that shortly. The town was named after Don Ignacio Martinez, who had 11 children and owned 17,000 acres here when California was part of Mexico

During the Gold Rush of 1848, miners would stop off in Martinez and drink something called the Martinez Special, a local concoction made of one part very dry sauterne wine and three parts gin. It was stirred in ice and finished with an olive. Over the years the Martinez Special became the martini special, then simply the martini.

Italian fishermen, including Joe DiMaggio's father, arrived shortly after the Gold Rush and kept their fishing fleets here. There is a Joe DiMaggio Street in Martinez and a Joe DiMaggio baseball park next to the bocce courts. Fisherman's Park is named in honor of the Italian fishermen of Martinez and, appropriately, is on Berrellessa Street.

But the town's real claim to fame these days is that it has become a mecca for bocce ball players—there are more players of the old Italian bowling game per square foot in Martinez, population 28,000, than anywhere else in the 50 states. The town has the largest organized bocce league in the U.S., 123 teams, with more than 1,200 regular players.

Ken "Barbarossa" Dothee, a public defender and former City Councilman is president of the U.S. Bocce Federation. His Italian nickname means Red Beard. He's not Italian, but of German descent.

United States Bocce, the official magazine of the game is published in Martinez. Donna Allen, like Dothee one of the town's better players, is editor. She works for the Contra Costa County Planning Commission. She isn't Italian, either.

National bocce championships have been played on the 12 permanent hard-compacted oyster shell courts at Shoreline Park in Martinez. "Our little town has the largest permanent bocce facility in America at Shoreline Park," noted Dothee. "There's no other layout like this in America." He explained that bocce was a game played traditionally by older gentlemen in Italian communities all over the United States. "It caught on here in Martinez in the mid 1970s and the face of the sport hasn't been the same since." Dothee said men, women and children of all nationalities are now playing the game. New leagues are springing up all over America.

Bocce dates to centuries before the birth of Christ. Julius Caesar and his soldiers lagged rocks at small target stones between campaigns. Bocce is the national sport of Italy and is popular as well in France, Switzerland and South America. *"Andiamo, a giocare le bocce,"* announces the "commish," the team leader in Martinez when league play begins. It means, "Let's go friends, and play bocce."

The courts at Shoreline Park are 85 feet long, 12 feet wide. The bocce is a wood composition or metal ball, softball-size, rolled down the court at a *pallino* or jack, the golf ball-size target ball. The object is to roll the bocce as close to the *pallino* as possible. In team play, eight balls are used, two per competitor. Points are scored for each team's throws closer to the *pallino* than the opponent's. Players also try to knock the other team's balls away from the *pallino*.

The Pope is a bocce player. So was Rudy Perpich, the longtime governor of Minnesota. And, says Allen, "People from all walks of life play bocce in Martinez. We have teams with four generations of the same family. We have all-women teams in addition to the all-men teams. Teams with husbands and wives, neighbors, co-workers, judges and garbage men, secretaries, cops, teachers, lawyers, doctors. The sport is a comer. We estimate that at least one million Americans play the game."

"As president of the U.S. Bocce Federation, established in 1977, my main job is to coordinate activities, to promote bocce, to get it accepted as a high school sport," said Dothee, who spearheaded the bocce movement in Martinez. "Bocce is in its adolescence in America. Our goal is to change that, to put it right up there with golf and tennis."

Dothee was introduced to the game as a youngster: "When I was a kid in San Francisco and rode my bike to the pier to go fishing, I'd pass the bocce courts on the waterfront. I was fascinated by the old men speaking in a foreign (Italian) language, bowling the balls and smoking cigars that smelled awful." Eventually, he took up the game himself, and in 1975 he and several others formed the first league in Martinez with eight teams. Said Al Milano, a surveyor, "Bocce is like abalone and calamari. Once only the Italians knew about it. Now, it's becoming popular all over the place."

EIGHT

DEL NORTE COUNTY

EASTER LILY CAPITAL OF THE WORLD

I F JAPAN hadn't bombed Pearl Harbor, Smith River, a tiny coastal town in Del Norte County, wouldn't be the Easter lily capital of the world today. Also, the town, population 500, wouldn't celebrate Easter twice a year—on the traditional day in spring and again on the second Sunday in July.

Ninety-nine percent of all Easter lilies, a "one-day" holiday plant peculiar to the United States and Canada, are grown in a 10-mile stretch of the Pacific Coast extending no more than a mile inland between Smith River, California, and Brookings, Oregon. Japan was the sole source of the holiday plant until Dec. 7, 1941. Pearl Harbor ended Japan's corner on the market.

For years Cecil Watt and a few others in the Smith River area had grown Easter lilies as a hobby but had never sold any commercially.

"The plants did exceptionally well in this relatively frost-free coastal area," said Watt, who was 88 in 1995. "When the source of Easter lily bulbs was suddenly shut off because of World War II, word spread that fortunes could be made in Smith River on 'white gold.'

"People came from everywhere. By the end of the war in 1945 there were nearly 1,000 growers producing Easter lily bulbs along the Northern California and Southern Oregon coast. Growers were getting $1 a bulb." But the boom became a bust for all but a handful of growers. Today there are nine growers producing 12 million Easter lily bulbs a year on about 700 acres of land, an industry that grosses roughly $8 million annually.

It takes three years for the tennis-ball size bulbs to be ready to be harvested early in October and shipped to greenhouses throughout the United States and Canada to be held in 40-degree temperatures for six weeks. Then, by regulating greenhouse temperatures the plants will bloom in time for Easter.

Easter lilies are a tradition dating back to 1890 when an amateur Philadelphia gardener brought bulbs back from a vacation visit to Bermuda. A Philadelphia nurseryman, William K. Harris, introduced the lilies to the florist trade and almost overnight the plants became identified with the religious holiday. Until World War I, all bulbs were imported from Bermuda. But a virus disease put the Bermuda growers out of business in 1917 and Japan—native home of the Easter lily—became the sole source. Then along came Pearl Harbor.

Strangers visiting Smith River the second Sunday in July do not believe what they are seeing, smelling, and hearing: People exchanging "Happy Easter!" greetings; signs pointing to "Easter Sunrise Service" on the banks of the river; kids on Easter egg hunts; women and girls promenading in Easter finery; the pungent scent of Easter lilies permeating the air, wafting from spectacular fields in bloom. Smith River celebrates its annual Easter-in-July festival because the lilies naturally bloom at that time of the year. "No, we haven't lost our marbles. We always celebrate two Easters in Smith River," said Etta Dahlstrom, as she stuck hundreds of Easter lilies on one of a dozen floats for the big Easter-in-July parade.

NINE

EL DORADO COUNTY

LAKE TAHOE DREAM CASTLE

THE VIKING CASTLE in the woods at the water's edge at Lake
Tahoe is open three months of the year—June, July and
August. Then it becomes a ghost castle. Empty. Boarded up.
Collecting dust.

Vikingsholm in Emerald Bay is called the finest example of Scandinavian architecture in the Western Hemisphere. It stands on the shores
of 22-mile-long, 12-mile-wide Lake Tahoe, Indian for "lake in the sky."
Lake Tahoe, on the California-Nevada border, is 6,229-feet high. Its
deepest point is 1,645 feet, the third deepest lake in North America.

The storybook castle was the dream house of heiress Lora
Josephine Knight for 16 summers, from 1930 until she died at the
castle in 1945. She designed and built Vikingsholm with the help of
Swedish architect Lennart Palme. They traveled to Norway, Finland,

Denmark and Sweden to gather ideas to incorporate into the 38-room stone structure, and to purchase rare pieces of art and antiques to decorate rooms in the castle.

Mrs. Knight was not of Scandinavian extraction. She was of English descent. But Emerald Bay reminded her of Norwegian fjords she had seen. She decided a replica of an 11th-century Scandinavian castle would be perfect on her Lake Tahoe property. When the snows melted in 1929 along the south shore of Lake Tahoe, Mrs. Knight employed an army of 200 men to construct Vikingsholm. The workmen lived in temporary barracks on the woman's 239-acre pristine estate. In 1930 Mrs. Knight moved into her dream castle, along with her staff of 15, five gardeners, a private secretary, personal maid, cook, assistant cook, pantry maid, serving maid, upstairs maid, chauffeur, assistant chauffeur and laundry woman.

Mrs. Knight's first husband, James Moore, and her father, Edward A. Small, held controlling interests in a number of America's leading companies including National Biscuit, Continental Can, Diamond Match, Union Pacific and Rock Island Railroad. She maintained palatial estates in Evanston, Ill., and Santa Barbara. Her only child, a son, died at age 25. She remarried after her husband's death in the early 1920s. The second marriage to Henry French Knight, a St. Louis stockbroker, was short-lived. In the wake of her divorce, she participated in the backing of Charles Lindbergh's flight across the Atlantic and embarked on building Vikingsholm, California's 11th-Century Scandinavian castle.

The castle is filled with 12th century armor, intricately carved dragon beams, dragon heads crossing roof peaks, and spikes protruding from gutters to ward off evil spirits. A Finnish clock features a human form for its base and a human face for the clock. Mrs. Knight's bed was a replica of a queen's bed found in an ancient Viking ship. She had a small fleet of boats with the largest, "Valkyrie," a mahogany cabin cruiser, kept in a boathouse.

Each year her entourage of gardeners, secretary, maids, cooks, chauffeurs and laundry woman came to Vikingsholm early in June, remaining until late September until the "Queen of Vikingsholm's" death at the age of 82.

Three visitors each summer to the castle were Mr. and Mrs. Benjamin Henry of Santa Barbara, longtime friends of Mrs. Knight, and the Henrys' daughter, Helen. "From my earliest memories until I was 14, when Mrs. Knight died, my summers were spent in the castle," recalled Helen Henry Smith.

After Mrs. Knight's death the castle and estate were sold. In 1953 wealthy lumberman Harvey West donated Vikingsholm to the state of California. It has been a been part of Emerald Bay State Park ever since. The castle is open to public visitation each year from Memorial Day weekend to Labor Day, open for tours seven days a week from 10 a.m. to 4 p.m. The castle is hidden deep in the woods, accessible by boat and also by foot on a steep mile-long trail, formerly Mrs. Knight's single-lane dirt road to Vikingsholm.

In 1968 Helen Henry Smith, who lived in the castle as a child, visited Vikingsholm with her husband, Peter W. Smith, president of the Western Gold and Platinum Company. "Because of my strong ties to the castle I was invited to live here and guide people through this enchanting place the three months it is open during summer," she explained. So, in 1969, Mrs. Smith became a summer, ranger-interpreter for the California Department of Parks and Recreation. The summer of 1997 was her 28th year as the mistress of the castle, her 42nd summer in Vikingsholm counting her 14 years there as a child. Mrs. Smith, with the help of other rangers, leads around 45,000 visitors on tours through the castle each summer. But, come Labor Day, storm shutters are placed on doors and windows, and Vikingsholm becomes California's ghost castle again until the following Memorial Day.

TEN

FRESNO COUNTY

A FERRY BOAT FOR HIKERS

W**HEN THE FERRYBOAT SIERRA QUEEN** is launched on 7,327-foot-high Florence Lake in Fresno County in time for the Fourth of July holiday, hikers in the High Sierra know summer has finally arrived. Sierra Queen is one of the most remote ferries in America, catering almost exclusively to backpackers hiking the Mexico-to-Canada Pacific Crest Trail and the John Muir Trail.

From July through the end of September, 3,000 to 4,000 hearty hikers each year in California's spectacular high country will have cruised across this three-mile-long lake on the 32-foot Sierra Queen. Ever since 1920 there has been ferry service for hikers on Florence Lake. There is also a store on the north shore to stock up on food and supplies and a place to camp nearby in Jackass Meadows.

The steel-hulled Sierra Queen, with a capacity of 25 passengers, is the latest in a series of ferryboats on the lake. Built in 1963, the boat first operated for two years as a State of California buoy tender in San Francisco Bay before being brought to Florence Lake.

Karl Smith bought the Sierra Queen for $5,000 in 1965 and trailered it up to the lake. He ran the Florence Lake Store and Ferry Service from 1947 until he died in 1981. His widow, Adeline, now owns it. When we rode the ferry, Adeline's daughter and son-in-law, Tom and Karla Hurley, were managing the store and operating the ferry. Smith's original 19 foot, 10-passenger ferryboat is a planter now standing on end in the Florence Lake Store. Dick Morrison previously owned the ferryboat and store. For years he spent winters alone at Florence Lake handcrafting boats while snowed in for up to eight months at a stretch.

Florence Lake is 100 miles northeast of Fresno, the last 21 miles a one-lane torturous road with scores of blind corners that winds up and down steep mountain slopes. Rearing up majestically from the south shore of Florence Lake is 11,200-foot Mt. Shinn. The lake is embraced by glacier-carved peaks, many crowned with snow year round, and by the John Muir Wilderness. It's one of the few places in the High Sierra where backpackers on the Pacific Crest and John Muir Trails have an opportunity to pick up food and supplies. There are, however, no phones to the outside. The nearest telephone is 10 miles from the lake. Many of the backpackers have been on the trail 10 days to two weeks without any contact with the outside world by the time they arrive at Florence Lake. The two-mile ride on the ferryboat takes 20 minutes.

"Backpackers are always a happy bunch, so excited to be in this marvelous pristine country away from the crowds and the cities and towns down below," said Pat Ferris, skipper of the Sierra Queen. She said she has yet to run across a grump on the boat.

What do the backpackers say they crave the most as they sail across the lake to the store on the other side, Ferris was asked. "Ice cream. They know or have heard the store has several different flavors of ice cream cones available. They really wolf up the ice cream." she replied.

ELEVEN

GLENN COUNTY

WILD GOOSE CHASE

WILDLIFE BIOLOGIST GREG MENSIK was sitting in his pickup truck atop a levee overlooking one of several huge ponds at the Sacramento National Wildlife Refuge in Glenn County near the Northern California town of Willows. "I have a Siberian bird dead center in the scope," he shouted. He jotted down 7C9 in his notebook, a number corresponding to markings on the bird's collar.

The big snowy-white waterfowl with black wing tips had flown thousands of miles south from Wrangel Island, Russia's remote, most northeastern Arctic Island. It was one of 75,000 to 100,000 snow geese that migrate south to California each winter. The cacophony of upwards of 10,000 raucous, honking snow geese and smaller Ross geese sitting on the pond in front of us was deafening.

"Another Wrangel Island goose, 0C4," said Mensik of the U.S.Fish and Wildlife Service, as he peered through his spotting scope and entered the identification code in his log. A minute later: "There's a black collar, 88A, a Canadian bird." A few minutes after that he spotted a goose with a blue collar marked TE42 from Alaska's North Slope.

Mensik is one of several wildlife biologists from the United States, Russia, Canada and Mexico keeping track of the far-flying flocks that nest and breed near the top of the world and winter in southern Canada, northern Washington, California and as far south as Mexico.

Snow geese are the most abundant of wintering geese in California with most found on Pacific Flyway refuges in the Central Valley north of Sacramento. An adult snow goose weighs about 6 pounds and has a 4-foot wing span.

Wrangel Island off the Siberian coast is home to Russia's only snow goose population. Called Ostrov Vrangelya by the Russians, the island was discovered by an American whaler in 1867. Later, Canada claimed Wrangel Island, but since 1924 it has been part of the Soviet Union and now Russia. The USSR government removed all the Eskimos and reindeer that once inhabited Wrangel Island to other parts of the Siberian mainland. The island is now a Russian national preserve.

The first major international effort to monitor the migration of snow geese began in 1990. "We're trying to sort out where the various colonies of snow geese fly to each winter. We have a pretty good idea that four-fifths of the snow geese from Wrangel Island wind up in California," said James C. Bartonek, Pacific Flyway representative from the U.S. Fish and Wildlife Service in Portland, Oregon.

Bartonek worked with Soviet scientists several years to forge an agreement to monitor the geese and to try to get an accurate count of the number of birds that make the journey. He shipped banding collars to Wrangel Island for placement on the Russian geese. "We made thousands of collars for Wrangel Island, Alaska and Canada," noted Bruce Deuel, assistant waterfowl coordinator for the California Department of Fish and Game. The collars with red letters and numbers signify snow geese from Wrangel, black numbers and letters from Canada and blue from Alaska. The greatest numbers of snow geese come from Canada's Arctic, mostly from Banks Island. Next are the Wrangel Island geese. The smallest numbers are from Alaska's Prudhoe Bay.

Dick Kerbes is Canada's snow goose expert, with the Canadian Wildlife Service in Saskatoon, Saskatchewan. Russian scientists spent time with Kerbes monitoring snow geese from Wrangel Island as they migrated through Canada. American and Canadian wildlife biologists have spent time studying Russian breeding and nesting populations of snow geese on Wrangel Island.

Snow geese mate for life and migrate in small family groups numbering from less than 100 to more than 10,000. The flocks travel at 50 miles an hour or more. Although various colonies of snow geese from Wrangel Island, Canada and Alaska mix on wintering grounds with one another and with Ross geese, they return to original breeding and nesting grounds in the Arctic in the spring.

"They remain in Glenn County from late October to March feeding by day on rice and grain stubble in the valley, leftovers after farmers harvest their crops," said biologist Mensik. The geese also feed on 300 acres of rice planted for them on the refuge. At night and during afternoons snow geese sleep on the ponds. There isn't a more spectacular sight than seeing great numbers of snow geese on ponds or flying above in huge flocks. I never tire of it," mused wildlife biologist Greg Mensik.

TWELVE

HUMBOLDT COUNTY

THE SAMOA COOKHOUSE

O N A PENINSULA, across Humboldt Bay from Eureka, is the tiny town of Samoa, home of the Samoa Cookhouse, one of the last of the old time lumber camp cookhouses left in the West. The cookhouse is located in the heart of a town owned by the Louisiana-Pacific Lumber Company in Northern California's Humboldt County.

Not much has changed at the Samoa Cookhouse since the turn of the century. Dozens of women in red and white aprons still serve up the same hearty homecooked meals on the old wooden, oilcloth covered tables as they did in 1900. Local lumberjacks and mill hands still sign their meal tickets for deduction from their paychecks.

One difference at the cookhouse since 1960 is the public is welcomed to join lumberjacks and mill hands at the 10-person tables. Another thing is different, too. In the early days only single women were employed at the cookhouse and they had to live in dorms above the huge dining room.

Prior to World War I, the cooks and waitresses were paid $30 a month, plus room and board. They worked from 6 a.m. to 7 p.m. with morning and afternoon breaks, seven days a week. They would work five weeks straight before getting a day off.

Old-timers in Samoa recall how the cookhouse girls had to be in their rooms each night at 10:30 p.m., when the doors were bolted shut. Some of the girls who came in after the curfew were known to squeeze through a narrow woodbox to get to their rooms. Samoa Cookhouse girls had a favorite game they played in their dorms called "pot sliding." They would slide their chamber pots down the halls bowling alley fashion. Cookhouse women today are wives and daughters of lumberjacks and mill workers living in surrounding communities.

The upstairs dorms are vacant now, but the rooms are still furnished as they were in the old days when the cookhouse girls lived there. Today diners eat what they get. Portions are enormous, served family style, and seconds can be had for the asking. And the menu changes every day. Homemade bread is served with every meal and homemade pie for dinner. Soup is always served and the cookhouse is open from 6 a.m. to 10 p.m. Prices are extremely reasonable. The Samoa Cookhouse is so popular that 85 women are employed in summer to prepare and serve meals. They can handle 500 people at a setting.

Off the main dining room is a lumber camp museum cluttered with tools and memorabilia of the timber industry—pickerel bars, grab hooks, timber dogs, spike hammers, splitting malls and an assortment of saws and antique cooking utensils from the cookhouse. Across from the cookhouse is a cluster of quaint short streets lined with 100 freshly painted company houses where Louisiana-Pacific employees pay $187 a month rent, including utilities, for three-bedroom homes.

BIGGEST FISHERMAN IN AMERICA

A 25-FOOT COPPER STATUE of a crusty, weather-beaten, bearded, mustachioed fisherman in high boots, flop hat and rumpled sou'westerly clothing overlooks the Pacific Ocean in Eureka. It's the largest figure of a fisherman in America, a memorial to the hundreds of men over the years who crossed the bar in Humboldt Bay, went to sea to fish and never returned.

The statue, by sculptor Dick Crane, was commissioned and dedicated by the Fishermen's Wives of Humboldt Bay in 1981. During the dedication ceremonies, wives of fishermen tossed garlands of flowers into the sea as Dale Hustler played the harmonica and sang the sea shanty he wrote for the fisherman: "O ho, you proud fishermen. I wish you luck and may the seas be good to you." Tears streaked leathery faces of veteran fishermen as the sea shanty echoed across the water. In his dedication prayer that day, the Rev. Darrell Kobs intoned, "This statue is a reminder of heroic deeds, of the pursuit of brave men after ever-elusive sea creatures."

Crane spent a year in his back yard creating "The Fisherman." The statue is at the west end of Woodley Island overlooking the New England-like town on the rugged north coast of California. It was the Fishermen's Wives of Humboldt Bay who sustained the sculptor in his work by holding fish fries and crab feeds to raise funds.

"Every time I look at this statue I remember my son," sighed Morgan Burlingame, as he stood arm-in-arm with his wife Anna Bell at the foot of the statue. Their son, Keith, was lost at sea while fishing.

"Dick Crane's statue is the greatest thing that ever happened to the fishermen and their families in Humboldt County," said Bev Haman. Her son, Steve, went to sea. A sudden storm overturned his boat. His body was never found.

The statue is Crane's impression of Ernie Lampella, who was 78 and a lifelong Eureka fisherman at the time "The Fisherman" was dedicated. "When you think of a fisherman, you think of Ernie. His hands rough from the many hours of work at sea. His face all wrinkled from salt spray and squinting at the sun. The statue is Ernie," said the sculptor. However, Ernie Lampella wasn't at the dedication. The fishermen and their wives knew he wouldn't be there. He was fishing. "Ernie is bashful and shy. He doesn't like to be the center of attention. He just likes to be out in his boat catching fish," said Crane.

Jan Scheffler, president of the Fishermen's Wives, called "The Fisherman" California's equivalent of the Statue of Liberty. "It sends chills up your back," declared Sue Williams, local civic leader, echoing the sentiments of all who remember the hearty fishermen who go down to the sea to catch fish, and to those who never come back.

THIRTEEN

IMPERIAL COUNTY

A REMOTE STATE PARK

PICACHIO STATE RECREATION AREA in Imperial County is one of the most inaccessible places in California's state park system. In the southeast corner of California on the west bank of the Colorado River, Picachio (pronounced Pea-kah-show) is 25 miles north of the town of Winterhaven. To get here by land is an 18 mile drive over a miserable, winding, one-lane dirt road that meanders through the hills, narrow gorges and valleys of the Chocolate Mountains.

"We are forever coming to the aid of people who get stranded and stuck on that awful road leading to the park," sighed seasonal ranger Dick Feia after a frustrating fall weekend, digging several cars out of the sand and muck on the only road into the park.

Estimates are that about 50,000 visitors find their way to Picacho each year, by land or river. Compared to other state parks that's a drop in the bucket. Most arrive in the park by boat as they sail down the Colorado River. And, those that come usually arrive between late October and mid April. The rest of the year Picacho is extremely hot. Days often go by in the heat of summer in this desert park with no one here except the ranger caretakers.

During our visit the park superintendent was ranger Steve Horvitz, who lived year round in the park with his wife, Sidona "Dodie", and their children, Nicole who was 8 at the time, and Ellie, 5. They had been living in Picacho a year. Horvitz asked to be stationed at Picacho because of the isolation and beauty of the place. His wife, a former state park ranger, wanted to be here for the same reasons.

Picacho is so remote that the two Horvitz girls received most of their schooling in the living room of their trailer home where they were taught by their mother. At the time they were the only children of state park rangers in California enrolled in a home-study program.

The 7,000-acre park is a rugged mountainous region with scenic formations dominated by 1,947-foot-high Picacho Peak, a volcanic outcropping that looks like a huge medieval castle. The area is alive with wildlife: quail, road-runners, red-tailed hawks, buzzards, wild burros, bighorn sheep, bobcats, raccoons, skunk, owls, bald eagles, deer and coyotes. "Coyotes are always howling in the middle of the night and waking us up," said Nicole Horvitz, as she pointed out animal tracks outside her home, including some from a mountain lion chasing a burro.

There are no telephones in the park. No concessions or stores. Electrical power is provided by generators. Water comes from a well. Horvitz noted, "The beauty of the river and the park, the remoteness and isolation, plus the low rent and free utilities serve as an incentive to rangers and their families to come to live in this far-away place. For many, this kind of lifestyle is not appealing. For us, Picacho is a paradise."

MOST LOW-DOWN PEOPLE IN AMERICA

THE MOST LOW-DOWN people in America live in Calipatria, a small Imperial County town in the southeast corner of California. Preachers have a standing joke about their parishioners in Calipatria: "People here pray a little harder, being that much closer to hell." At 184 feet below sea level, Calipatria is the lowest incorporated town in the Western Hemisphere. The lowest place in the United States is Bad Water in Death Valley at 282 feet below sea level. But nobody lives at Bad Water.

Calipatria, population 3,228, is a farm center. Since 1992 it is also home of a state maximum security prison with 4,000 inmates. You could say the most low down convicts in the Western Hemisphere live in Calipatria.

The people of Calipatria are particularly proud of what they believe is the world's tallest flagpole. "Our 16-story flagpole keeps us in the Union," said mayor Ed Rademacher. "It stretches 184 feet into the atmosphere, clear up to sea level." The flagpole brought worldwide attention to the small town when it was erected in 1958.

The flagpole came about like this: Before World War II, Takeo "Harry" Momita, a native of Japan, was the town druggist. When the War came along, Momita and his family were sent to a relocation camp for three years. They returned to Calipatria after the war and reopened the drugstore. Later, Momita and his wife, Helen, were visiting Los Angeles when they were involved in an auto accident. Mrs. Momita was killed. The town came to the aid of the family, operating the drugstore for Momita while he regained his health. Individuals donated a total of $500 to Momita in memory of his wife.

Momita decided to erect the tallest flagpole in the world to show his appreciation for his life in America, despite time in the relocation camp, and to show his affection for the people of Calipatria who rallied to his help. He matched the $500 from his own funds. $10,000 for the flagpole poured in from all over the country and from many foreign nations after wire services carried the story about Harry Momita. Each Christmas hundreds of colored lights are strung up the flagpole from the bottom of Calipatria to sea level—making it, the town insists, also the tallest Christmas tree in America.

FOURTEEN

INYO COUNTY

HOTTEST PLACE ON EARTH

I
T'S SO HOT IN DEATH VALLEY (in summer the hottest, driest spot on earth!) that swallows, ravens and other birds seldom fly during the day. The birds take cover in the shade, standing like statues, mouths open, breathing heavily. Why, it's so hot, that when dogs chase cats, both animals walk.

Death Valley is a blast furnace in summer—Dante's View, Devil's Golfcourse, Funeral Mountains, Furnace Creek, Hell's Gate, Stovepipe Well are some of the place names here attesting to the summer inferno. "Heat Wave" is the name of the in-house paper published by Death Valley rangers. The few people who work outside in Death Valley in summer consume an average of five gallons of water a day—that's right, *five gallons!* "If we didn't stop and drink regularly we would die," said Kenneth Pye, working on a road construction project.

Death Valley, in California's Inyo County, has had temperatures in excess of 100 degrees for 126 consecutive days—over 110 degrees for 65 consecutive days. It has been as hot as 134 degrees here. The lowest temperature recorded on some days has been 110. It is 10% hotter in Death Valley in July—the hottest month of the year—than in Azizia, Libya, hottest of the African deserts. The summer ground temperature in Death Valley—the heat of the ground when you touch it—is a sizzling 170 to 190 degrees. The air is like an oven from sunup to sundown and through the night. Stick your hand out a car window when driving and your fingers burn. Grave markers litter the valley floor with epitaphs of those who perished in the heat.

But, despite the incredible hot weather, about 200 men, women and children live in this below sea level, 140-mile long, 4-to-16-mile wide furnace. A skeleton crew of National Park Service personnel and their families stick it out in the sizzling summer. There are also a Highway Patrol officer, a deputy sheriff, the postmaster, a few miners, the gas station attendants, those who work in the general store, in the gift shop, at the Furnace Creek Ranch Motel, at the saloon and at two restaurants. That's it.

"Death Valley isn't the Siberia of the National Park system, as some might think," insisted Homer P. Leach, chief ranger. Added chief naturalist Pete Sanchez, "We're really not here because we're being punished for goofing off, we're here because we like it." Leach's wife, Beth, admitted that during one's first summer in the valley "everyone holds his breath and wonders how he's going to make it. We have three months of this unbelievable heat, then nine months of perfect weather. In summer it's like living in a sauna if you go outside. We stay indoors in our air-conditioned homes." There are no fat rangers in Death Valley National Park.

In summer, water heaters are turned off, because water heaters keep water cooler than that out of cold water faucets. So, everyone turns on "cold" when he wants hot water and "hot" when he wants water not quite as hot. When people stagger into the store or gas station at Furnace Creek Ranch, the first remark to those working in the establishments seems like it is always the same: "My God, how do you people stand it?"

A man dressed in a black pin-stripe suit, waistcoat, white shirt, tie and bowler hat strolled out of the 120-degree heat into the store and asked Jean Mackey, who worked there, if he could borrow her dog. He said he was from the London Times and was going to have his picture taken at the Salt Flats. The man told her the newspaper planned to run the photo captioned: "Only mad dogs and Englishmen go out in the midday sun in Death Valley in summer."

Vern Rulison, caretaker for the plush Furnace Creek Inn, when it is boarded up for the summer because of the sizzling temperatures, said "it's so hot when I go inside to make sure everything is OK, that 120 on the outside seems cool." Rulison flushes every toilet in the inn a couple of times a week because the water in the bowls evaporates.

On a typical summer day in Death Valley, the highest temperature was 124 degrees. But the U.S.Weather Bureau reported the 114 recorded at Blythe, California, was the highest in the nation. It happens all the time. "If we repeated day after day that Death Valley was the hottest place in the country, it would get pretty monotonous," explained Bob Grebe, U.S. Weather Bureau meteorologist in Los Angeles. So, the Weather Bureau lies.

DEATH VALLEY'S GOOD SAMARITAN

As a CALIFORNIA HIGHWAY PATROLMAN responsible for 5,000 square miles in America's hottest national park, Dave Flegel was known to many as Death Valley's good Samaritan. He had been the lone CHP officer in Death Valley for eight years when we spent a sizzling summer day on patrol with him in the hottest place on earth. Every week during the scorching summer months he rescues dozens of travelers stranded when their cars break down.

"The heat plays hell with tires, hoses and fan belts. Many people think their cars are in tip-top shape mechanically. Yet many come unglued in the heat," said Flegel. He handles several heat exhaustion cases each week. "I carry eight gallons of water in my trunk for overheating radiators or for people to drink. I drink two gallons a day myself," he related, wiping the perspiration from his forehead and off his glasses. He encountered two suicide victims on isolated stretches of road and handled 40 fatalities from vehicle accidents.

While stopped at Bad Water to make sure everyone was all right, the temperature on the hood of his CHP car read 116 degrees. It's the only CHP car in the state with a thermometer on the hood. "I put it there because people are forever asking: 'How hot is it?'"

He regularly patrolled hundreds of miles of state highways and paved and dirt roads in the national park and southeastern Inyo County, driving 200 to 400 miles during an eight-hour stint and was on call around the clock for emergencies.

FOREIGNERS FLOCK TO DEATH VALLEY

A BLISTERING MIDDAY SUN shimmered eerily in all directions across the vast emptiness of Death Valley. Despite the 120-degree heat, people poured from rented cars and chartered buses at Bad Water, speaking a cacophony of languages—German, French, Spanish, Dutch, Chinese, Japanese, Italian, Korean, Hungarian. Obviously, they were all from foreign lands, where travel agents in their home countries sell package excursions to California featuring "a visit to Death Valley in the summer, the hottest place in the world, an experience you will never forget." In July and August, Death Valley isn't an American national park, it belongs to foreign tourists.

Going to Death Valley at the hottest time of the year is a great adventure for foreigners, who want it to be as scorching as possible so they can return home and tell their friends what itís like to spend a couple days in an oven. It's the type of "adventure" that most Americans avoid. "All Germans know Taldestodes (Death Valley, in German) as one of the world's most mysterious places," said Juergen Philipper, of Neuss, Germany. His wife, Illy, added, "My boss said we must go to Death Valley. There's no experience in the world like it, he said. And he was right." Others in the sweating, multinational crowd agreed.

FIFTEEN

KERN COUNTY

TUBATALABULS

Time is running out for the Tubatalabuls—a native California tribe, who speak one of the "happiest" languages on earth, a distinct language, spoken for centuries by thousands of Indians who lived in a remote mountain valley in Kern County. Now there are only 22 men and women fluent in Tubatalabul (too-bot-a-lobble), one of 180 different Indian languages still spoken in America, and one of 50 living Indian languages in California.

"Whenever Tubatalabuls get together and talk Tubatalabul, everyone roars with laughter, " said Chanza Andreas, explaining: "Other Indian languages aren't like that and people don't bend over in stitches when someone starts talking English. But when something is said in Tubatalabul it always sounds so funny. Even the name of our people and our language, Tubatalabul, makes us laugh. It's hard to pronounce but when you say it, it makes you feel good —too-bot-a-lobble.

Especially if you say it fast like we do. It's a real mouthful." The name means "a people that go to the forest to gather tubat (pinon nuts)."

For centuries Tubatalabuls lived in what was a remote 15-mile-long, 2-to-4-mile-wide verdant valley where the North and South Forks of Kern River spill down from the High Sierra. In recent years the rivers were dammed and today half the valley is the Lake Isabella Recreation Area 50 miles east of Bakersfield.

There are less than 100 of the tribe left, and less than a fourth of them, all over 60, speak the language. "It's all over for the Tubatalabuls," sighed Tony Pablo. "Soon nobody will speak the language." Today only a handful of them are left in the valley—a few ranchers living in Weldon and Onyx, two hamlets at the east end. "Tubatalabuls were everywhere in this valley when my grandparents and their grandparents lived here," said Pablo. "They lived off the land, fished in the rivers and streams and hunted in the mountains that surround us."

Mrs. Andreas said that when she was a child there were about 200 Tubatalabuls fluent in the language in the valley. "They were the happiest people I've ever seen, laughing all the time," she recalled. To this day the Tubatalabuls seem to have built-in smiles, like dolphins in the sea. "It's because we have always been such a happy people with this wonderfully funny language of ours," insisted Mrs. Andreas. "Stories handed down in our families say the Tubatalabuls were always a content people living at peace in this little valley. Protected by high mountains all around they had little contact with outside Indians. The Spanish were the first non-Indians to come through. That's how we came by the names we have today. None of us have the old Tubatalabul names."

Chanza Andreas said her people did not want to mix. "They were always proud of their blood lines. They never mixed with other Indians. They didn't mix with the Spaniards or Mexicans. Some people say all Indians look alike. That's not true at all. Each tribe or group has its own facial or physical characteristics, unless the blood lines have been mixed extensively.

"We finally ran out of Tubatalabuls. There weren't enough to go round. Now, many of my grandchildren and many grandchildren of the few of us that are left have blonde hair and green eyes. It is nearly at an end. My generation is about the last of a beautiful culture. It's really sad. But with so few speaking the language, it is not practical for the young ones to retain it."

Pablo, Mrs. Andreas and other Tubatalabuls in the valley took count of those still speaking the language. In Weldon and Onyx there were only eight still fluent in it. The others still speaking the ancient language included eight Tubatalabuls in Bakersfield, two in Tracy, one in Porterville and one in Los Angeles.

"There are so many things to tell about Tubatalabul," said Mrs. Andreas. "We have no swear words. When someone gets mad at somebody else, they call that person a dog, a rat or a mouse. Even those words are fun words." Tony Pablo climbed onto his horse to ride out and check his cattle. He contributed a parting observation: "When we say good morning, we simply say 'Ma'—just like the sound an old cow would make." Then he laughed in typical Tubatalabul fashion, almost falling off his horse as he rode off into the sunset.

BEAUTIFYING THE DESERT

As THE FIVE WOMEN were planting flowers on the grounds of the new Ridgecrest City Hall in the northeastern corner of Kern County, the lawn sprinklers suddenly went on. The women screamed and ran. They were drenched. "You never know what's going to happen next," laughed Bernice Butler, 84.

The women belong to the Desert Planters, a local garden club whose 35 members, mostly women between 65 and 85, have a goal "to make Ridgecrest the most beautiful desert city on earth by the year 2013." Desert Planters have a 2013 Committee to achieve that ambitious distinction. Why the year 2013? Because that will be the 50th anniversary of the incorporation of Ridgecrest, 150 miles north of Los Angeles on the Mojave Desert in the shadows of the towering High Sierra, and the 50th anniversary of the Desert Planters as well. "It's not just rhetoric. We're well on our way," insisted Dorothy Bennett, 55, the club president.

Everywhere you go in Ridgecrest, population 31,000, one sees evidence of the volunteer beautification work by the Desert Planters. There are thousands of trees and gardens planted at public buildings, schools, the local college, the library, cemeteries, parkways and business districts. "We plant anywhere they will let us. We encourage all homeowners to have gardens, trees and manicured lawns," explained Alice Hirsch, the club's founding president.

The Desert Planters were on a daffodil kick. They pushed a wheelbarrow full of daffodil bulbs into the City Council chambers recently and later planted them in front of the City Hall. "We're trying to get people all over town to plant daffodils in their yards to brighten up Ridgecrest and give it a cheerful yellow glow," noted Marge Daiber, 82, one of the group's past presidents. She is one of three members of the local garden club who have been president of the California Garden Clubs, a statewide organization of 286 clubs with 13,500 members.

Desert Planters sponsor garden contests, public awareness programs, planting demonstrations, an annual garden show, an annual cleanup day, and a landscape school featuring leading landscape architects from throughout the West. It is one of the most active garden clubs in the nation, winning numerous local, state and national accolades.

Several Desert Planters were sitting in Dorothy Bennett's living room, recalling what Ridgecrest was like before their organization. "There were no flowers, no trees anywhere in town. Not even a blade of grass. Just bare desert with lots of tumbleweeds," sighed Alice Hirsch, who was the first president, from 1963 to 1966, and president again from 1987 to 1989.

The Desert Planters have come a long way. The town's motto is "Cleaner and Greener Ridgecrest." "Just look at other desert communities, they don't have near the plantings we have," observed ex-president Edna Pierce, 78. "When we say Ridgecrest will be the most beautiful desert city on earth by the year 2013, we're not just whistling Dixie," allowed Vera Appleton, 77. If their past record is any criteria, the ambitious goal of the Desert Planters may well come to fruition.

SIXTEEN

KINGS COUNTY

CHEF SAVES CHINATOWN

CHINA ALLEY, the charming 19th-Century Chinatown in Hanford, a small farm center just west of Tulare and south of Fresno, was saved by a chef *extraordinaire* and his family. Presidents Eisenhower and Truman, the king of England and other heads of state, including Mao Tse-tung and Chiang Kai-shek, have sent people to this cow town to eat. A group of wealthy businessmen flies here four times a year from New York, round trip, first class, just to savor one of Chef Richard Wing's superb gourmet meals. Some of the outstanding feasts in the West—annual Escoffier, Food and Wine Societe and Chef de Cuisine banquets--take place at Wing's Imperial Dynasty Restaurant.

The restaurant is one of several old structures with faded Oriental markings on the block-long back street. It is here that Richard Wing's grandfather, Chow Gong Wing, began selling noodles for 5 cents a bowl in 1883.

Hanford then was the second-largest Chinese community in California—a huge camp of 15,000 railroad laborers who were left without jobs with the completion of a railroad roadbed. The town's population today is the same as it was when Chow Gong Wing arrived after a nine-month voyage on a sailing vessel from China. But today fewer than 100 who live here are Chinese.

With the exodus of the Chinese from Hanford over the years, the old buildings in Chinatown deteriorated. Eventually, they collapsed or were torn down, except those fronting China Alley and the Chinese School a block away. Wing and his family purchased the property on China Alley to save it from the bulldozers. What had been an herb store, a gambling house, an opium den and the headquarters of a local tong is now the Imperial Dynasty.

The *Wine Spectator* presented the Imperial Dynasty with its Grand Award for having "one of the greatest wine cellars in the world." "Only 10% of our guests on an average night at the Imperial Dynasty are from the Hanford area," explained Wing. "The rest come here from long distances." Gourmets come to this tiny town not for Wing's Chinese food, but for his Chinoise style of cooking—the culinary combination of two great cuisines, French haute with a Chinese accent.

A sampling: Richard Wing's Essence of Pigonneaux, Chasseur Potage—a rich aromatic, double consommé prepared from a unique stock of squabs, guinea hens, frog legs, ducks and pheasants. His escargots have won the coveted Cordon Bleu award for two consecutive years. Snails in the shells delectably flavored with garlic butter, minced Cornish hen, cashew spread, shallots, herbs and fragrance of Chablis wine--bedecked with garlands of sliced onions.

Wing's Eperlans farcis aux fruits de mer: A stunning fish dish. Two delicate boned silver smelts—filled with an exquisitely flavored forcemeat of lobster, shrimp, perch, truffle, and an elusive touch of cognac. Lightly coated with a mixture of waterchestnut flour and almond powder. Then gently poached in vermouth and butter. Presented floating on a grapefruit cup of sauce normande. The dessert is the grand finale: baked apple filled with cream cheese on foundations of almond cake, embraced by a noble sauce of mashed banana, orange juice and Grand Marnier.

Wing's grandfather Chow Gong Wing operated a restaurant in Hanford until he died in 1923. He was a famous chef in his own right, introducing dishes that have become everyday entrees in Chinese restaurants all over America. Chow Wing's son, Henry Chow Wing, also a widely known Chinese chef, succeeded his father. Now Richard Wing, 76 in 1997, carries on the more than century-old family tradition with the help of 22 members of the Wing clan.

Richard Wing has traveled the world cooking for and dining with heads of states on all continents. During World War II he was General George C. Marshall's personal aide. He was in Moscow when Marshall met with Stalin and in China for meetings with Mao and Chiang Kai-shek. He ate with and cooked for Harry Truman, Dwight Eisenhower, Winston Churchill and leaders of many nations. Wing was trained in intelligence. He was Marshall's second pair of eyes and ears. But ostensibly he was the general's aide, cook and food taster. Those four years were Wing's training ground—that and the family tradition.

World leaders knew and respected Wing's wizardry in the kitchen, and when the war was over, made certain that emissaries from their countries visiting California dine with this chef *extraordinaire*. Wing insists, "A chef has a sacred duty to help sustain, maintain, restore and revitalize the body."

SEVENTEEN

LAKE COUNTY

ONE-ROUND HOGAN & AMERICA'S NICE TOWN

THERE ARE NO NICE CHURCHES, Nice Libraries, Nice policemen, Nice newspapers, or Nice jails on the north shore of Clear Lake in Lake County. But there are 2,126 Nice people, when counted in the mid-1990s, in the quaint town of Nice, 121 miles north of San Francisco.

It's the only town in America with a Nice Fire Department and a Nice Post Office. There's also a Nice Market and a Nice Garage and a Nice Park. Which is all very nice except: "We don't like to be called Nice, rhyming it with mice, vice or lice," snapped Helen Barkley Bayne, during our first visit to Nice many years ago. Helen has since died, as had her husband, Charles W. Bayne, better known as "One Round Hogan," his nickname when he was a professional boxer. "One Round Hogan" gave the town its name.

"It's Nice (Neece), as in Nice, France," Helen explained. "When strangers come here they always laugh and say: 'It's nice to be in Nice.' We tell 'em: 'It's nice to be in Nice (Neece).' We shudder, absolutely shudder, when people call us Nice." Mrs. Bayne served 20 years as postmaster of Nice, one of a dozen towns on the shores of 20-mile long, 1-to-8-miles-wide Clear Lake, the largest body of fresh water entirely in California. (Lake Tahoe has the California-Nevada border running right through it.)

Her husband came by his nickname, Helen explained, "because it usually only took one round to knock him out. He may not have been much of a fighter, but he was a wonderful man, and to his credit he will always be remembered as the man who gave Nice, California, its name." When the Baynes came to Nice in 1923 it was called The Villas.

"Five years after we settled here the government gave us our post office," continued Mrs. Bayne. "My husband and three other men in the community figured we needed a catchy name for the post office and the town. Max Maireder, who ran the general store at the time, wanted to name it Lakemont to describe the way the mountains spill into the lake here. But my husband held off for a fancier name. The town next to us is Lucerne, named after Lucerne, Switzerland. So 'One Round Hogan,' Max and the others agreed to call it Nice (Neece) after the resort on the French Riviera where the Maritime Alps spill into the Mediterranean, just as Bartlett Mountain spills into Clear Lake at Nice."

Maireder was the first Nice postmaster and Mrs. Bayne, the second. Michael Wilbur, named Nice postmaster in 1993, still the only Nice postmaster in America, says his post office continues to receive stamped, self-addressed envelopes from people across the country requesting copies of the country's only Nice postmark.

"We get a lot of missent European mail in this small town," noted Matt Gardner, long time senior clerk at the Nice Post Office. "One of the longest streets in Nice, France is De California. Sometimes someone addresses a letter to a person living on De California in Nice and forgets to add France. A postman spots the De California address, checks the postal guide, sees that there is a Nice, California, and we get it." That's life in the "neecest" town in America.

EIGHTEEN

LASSEN COUNTY

RAILS-TO-TRAILS

FOR 50 YEARS, steam locomotives pulling flatcars stacked with timber snaked through the woods along the banks of fast-flowing Susan River in Lassen County. Now, instead of trains, joggers, hikers, equestrians and cyclists wind their way along the 25-mile, single-track railbed called the Bizz Johnson Trail.

One of the first of its kind in the West, this linear "rails-to-trails" park between Westwood and Sunsanville in Northern California was dedicated in 1986. The old railbed cuts through the Lower Cascade Mountains in two huge tunnels—one 800 feet long, the other 450 feet—and crosses and recrosses the river on 11 trestles. Flanked by steep cliffs, the trail traverses wild river and pine forest varying in elevation from 4,214 feet at Sunsanville to 5,520 feet at Westwood. There are quiet pools in the river for swimming, and choice spots for trout fishing.

The trail system is the brainchild of an alliance of environmental and recreational groups that launched the Rails-to-Trails Conservancy in 1986. That year there were 85 abandoned railbeds converted to narrow parks, nearly all in the East and the Midwest. By 1995 there were 715 trails converted from abandoned railbeds totaling 7,275 miles, with the longest Rails-to-Trails linear park, the Katy Trail State Park in Missouri, 200 miles long, and the shortest, the two-block-long Watts Tower Crescent Greenway Park in Los Angeles created from an old railbed.

Within nine years after the Bizz Johnson Trail became the first Rails-to-Trails park in California there were 46 former railbeds transformed into parks totaling 191 miles in 21 of California's counties. Orange County with eight of the trail parks has more than any other county in the state. The Rails-to-Trails Conservancy was created to halt the piecemeal sale of old railbeds that stretch for tens of thousands of miles through every state, and to develop the land into bicycling, horseback riding and hiking paths.

It took eight years to acquire the abandoned roadbed of the old Fernley & Lassen Railroad and convert it to the Bizz Johnson Trail. Stan Bales, U.S. Bureau of Land Management outdoor recreation planner, headed the project from its inception. Sections of the railbed owned by the Southern Pacific Railroad, timber companies and private parties were bought or easement rights were obtained in years of negotiations. In some instances, federal lands in nearby areas were exchanged for the railbed. The largest land exchange—involving 1,200 acres and 4.2 miles of railbed—completed the acquisition project, enabling the BLM and the U.S. Forest Service to convert the old railbed into the trail named after the late Harold T. (Bizz) Johnson of Roseville, who served in the U.S. House of Representatives from 1958 to 1980. It was Johnson who obtained federal funds to purchase the land and build the trail. He also helped with the negotiations in acquiring the property.

Fernley & Lassen Railroad was built by the Red River Lumber Company, in 1914 to link the timber concern's large mill at Westwood with Southern Pacific's mainline at Fernley, Nevada. The Interstate Commerce Commission granted Southern Pacific's petition for abandoning the then-defunct Sunsanville-to-Westwood part of the line in 1978. That part of the line was used for the trail.

No motorized vehicles are permitted on the trail. It has become the biggest visitor attraction in Lassen County with an estimated 30,000 users a year, 40% of them cyclists and 60% hikers with a small percentage of horseback riders. The trail is a popular cross country ski trail in winter.

The first Rails-to-Trails park in America is the 35-mile long Illinois Prairie Path, converted from the Chicago, Aurora & Elgin Railroad in 1968. These long, narrow parks are now located in all the states except Delaware and Hawaii and are federal, state, county and city parks. The Rails-to-Trails Conservancy is headquartered at Suite 300, 1400 16th St., N.W., Washington, D.C., 20036, and is supported solely by member dues and donations. The organization has 70,000 members who receive the Rails-to-Trails Quarterly and a discount on the organization's publications. *Seven Hundred Great Trails,* its most popular book, describes the 700 first Rails-to-Trails.

"At the turn of the century there were 300,000 miles of railroad corridors in America. Today there are less than 140,000 miles of corridors being used, with 3,000 miles of lines being abandoned a year," noted Greg Smith, Rails-to-Trails research coordinator, adding, "The abandoned railbeds are a wonderful resource. Yet, it is being lost at an incredible rate, with about 150,000 miles split up and sold to adjacent landowners, potential trail paths are lost forever. But the Rails-to-Trails movement has caught on and is gaining momentum. In addition to the 715 Rails-to-Trails parks already established, totaling 7,275 miles in length, there are another 950 projects underway which will add another 12,690 miles of hiking and cycling pathways across the nation."

Rails-to-Trails Conservancy is not involved in managing any of the trails but it does provide free technical assistance to individuals or governmental agencies in helping acquire the railbeds. It takes years to negotiate and complete the acquisition projects once a railroad decides to abandon a rail line. In California, the Bizz Johnson Trail in Lassen County blazed the way for establishing a state-wide system of linear parks treasured by cyclists, equestrians and hikers.

NINETEEN

LOS ANGELES COUNTY

MR. GRIFFITH'S PRESENT

N o AMERICAN city ever received a Christmas present as large and as valuable as that given to Los Angeles in 1896—a mountain, with its 3,015 acres of ridges, slopes, cliffs, canyons and meadows in the heart of the city.

"I wish to make this gift while I am still in the full vigor of life," said Griffith J. Griffith, addressing the mayor, City Council, and a large gathering at City Hall on Dec. 17, 1896. "It must be made a place of recreation and rest for the masses, a resort for the rank and file of the plain people. I have but one request that the public—the whole public—should enjoy with me this beautiful spot." To this day the gift by the Welsh immigrant who became a millionaire is the largest city park in the United States.

Seven years after Griffith gave the city the acreage that was to carry his name, Griffith Park, he was in San Quentin serving a two-year sentence for shooting his wife on Sept. 3, 1903, while they were alone in a room in Santa Monica's Arcadia Hotel. Newspapers carried front page stories for months following the shooting and the subsequent trial and sentencing of Griffith. His wife, socially prominent Mary Agnes Mesmer Griffith, daughter of the owner of one of the city's finest hotels, The United States, recovered and, no surprise, divorced Griffith.

Once out of prison, Griffith resumed his role as one of the city's leading citizens. On Dec. 22, 1912, he appeared at City Hall, this time to announced he wanted to present the people of Los Angeles with another Christmas present—$100,000 for an observatory on 1,652-foot-high Mt. Hollywood in the center of Griffith Park. "I consider it my obligation to make Los Angeles a happier, cleaner and finer city. I wish to pay my debt of duty in this way to the community in which I have prospered," Griffith declared. The offer was immediately accepted by the City Council but objections were voiced by many citizens and public officials.

"On behalf of the rising generation of girls and boys we protest against the acceptance of this bribe," a prominent member of the community wrote in a letter printed on the front page of one local newspaper. "What sort of ideal are you placing before them? Are you prepared to say to them that if a man is a millionaire he can commit a crime, and then with his wealth bribe the community to receive him back into fellowship merely because of that bribe," the letter continued. "This community is neither so poor nor so lost to sense of public decency that it can afford to accept this money, and if you insist on accepting it, let us have a referendum." Members of the Park Commission turned down the $100,000, and later instituted a court action restraining Griffith from proceeding in the fulfilling of his offer.

Griffith died July 6, 1919, at the age of 69. His second major Christmas present to the city, the observatory, had still not been accepted. But he did live to see his vast estate, El Rancho de Los Feliz—his first Christmas gift to the city—become one of the finest city parks in America.

Griffith Jenkins Griffith was born January 4, 1850, on a farm in Glamorganshire, South Wales. He came to America in 1865 settling in Ashland, Pennsylvania. In 1873 he came to California where he was a reporter for the Alta California, an early-day San Francisco newspaper. He covered the gold fields of this state and Nevada, becoming a nationally recognized authority on mining in the West. In time he became an official of a mining syndicate and made a fortune. He moved to Los Angeles in 1882 and invested a great deal of his money in real estate, purchasing the old Spanish land grant, El Rancho de Los Feliz.

Griffith allied himself with the best business and reform movements in the city. He was an officer in the Citizens' League, organized to secure honest administrations of the city and county governments. He was a director of the Merchants and Manufacturers Assn. He was active in the formation of the Pioneer Fruit Growers Association. There was a great deal of discussion by civic leaders in Los Angeles during the mid-1890s regarding the need for city parks. Griffith reacted by presenting the city with his huge estate as a Christmas present.

Undaunted by the city's refusal to accept his second Christmas gift, he left $750,000 in his will for the construction of a Greek Theater and the observatory. "I want the masses to be attracted there and be given something that will entertain them and at the same time make them think, something that will lift them above their troubles and turn them to higher things. I want them to look up instead of down, to count the stars instead of counting their beads," he wrote, explaining why he left the money for the observatory.

The Griffith Park Observatory, with one of the finest planetariums in the world, was finally accepted by the city in accordance with the stipulations of Griffith's will. It was completed and opened May 14, 1935. The Greek Theater had its premiere performance Sept. 25, 1930.

Griffith's park has grown through the years to its present size of 4,064 acres. Three-fourths of the park is rugged mountainous terrain. Park features in addition to the Greek Theater and Observatory, include four golf courses, the Los Angeles Zoo, the Children's Zoo, Ferndell, Travel Town, a bird sanctuary, miles of scenic mountain drives, 43 miles of bridle trails and 53 miles of hiking trails. There are tennis courts, baseball diamonds, touch football fields, a swimming pool, 35 picnic areas, croquet, volleyball and horseshoe courts, two hockey fields and a cricket field. For small children, there are pony rides, a miniature train ride and a merry-go-round.

It is one of the few parks in the heart of a major city where youngsters camp out in a wilderness setting, living in cabins tucked into sharply rising canyon walls. And, Los Angeles is one of the few cities with a natural wildlife area in its backyard. Deer, quail and many forms of wild life roam in rugged mountain terrain surrounded on all sides by busy metropolitan areas.

The park is also noted for its statuary, including the 40-foot-high "Astronomers' Monument" by the Observatory. This mammoth work of art, a Works Project Administration creation, unveiled Nov. 18, 1934, features statues of the world's six greatest astronomers—Copernicus, Newton, Galileo, Hipparchus, Kepler and Herschel. President Franklin D. Roosevelt unveiled the famed "Civilian Conservation Worker" statue created by unemployed sculptors during the Great Depression.

To this day, Griffith Park fulfills the fondest wish of Griffith J. Griffith, who gave it to the city to "be made a place of recreation and rest for the masses."

WHAT IS L.A.'S HIGHEST POINT?

I N 1961 on trying to learn the highest point in the city of Los Angeles for a story, I discovered conflicting information: Checking map books, encyclopedias, gazetteers, and calling City Hall, I found a ready answer at each source, but a different one each time. Some said Verdugo Mountain, elevation 2,811 feet, others another mountain top 3,275 feet high. There were sources that reported a 4,150 foot peak. Some said Mt. Wilson, which isn't even in the city.

Alfred H. Boysen, senior survey supervisor in the city's bureau of engineering and others on his staff searched maps and records. The County Engineering Department and U.S. Forest Service were consulted. After an exhaustive study to be certain of accuracy, a definite point was finally named as the highest spot in the city of Los Angeles, Sister Elsie Peak, elevation 5,082 feet. The Peak, named after a Catholic nun, lies within both the city limits and Angeles National Forest.

Bill Dresser, assistant supervisor of Angeles National Forest at the time became interested in the project, and had an appropriate sign made. On June 4, 1961, Dresser, Boysen, Los Angeles Times photographer John Malmin and I hiked up Mt. Lukens Fire Road and the old Sister Elsie Trail to the top of the mountain, where Dresser's large wooden marker was cemented into the ground. It reads:

SISTER ELSIE PEAK—ELEVATON 5082 FEET
HIGHEST POINT IN THE CITY OF LOS ANGELES
THIS PEAK IS A PART OF MT. LUKENS.

Johnny Malmin shot a picture of Bill Dresser holding the shovel he used to plant the sign and Al Boysen and myself standing next to the sign for the story. Ever since, map books, encyclopedias, gazetteers, and official records of the city duly note that Sister Elsie Peak is the highest point in Los Angeles.

PACK TRAIN IN THE CITY

A TEEMING CITY. Fifteen million people living in its metropolitan area. A network of freeways jammed with vehicles day and night. Yet, 20 miles from the Los Angeles City Hall, bears, deer, bob cats and mountain lions run wild. And what is believed to be the only daily pack train operated year round in America carries food and supplies to isolated cabins in Angeles National Forest.

It was a typical day in the fall of 1996 for packer Dennis Lonergan as he led a string of animals on his horse slowly through the Big Santa Anita Canyon, as packers have been doing along the trail ever since 1893. Hugging the sides of the steep cliffs, the sure-footed burros, mules and donkeys were carrying 1,000 pounds of food and supplies. No roads lead into the canyon, so these carefully loaded beasts, the latest edition of the century-old pack train, are still the lifeline to the outside world for 81 remote cabins and a church camp above Arcadia.

None of the modest, stone-and-wood cabins have electricity or indoor plumbing. Cabin owners use kerosene lanterns for lights, propane or wood for cooking. They fetch water from nearby springs or have five gallon jugs packed in.

This trip was to Camp Sturtevant, deep in the woods, 4½ miles from the trail head and a climb of 1,500 feet. The eight pack animals were carrying provisions for a youth group that hiked into the church camp ahead of the pack train.

"What cabin owners can't or don't want to carry in on their backs we bring in on the animals," explained Dennis Lonergan, 40, operator of the pack train since 1984 with his wife, Jody. "Last month we carried a piano to one cabin," he recalled. Lonergan looked the part. He had a wad of chewing tobacco wedged in his mouth as he led the string of animals. He is six-feet tall, sprouts a wild mustache and mutton-chop sideburns. His wife, astride her horse, Dakota, is 5-foot-9, brown-haired and blue-eyed. Dennis' uncle, Bill Adams, owned and operated the pack train for 40 years until he sold it to the couple in 1984.

It was a vastly different world from the city below. The trail meandered beside Big Santa Anita Creek, traversing a dense forest of oak, pine and spruce. Squirrels and lizards skittered in front of the pack train. Fresh coyote, fox , bear and deer tracks etched the path. The soothing sounds of the rushing creek filled the air, growing increasingly louder as the trail neared the 75-foot drop of Sturtevant Falls. Only 3½ miles down the mountain from the trail head the air was rent with the loud cacophony of thousands of cars and trucks speeding along Foothill Freeway in the hectic rush of daily life in the city.

"I have had horses all my life. Denny has been leading pack trains up this canyon with his uncle ever since he was 12. We love every minute we're in here," said Jody Lonergan as the animals gingerly made their way around the bend of a cliff where the trail hung precariously over a nearly straight drop.

"Take it easy, Moonbeam! Watch it, Sugarfoot!" Dennis shouted to the pack animals. The shoulder of the trail gave way at this point a couple months ago and a donkey named Mac rolled 100 feet down the cliff. "It really shook Mac up, but luckily he was carrying a load of sleeping bags and was well padded. I went down and got him, cut a scratch trail up the cliff and we were on our way again with Mac bruised and battered but able to make it," the packer recalled. "A donkey carries a maximum load of 125 pounds, a mule can take 300 pounds," Jody noted.

Cabin owners and operators of Camp Sturtevant let the Lonergans know when they will need food and supplies, and since there are no phones in the canyon, they will often alert the packers when they pass by that they will soon be needing help. The cabins, built between 1910 and 1930 on land leased from the federal government, are owned by a mix of people—firemen, policemen, doctors, teachers, lawyers and retirees. Once there were more than 300 recreational cabins in the canyon, but floods and fires destroyed all but the 81 still standing. No leases for new cabins have been issued by the Forest Service in over 60 years.

Twins Pat Chasteen and Muriel Carlson bought their cabin for $65 in a sealed bid in 1930 when they were 21. "My sister and I still like to spend a few days at our cabin every month," said Pat Chasteen. "We couldn't exist without that pack train," insisted Chasteen. "Why earlier this summer we had to pack in the roofing to renew our roof. We love to see the pack animals moving through the canyon."

Sometimes the packers will make two or three trips in and out of the canyon in one day with their string of animals. Other times they will make only three or four trips a week. It all depends upon demand. "You never know," Dennis Lonergan said. "We may make one trip taking care of the needs of four cabin owners, or we may make 50 trips to one cabin bringing in building materials for an addition."

The packers charge 25 cents a pound for freight. The nearest cabin is less than a mile from the trail head. Camp Sturtevant, $4^{1}/_{2}$ miles in, is at the end of the line. A typical round trip all the way to Camp Sturtevant takes about 5 hours, two hours in, two hours out and an hour to unload and rest the animals.

The Lonergans run the pack train, operate a small refreshment stand at the trail head and have a contract with the U.S. Forest Service to maintain camp grounds and picnic facilities in Big Santa Anita Canyon. Their home is at the pack station at Chantry Flat. Bill Adams and his wife, Lila, fill in for them and operate the pack train on rare occasions when the Lonergans take time off. "We're not getting rich," Jody said, "but we would rather be happy than rich. We plan to run the pack train until we're old enough to retire."

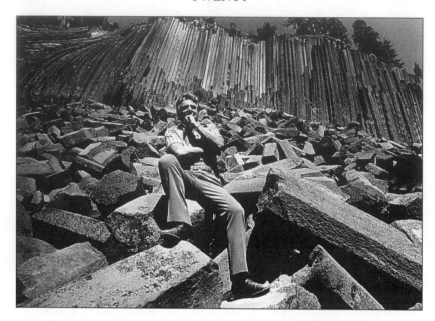

TWENTY

MADERA COUNTY

THE EXACT CENTER OF THE STATE

W**HERE'S THE GEOGRAPHIC CENTER OF CALIFORNIA?** City fathers in Madera, seat of Madera County, deposited a four-ton, six foot high, four-foot wide, white granite rock in Courthouse Park in the heart of downtown Madera. On May 18, 1968 a huge ceremony was held with the unveiling of a plaque on the giant rock that proclaimed Madera to be the geographic center of California. City, county and state officials spoke at the dedication. The Thomas Jefferson Junior High School band played.

"This makes it official. This spot is the geographic center of California," declared Richard M. Shearer, manager of the Security Title Insurance Company's Madera branch, donors of the plaque. "And nobody's going to steal this monument and haul it off to the hills," chimed in Ralph Baraldi, chairman of the county's diamond jubilee then in progress. "We're anchoring it into a concrete foundation. The point is, everybody agrees the geographic center is somewhere in Madera County. Since the city of Madera is the center of activities in this county we feel this is the proper place for this monument."

There was an uproar about the monument's location by people in a dozen Madera County mountain hamlets. "They're putting it in the wrong place," insisted Darlene Murray, who with her husband, Larry, operated a gas station and garage in North Fork. "California's true geographic center is within spittin' distance of North Fork, and we're 43 miles up the hill from Madera."

Dedication of the monument and plaque in the downtown Madera park was protested by Indians, miners, lumberjacks, U.S. Forestry officials, and hundreds of other mountain folk in eastern Madera County. The people of North Fork were particularly incensed about placing the monument and plaque in Madera. Residents of Nippin-nawassee, Sugar Pine, Ahwahnee, Grub Gulch, Oakhurst, Bass Lake, Wishon, Coarse Gold, Fine Gold and O'Neals were equally upset. They weren't sure exactly where the state's geographic center was located, but they were certain it sure wasn't in the county seat.

In 1997, the four-ton white granite monument was still in Court-house Park. Nobody had hauled it off into the mountains. But the "Center of California" plaque had been missing from the rock for years. "Vandals removed the plaque," said a spokeswoman for the Madera County Historical Society.

The location of the geographic center of California has been an historically controversial issue ever since 1930 when the U.S. Coast and Geodetic Survey marked the spot in the hills east of Madera. When the monument was dedicated in Courthouse Park, Rosalie Bethel, a Mono Indian, recalled: "My father and his father before him always said we lived in the geographic center of the state." She said when she was a little girl her father often pointed out three rocks along the road from North Fork to O'Neals and told her that was the exact place.

Nothing much happened about the controversy until 1994 when the North Fork History Group decided it was high time to clear up the matter once and for all. Phil Ellis, a retired Madera County deputy sheriff who runs a sawmill in North Fork, contacted Fresno State University's engineering department for help. Leonard Gabrielson took on the project as the subject of his thesis for graduation, and in the summer of 1995 found the old U.S. Coast and Geodetic Survey markers and pinpointed the exact geographic center of California—It is 100 feet up a steep hill from Italian Bar Road 4.7 miles north of North Fork.

"This is very exciting for our little town. Our North Fork History Group has had special 'North Fork, Exact Center of California' license plates made. We have asked county and state officials for money to erect an appropriate monument," said Ellis.

DEVILS POSTPILE

I F MINING COMPANIES HAD THEIR WAY, Devils Postpile National Monument in Madera County, a freak of nature, would have been blown apart years ago. But Devils Postpile is still here—one of California's lesser known natural phenomena.

In 1911 several mining companies decided to blast apart hundreds of the strange towering lava pillars to form a rock-filled dam in the nearby middle fork of the San Joaquin River. President William Howard Taft told the mining companies to forget it. To prevent the lava columns from being destroyed for material to build the dam, Taft, on July 6, 1911, set aside Devils Postpile as a national monument.

Ever since, people have been hiking into this 7,600-foot-high wilderness in the High Sierra, 15 miles west of Mammoth Lakes, the last five miles of which is a rough unpaved road, to stand in awe at the remarkable columns created by fire and etched by ice, formed nearly a million years ago during a volcanic eruption that spewed lava into the area— lava that cooled into the vertical 60-foot columns, averaging 2 to 3½ feet in diameter. Only Giant's Causeway in Ireland and Fingal's Cave in Scotland have similar multisided lava columns of this magnitude.

After the columns were formed, a glacier from the north moved through the area, polishing and scouring the tops of the rock columns, to form a plateau resembling a giant floor of polygonal and hexagonal tiles—their shining surfaces polished by fine silt during the ice age. At the foot of the columns is a huge debris pile, containing shattered sections of hundreds of pillars that fell through the centuries.

"A column will topple and break into pieces on extremely rare occasions," explained Wymond Eckhardt, chief ranger at Devils Postpile for many years. Old photos show only a handful of pillars have fallen during the last century--one being pushed over some years ago by a group of young men, an act that can draw a heavy fine.

Eckhardt, a professor at California State University, Fresno, when not a National Park Service ranger in summers at Devils Postpile, said two percent of the lava posts are 4 sided, 37% are 5 sided, 55% are 6 sided and 5% are 7 sided. Some are round and only a few have three sides. Outcroppings of the pillars on the plateau extend for a mile back from the cliffs of lava columns. When miners first discovered the odd formation 100 years ago, they called it the Devils Woodpile. It is one of more than 150 places in California carrying the Devil's name, including Devil's Kitchen in Lassen National Park and Devils Punchbowl in Los Angeles County.

It is a favorite area for field trips by college geology classes. On one such trip, 13 students from Saddleback College in Mission Viejo, led by Professor John Minch, visited Devils Postpile. "We're visiting nine national parks and monuments in the West to study geological formations," explained Minch. "We came here because this is the classic example of cooling lava forming into vertical columns."

Ranger Eckhardt stood on the huge talus pile of broken posts, relating the history of Devils Postpile to the Mission Viejo students. "If President Taft had not created this national monument and spared these strange soaring pillars, we would never have been able to stand on this spot." related the ranger. "It would have been under the waters of Devils Postpile Lake."

TWENTY-ONE

MARIN COUNTY

ANGEL ISLAND: BEAUTIFUL PARK IN THE BAY

T HERE ARE NO CARS ON ANGEL ISLAND, just across from San Francisco, only foot and bike trails. The island, a tranquil treasure near the mouth of San Francisco Bay is one of the most historic spots in the West: Indians lived here for centuries before the coming of the Spaniards. Russians hunted sea otters on the island at the turn of the 19th century. In 1850, the 640-acre island became a military fortress. One of the first Army groups based here was the famed all-Black regiment, the 48th Volunteers.

During the Civil War in 1863, Fort McDowell was erected on the west end. The Civil War military installation is still here—the old parade grounds, moss-covered barracks, hospital and headquarters building. In later years it was renamed Camp Reynolds. It's a ghost fort now.

For years Angel Island was the Ellis Island of the West, the first place immigrants from the Orient stayed upon landing in the United States. A huge Army hospital was constructed on the north end of the island in 1910, later housing, among others, men who had contacted malaria while building the Panama Canal. It was subsequently an important Army base during World War I, and served as a staging area during the war for overseas replacements.

Prisoners of war were held here during both world wars. The first Japanese prisoner of war in 1941, captured at Pearl Harbor in a one-man submarine, was among prisoners on Angel Island during World War II. Visitors from Japan still come to Angel Island to see where Japanese prisoners were held during the war.

One section of the island is known as Alcatraz Gardens. For years convicts serving time on Alcatraz were brought by boat to Angel Island to grow vegetables for fellow prisoners on "the rock."

At one time, the island was seriously considered as the site for the United Nations headquarters. But since 1963, Angel Island has been a California state park, its 640 acres contained within five miles around, with its highest point 776 feet. Now, upwards of 200,000 men, women and children a year come to the island to picnic, to hike, bike and to visit the many historic sites.

Groups of 5th and 6th graders camp out overnight on the island as part of environmental living programs. Reenactment organizations portray historical events that occurred on Angel Island. All come by private boat or by ferry from Tiburon, a 10-minute ride, or from San Francisco, three miles and 45 minutes away.

Angel Island is covered with towering pines and eucalyptus, with wild flowers and shrubs, criss-crossed with hiking and cycling trails. It's a quiet island disturbed only by the sounds of bell buoys and foghorns, of seals at play on surrounding rocks, of thousands of seagulls, cormorants and brown pelicans. Its turbulent past now a peaceful sanctuary.

ELLIS ISLAND OF THE WEST

P AUL CHOW made his way slowly along the narrow path leading through dense brush and thick woods on Angel Island until finally he came to an old, wooden two-story barracks. "This is our Plymouth Rock," he declared. "This is where it all began for thousands of Chinese-Americans." The tiny island was the Ellis Island of the West Coast for immigrants who passed through here from 1909, when the barracks were erected, until 1940.

Chow unlocked a gate in the high fence surrounding the weather-beaten barracks. He opened two locks on the main entrance door. For Chinese-Americans, this old building represents one of the most significant chapters of their history. Chow, who conducts tours through the barracks in English and Chinese as a State Park volunteer, walked down a dark, dank hallway shining his flashlight ahead, then turned a corner into a huge room filled with iron poles that once held three tiers of bunks.

The walls are covered with Chinese calligraphy--writings and poems scrawled and carved by immigrants who waited days, weeks, months and sometimes as long as one, two or three years before being accepted into America or being deported back to China. There are poignant expressions of hope, anger, despair:

"My fellow countrymen are rejoicing with me as I say good-bye to this house."

"I will not be yielding. If I ever get out of this place I shall return and burn it to the ground."

"I am lonely and want to go home."

The barracks were not pleasant for the immigrants. Men stayed in one section, women in another, 24 hours a day, never leaving the one room where their bunks were until their case was cleared. In the women's section, where sometimes as many as 500 were housed, there still stand the one shower and a dozen toilets side by side with no partitions. "The women called using the toilet 'paper bag solitude,'" Chow noted. "They called it that because, being modest, they would put paper bags over their heads when they used the commodes."

There were suicides, especially of women, who, on learning they were to be deported, would hang themselves from the shower stall rather than return to China. "To get here they borrowed, begged and sometimes stole enough money for their passage. Men on being deported would work their way back to China on ships as cooks or stewards," said Chow. "The only way women could work their way back in most instances was to serve as prostitutes for the crew. Knowing this, some women chose to take their own lives on hearing the bad news."

Thousands of Japanese were processed through the immigration station as well. But the Japanese came better prepared, with their papers checked by American immigration personnel stationed in Japan through a treaty with the Japanese government. Filipinos, Koreans and other Asians also passed through Angel Island but they too, for the most part, were not detained in the immigration barracks as were the Chinese. The Chinese government had no treaty with the United States on immigration procedure. It was a haphazard system at best.

The second floor of the barracks served from the outset as a federal prison. During World War II, Japanese, German and Italian prisoners of war were housed here. Among the Japanese writings on the second floor walls is one message that declares, in translation: Down with America. *Down with Britain. Our Imperial Navy will soon land on these shores!*

After World War II, the U.S. government changed its policy on Chinese immigrants and the barracks were no longer used. A master plan for developing Angel Island State Park in 1974 called for razing the barracks and turning the 14-acre site at China Cove into campsites. That was when Chow, a highway engineer for the California Department of Transportation, and nine other residents of San Francisco's Chinatown formed the Angel Island Immigration Station Historical Advisory Committee. The committee went to work to save and restore the barracks. It filed a report with the Legislature recommending Angel Island Immigration Station "be enshrined as a national monument to commemorate Asian immigration to America in the same way Ellis Island has been set aside to commemorate European immigration to this nation." A bill allocating $250,000 of state park funds toward the restoration of the building as a historical landmark and museum was passed by the Legislature and signed by the governor in August, 1976.

When the Chinatown Committee was formed, state park rangers on the island suggested someone from the committee give tours of the barracks. Chow, whose father spent four weeks in the barracks in the 1920s, his mother four months in 1940, volunteered to be a guide on weekends without pay early in 1975. By 1995, some 20 years later, he was still conducting tours of the barracks.

"Many elderly men and women, who started their lives in America here, take a sentimental journey on the ferryboats to the island," said Chow. "It isn't easy for them. They have to walk a mile up one steep hill and down another and another mile back to the boat. But they insist it is worth it. Angel Island has great emotional feeling for tens of thousands of Chinese-Americans," he mused.

LONG-TERM RELATIONSHIP, WITH A SEA ANEMONE

FOR 33 YEARS marine biologist Gordon L. Chan had been observing and feeding an individual sea anemone, named Tony, in a tidepool at Bolinas. "I believe it is the longest observed single organism off the Pacific Coast," said Chan. "For me it has been a fascinating friendship. I wade out into the water and visit Tony at least once a month and always bring him a mussel or two to eat. I stick my hand into the anemone's mouth between its array of tentacles and feed him. He eats the mussel and burps up its shell after a period of time. When the tide is low, I crouch down in the shallow water and feed Tony. He quivers. Maybe he knows me," mused the scientist.

Chan noted that every time he went to the tidepool the sea anemone was in the same spot. "Nobody knows how long sea anemones live," he continued. Tony the anemone lived in Duxbury Reef Reserve, 20 miles north of San Francisco.

It was through Chan's effors that Duxbury, one of the largest intertidal reefs on the Pacific Coast, was set aside by the California Legislature as a reserve. Duxbury, three miles long and jutting a half mile out to sea, was named after a ship that sunk in the shallow waters there in 1849. It is one of three such reef reserves in the state, and all marine life in the reefs is protected by state law.

Chan, professor of marine biology at the College of Marin in Kentfield, had been studying and writing about the rich marine life in Duxbury Reef since 1949. Two of his former students, who went on to become prominent marine biologists themselves, discovered a species of sea slug in the reef never previously recorded. In a scientific paper describing and naming the new species, an inch long, lemon-yellow sea slug with eight maroon spots, Terrence Gosliner and Gary Williams wrote: "We name this species *Hallaxa chani* in honor of Dr. Gordon L. Chan, for initially inspiring our interest in marine biology, for his continued enthusiasm in marine science education, and for his efforts in establishing Duxbury Reef as a marine reserve."

Chan, a Chinese-American born in Seattle, was a halfback on the Stanford football teams from 1948 to 1951. He earned his BA and MA at Stanford and his Ph.D at University of California at Berkeley. He is the author of numerous scientific papers about marine life in the Pacific. He is also noted for his publications on oil spill data along the Marin County coast. In 1971 a Standard Oil tanker spilled 800,000 gallons under the Golden Gate Bridge. The fuel moved along the Marin coastline wiping out whole populations of marine organisms on Duxbury Reef. But the reef made a remarkable recovery and within four years re-established itself without losing any species. None that they know of, that is.

Gordon Chan operates the College of Marin marine lab at Bolinas. He is often seen wading in the shallow waters of the reef with school children, who come to view and learn about the myriad sealife in the tidal zone. Of all the amazing creatures in the sea that Chan has come to know, however, his all-time favorite is Tony, his friend of 33 years.

TWENTY-TWO

MARIPOSA COUNTY

CHRISTMAS IN YOSEMITE

C HRISTMAS in the majestic splendor of Yosemite has been a California tradition for more than a century. Awaiting the thousands who make the trek from all corners of the state is a dazzling winter wonderland—towering peaks, granite spires and domes, and lofty alpine meadows crowned with deep snow.

Throughout Christmas week in the mile-deep, seven-mile-long, mile-wide Yosemite Valley—the heart of the national park—villagers march along footpaths after dark singing Christmas carols. In the evenings, skaters at the huge outdoor rink with Half Dome as a backdrop, warm themselves around log fires, roasting marshmallows and hot dogs. On Christmas Eve, many attend nondenominational services at the church in the valley.

Hundreds of cross-country skiers spend Christmas Day in the

snowy wilderness of Yosemite, some on a day's outing, others in the pristine back country for a week, two weeks, even a month or more. The sparkling, snow-covered slopes at 8,000-foot high Badger Pass are filled with joyous holiday downhill skiers.

Even Santa spends Christmas skiing the steep slopes of the Pass, stopping now and then to pass out candy canes and gifts to young-sters on skis pausing during or after downhill runs. Nic Fiore, 74, has been Yosemite's skiing Santa Claus at Badger Pass every Christmas Day since 1947.

Yosemite was set aside as a state park in 1864 and as a national park in 1890. Badger Pass is California's oldest established downhill ski area and the Yosemite Ski School, dating back to 1928, is the old-est ski school in the West. Each morning and each afternoon Nic Fiore rings the big bell at the bottom of the Badger Pass ski runs sum-moning his students to class. Fiore has directed the ski school since 1947. His colleagues say he has introduced more people to skiing than any other instructor in the West—more than 100,000 men, women and children.

High point of the holiday in the park for 1,650 lucky visitors is the reenactment of an 18th-Century English baronial Christmas feast lift-ed from the pages of Washington Irving's "Sketchbook." So many want to attend that a lottery determines who goes. Each year since 1927, in the candlelit medieval-like setting of the great dining hall of the Ahwahnee Hotel, the Bracebridge Christmas Dinner has sprung to life from the pages of Irving's story.

Trumpets sound the guests to the five settings of Squire Brace-bridge's three-hour feasts of food, music and pageantry over a three-day period in the famed mountain inn. Diners come dressed in tuxedos and gorgeous gowns. The 125 actors, singers and musicians wear Tudor costumes. Carols and ancient ballads are sung throughout the hearty feasts. Narration is all in rhyme. Jesters cavort. Minstrels strum and sing. A great fish, a peacock pie, a boar's head, a baron of beef—knighted Sir Loin by the squire—and a flaming wassail bowl and huge plum pudding are borne through the dining room on litters.

While many families stay at the Ahwahnee, Yosemite Lodge and Curry Village, others camp out in tents on the valley floor and in snow houses and snow caves at higher elevations. In the white wilderness near Glacier Point, Herb Davis spent two hours the day before Christmas constructing a snow house in which to spend the night. He shoveled snow, stacking it 6 feet high and compacting it by jumping on the snowpile in his snowshoes. Then he hollowed out the inside. "Snow houses are warmer than tents," he explained.

At least 500 cross-country skiers spend the Christmas holidays skiing through the upper reaches of the 1,200-square-mile national park, ranging in elevation from 2,000 feet to more than 13,000 feet. "Some of the skiers stash food caches in metal cans in trees as long ago as the previous summer preparing for their long-distance tours," explained Lloyd Price, director of cross-country skiing in Yosemite. Long-distance, cross-country skiers often will cover upwards of 250 miles on a month-long trip. Many sleep in snow houses and snow caves they construct as they move from place to place.

Park rangers lead two-hour snowshoe treks daily and five-hour cross-country ski tours on weekends from Badger Pass through the back country. The park has 90 miles of marked ski trails and a two-story stone hut at Lake Ostrander where 25 cross-country skiers can be accommodated overnight.

Eerie, gun-metal gray clouds lend added grandeur to Half Dome, El Capitan, Glacier Point. Towering Yosemite Falls, nine times as high as Niagara, and other giant waterfalls spill into and through clouds hovering low over the valley. Everywhere, the vistas are breathtaking, the trees heavily laden with snow, the snowy mountains and meadows mirroring Christmas scenes. Each year Christmas adds another page to a cherished California tradition dating back to the late 1880s.

EVERYTHING'S OLD TIME IN MARIPOSA

"EVERYTHING'S OLD TIME IN THIS COUNTY," Kay Olsen mused, "and we kinda like it that way. Oldest courthouse still in use west of the Mississippi. One of the oldest continuously published weekly newspaper in the West...." Kay noted the claims of antiquity while standing on the Mariposa County Courthouse lawn holding Vol. 1, No. 1, of the Mariposa Chronicle, dated January 20, 1854, the same year the courthouse was completed.

Mariposa County, population 16,400, is a slow-paced Mother Lode county in the foothills of the Sierra Nevada just east of Merced and spreading into Yosemite National Park. When California achieved statehood in 1850, Mariposa was the largest of the state's original 27 counties. It extended as far south as present-day Los Angeles County, occupying one-fifth of the entire state. The county when first created was an awesome 30,000 square miles. Over the years it has shrunk to a mere 1,455 square miles. What was Mariposa in the beginning is now all or part of 11 other counties, earning it the nickname of Mother of California Counties.

The Chronicle changed its name to the Mariposa Gazette in 1855 and has been the Gazette ever since. Mrs. Olsen's mother and father, Kate and John Dexter, published the paper from 1918 until their deaths in 1947. Since then the weekly has been published by Kay and her sister Marguerite Campbell, and in recent years by Marguerite's son and daughter-in-law, Dalmar and Ruth Campbell. "In Mariposa County Everybody Reads the Gazette," proclaims the Gazette's masthead. And they do.

On election nights residents and candidates from all over the county gather outside the Gazette office in a tradition going back to 1854, the year the paper was first published, to read election results posted on the front door. "We don't have radio or television stations up here in the boondocks," explained Kay Olsen. "We get the results and post them as each precinct reports."

The old County Courthouse underwent major renovation in 1988. "Nothing was changed," emphasized county historian Scott Pinkerton, who headed a local committee to make certain that the historic integrity of the building remained intact. Because of the courthouse's historic significance, two grants were awarded by the State Department of Parks and Recreation and another by the county for the restoration.

The original rock foundation was shored up with cement to ensure continuing stability of the old structure. Torn wallpaper hung in 1912 was replaced with wallpaper of similar design. Studs and framing in the building are still held together with wooden pegs, not nails. The original clapboard on the outside and siding on the inside are fastened with square nails. The building was repainted inside and out in its original colors. The potbellied stove, the Seth Thomas clock, the 1854 court benches, the original furniture and furnishings in the Board of Supervisors' room, the county clerk's office and the law library were all refinished in 1988. A small museum in the courthouse includes an exhibit of early Mariposa County cattle brands.

"With only a handful of people, compared to nearly all other counties in the state, and no incorporated cities, Mariposa and its courthouse are tied very much to the past," observed long time County Supervisor Eugene Dalton. "We know practically everyone by first name. People call us at home if they have a problem. Everything here is so informal."

TWENTY-THREE

MENDOCINO COUNTY

BOONTLING SPOKEN HERE

A KNOT OF PEOPLE in Boonville, a Mendocino County hamlet, were "cuttin' buckeye and harpin' a slib of boontling" in front of Anderson's General Store. Karen Ottoboni, who "ottoins" at the "Bahl Gorms" down the street, greeted the Boonters and ducked into the "Buckey Walter" to ring her "nook." It may sound like Greek to you but actually it is a bit of Boontling, the century-old language of Boonville, a town of about 1,000, surrounded by apple orchards and sheep ranches in a long, narrow valley 125 miles northwest of San Francisco.

"Cuttin' buckeye" means taking it easy in Boontling. "Harping a slib" means idle chatter. "Ottoins" means working. "Bahl Gorms" is the name of a drive-in and means good food. Boonters are people who live in Boonville. A "Buckey Walter" is a pay phone and a "nook" is home.

In a cookbook entitled "Bahl Gorms in Boont," Boonter Edna Sanders explained in the foreword, written in boontling: "Boontling originated in the 1880s around a huge jeffer at mowkeef time, at hobs, at boshin' tidricks, at sharshin' matches, at the Anytime Saloon and wherever kimmies tidricked." Translated, that means: Boontling originated in the 1880s around a big fire at hay-making time, at dances, at deer hunts, at sheep-shearing sessions, at the Anytime Saloon and wherever people gathered.

Edna's cookbook is written in both Boontling and English. There's a glossary to help the uninitiated. Easter means egg. Dumplin' dust is flour. Doolsey is sugar. Zeese is coffee. Boarp is pork. Boo is potatoes. French boos are French friend potatoes.

Mrs. Sanders was a Boonville school teacher. For years she taught Boontling to third graders, taught Boontling in the local high school and also taught college courses on the subject. "My idea in teaching Boontling to third graders was it helped them better understand the strange second language of their parents, helped motivate them and applied the use of phonetics," explained the teacher known far and wide by her Boontling name "Schoolch." All Boonters have Boontling nicknames.

A teacher in nearby Ukiah, over the Drearies (the local bald mountains) and 20 miles northeast of Boonville, wrote her master's thesis several years ago comparing the general progress of third graders in Ukiah with that of third graders in Boonville. "The results showed that children in my class were not handicapped in any way by being bilingual in the local lingo," insisted Schoolch during an interview with the author. "On the contrary, they did much better in all their classes, including English."

According to Jack "Wee Fuz" June, forester, apple orchard owner, and lifelong Boonter: "Boontling has all the forms, background, everything of a regular language. It was the secret language of this small town originated by local men while shearing their sheep and harvesting hops. At first it was a way of talking without the kids standing around understanding what was being said. Women picked up on it and so did the kids in time. It proved to be handy to talk around strangers. When the Boonters would go shopping in Ukiah or

San Francisco, nobody had the slightest idea of what they were saying. There was always someone around who could understand German, Spanish, French or Italian but no one could ever harp Boontling unless they were from here. The language caught on and just grew and grew."

Edna Sanders was very important in keeping the small town language alive among the young people of Boonville during the 1940s, 50s, 60s and until she retired from teaching in 1971. She died at the age of 81 in 1992. "Schoolch is sorely missed in these parts. Her classes in Bootling were sanctioned by the State of California and praised by school officials as a great reading aid. The children loved it," recalled Bobby (Chipmunk) Glover, lifelong Boonter.

Glover, a water developer, inherited his Boontling nickname from his grandfather. He was one of perhaps less than 100 fluent in Boontling by the late 1990s. "Boontling was universally spoken and understood not only in Boonville but in the other small towns of Anderson Valley from the turn of the century through the 1930s," noted Glover. "But I'm sorry to say now it's being kept alive only by old-timers like myself who harp a slib whenever we get together."

A scholarly book, *Boontling, An American Lingo,* written by Charles C. Adams, professor of English at California State University, Chico, was published by the University of Texas Press. It traces the history and development of the language and includes a dictionary of 1,000 Boontling words and expressions.

For years Homer Mannix, publisher, editor, chief reporter, and sole photographer of the *Anderson Valley Advertiser,* the local weekly newspaper, published stories, columns, and letters from readers written in Boontling. Mannix was known as the Boonville Greeley. A greeley (from Horace Greeley) is Boontling for newsman. When the first astronauts landed on the moon in 1969, Mannix duly noted in a banner: "Kimmey Puts Cloudies on Green Tedessel." Boonters all knew that meant man had set foot on the moon.

Mannix's paper had about 1,000 subscribers living in Boont (Boonville) and the other nearby towns in the Land of the Boontling, including Poleeko (Philo), Belk (Bell Valley), Land of the Maypoles (Peachwood), Deep End (Navarro) and High Rollers Region

(Yorkville). Yorkville is the high country of the valley. Navarro is at the deep end. The Boonville Greeley was not only publisher of the local gazette, he was also Boonville's judge for seven years, same time as he published the paper, as well as the valley's long-time fire chief.

There are words in Boontling for many things. Heese is a high school and wee heese is an elementary school. A preacher is a skipe (sky pilot), the ocean is the briney and a lighthouse is a briney glimmer. And on and on and on. The first word in Professor Adams' Boontling dictionary is ab, meaning to crowd into a line. The last word is zeese, which you've learned means coffee. A high heeler is a judge, a shoveltooth is a doctor.

Many of the words come from the names of people who have lived in the valley and had peculiar characteristics. Bill Nunn, for example, always used a lot of syrup on food, so syrup in Bootling is Bill Nunn. A onetime judge had one leg shorter than the other and wore one shoe built up; thus the term high heeler for judge. An early day doctor had protruding teeth. All the doctors since have been called a shoveltooth.

"I've been harpin' Boontling ever since I was a wee tweed (little kid)," said Bobby Glover who was 74 in 1995. "I grew up with it, used it all my life and will continue to speak it as my second language until the day I die."

MENDOCINO MUSHROOMING

THE CHARTER BUS slowly wound its way on Highway 1 along the rugged Northern California coast in Mendocino County filled with adventurers on a weekend expedition to a rain forest. As the bus maneuvered around tight curves on steep seacliffs and across high bridges over estuaries, inlets and bays, the expedition leader, Dr. Robert T. Orr, an internationally known mycologist (mushroom expert), enchanted the passengers with fascinating tales about mushrooms and fungi.

Orr spoke of the many deadly species of wild mushrooms. "Graveyards are full of people who believed old wives' tales about the silver spoon turning black and other fables," cautioned the mycologist. He noted that there are at least 70,000 species of fungi on earth, with at least 15,000 of them mushrooms.

There were 30 aboard the bus destined for a never-to-be-forgotten foray of "Mendocino Mushrooming." They left San Francisco a little after noon on a Friday to drive the 200 miles north to prime mushroom-hunting grounds in coastal rain forests of Mendocino County. Those aboard included a university professor, a data processor, a grade school teacher, a school administrator, a fireman, a podiatrist, an orthodontist, a dentist, a housewife, several retired couples, a chemist, a student, a naval architect, an artist, a retired airline pilot, a telephone technician, and this writer—all strangers brought together by a fascination for mushrooms.

There were newlyweds Libby, 76, and Holbrook Working, 83, a Stanford economist the past 53 years. "I came because my wife wanted to go," explained Working. "I've been gathering mushrooms ever since I was 11 on a rainy day in Maine when my mother said, 'For goodness sake, Libby, why don't you go out into the woods and collect mushrooms,'" laughed Mrs. Working, who added mischievously, "I'm really an old witch who likes mushrooms, toads and snakes."

For San Francisco artist Norma Novy, "Mendocino Mushrooming," meant going "houby" hunting. "Houby is a Czech word for mushrooms," she explained. "Mushrooms are a big thing for Bohemians. All my old relatives had secret spots in the woods where they collected their wild mushrooms. I've come along to find my secret place for houby hunting...."

Dr. Orr, one of the world's foremost mushroom experts, was leading one of his annual mushrooming expeditions. He has hunted mushrooms all over the earth, including Asia, Africa, Europe, North and South America, Australia, the Gobi Desert and the Galapagos Islands. He wrote two of the most popular textbooks on California mushrooms and is author of the University of California Press *Guide to the Fungi of Western North America.*

The "Mendocino Mushroomers" overnighted at the charming Little River Inn on Friday and Saturday nights. Rising at dawn Saturday and Sunday, dressed in several layers of clothes, knitted caps and boots, the intrepid group entered the dank, dark, dense coastal forest of Van Damme State Park and nearby environs—some of the richest mushroom grounds in the state. They remained in these forests collecting mushrooms both days, stopping only to feast on boxed lunches and local wine.

Some were novices knowing little or nothing about mushrooms. Others, like Orr and the mycologist's wife, Margaret, have tramped the world in pursuit of the intriguing, tiny umbrella-like fleshy fungi. Orr noted that there is no rule of thumb for distinguishing edible and poisonous wild mushrooms. "It is a matter of learning to identify each species and getting to know those that are good to eat and those that have horrible flavors and those that would make you very sick or even kill you." We were here to see and learn about the amazing variety of mushrooms in the forest and to take home and prepare the edible mushrooms for later gourmet's delights.

The first mushrooms were gathered moments after the hardy group of ground-watchers left the bus Saturday morning and ventured up a narrow trail through a spectacular fern canyon. "Keep looking down," Orr told the group. "At first you won't see them for all the dense foliage and leaves, but they'll begin to jump out at you." And, sure enough, the forest sprang alive with mushrooms, fungi and lichens of all colors, shapes, sizes and descriptions at the foot of trees, on fallen logs, stumps and snags and scattered in clumps here, there and everywhere on the floor of the woods. Orr bent over and scooped up a medium-sized mushroom, smelled and declared, "Aha, a Coprinus comatus or shaggy mane." Then he plucked another, an oak-loving mushroom at the foot of an oak tree.

The "Mendocino Mushroomers" scattered to gather and to rush back to the knowledgeable mycologist to show their finds and learn their identification: There were surrey-with-the-fringe-on-top mushrooms, puffballs, bird's nests, artist's conks, orange peels, pig's ear, fly and meadow mushrooms and on and on and on, purple, pink, coral, golden, brown, red mushrooms. Giant mushrooms and barely visible mushrooms. Poisonous and edible mushrooms. Stumps covered with hundreds of glistening white teeth-like fungi and dead man's fingers fungi—fungi eerily shaped like a human, and encrusted with flaky snow-like fungi.

TWENTY-FOUR

MERCED COUNTY

THE SWEET POTATO CAPITAL

L IVINGSTON, a small farm center 65 miles north of Fresno in Merced County is the sweet potato capital of California—within a 15-mile radius of Livingston, 80% of the state's sweet potatoes are grown. Farmers have been growing sweet potatoes around here since the 1860s.

"The best-looking, best-tasting sweet potatoes in America come from California. Yet, few Californians are aware sweet potatoes grow in this state," noted Bob Scheuerman, 63, a University of California farm adviser and California's official sweet potato expert for 33 years. Scheuerman wore a cap that proclaimed "I Yam a Sweet Potato Man." "There is a lot of confusion over the names yam and sweet potato," said Scheuerman, explaining the message on his cap. "They're both sweet potatoes. A yam is a sweet potato with red, purple or copper-colored skin and moist orange flesh after cooking. The creamy-colored potato with yellow dry flesh after cooking is commonly called the sweet potato."

Scheuerman works closely with sweet potato growers and processors. He has an experimental plot in Livingston, where he grows different varieties of sweet potatoes in his never-ending search for the perfect potato. About 100 farmers grow sweet potatoes in the area. The smallest farm is six acres, the largest 400 acres. Sweet potatoes are a $30 million crop for California farmers.

One of those farmers is "Sweet Potato Joe" Alvernaz, 74, and no "small potatoes" when it comes to sweet potatoes. He grows more than 7 million a year on his Livingston farm, planting his potatoes according to phases of the moon. "It's based on centuries of observation by Portuguese sweet potato growers in the Azores," explained Alvernaz, a descendant of growers who migrated to the San Joaquin Valley from Pico Island in the Azores. "I never put a potato in the ground without consulting the *Farmers Almanac and Moon Book,*" said Alvernaz. "And it works!"

He has been known as "Sweet Potato Joe" ever since his high school days and he carried the nickname all over the South Pacific for three years during World War II as a tailgunner on Marine dive bombers. He's also a firm believer in the power of positive suggestions as he walks through his rows of sweet potatoes. "I always think good thoughts every time I pass my plants. Other growers think I'm nuts, but I honestly think plants react to the way you feel toward them." He also insists workers on his farm keep their fingernails trim so they do not scratch the yams.

"One of the problems with sweet potatoes is that even rutabagas have more sex appeal," allowed Sweet Potato Joe. "We should, but don't, have a promotional campaign. We should stick up big billboards along the freeways showing a sweet potato smothered in melting butter."

North Carolina is the No. 1 sweet potato state, with 35,000 acres devoted to the crop. Louisiana is second with 19,000 acres, and California third with 8,000 acres. Sweet potatoes are raised on 94,000 acres in a dozen states. "In Louisiana most of the growers are of French descent," noted Alvernaz. "Here in California sweet potatoes are produced primarily by Japanese, Portuguese and German Mennonite farmers. In New Jersey, a big sweet potato state, growers are mostly

Italian. And in North Carolina they're all Baptists." The interview with Sweet Potato Joe was out in the field. The moon was just right. He and his crew were planting. "Smile and think good thoughts," he declared.

Scheuerman is a member of state and national Sweet Potato Councils and of the National Sweet Potato Collaborators, a research group of about 100 sweet potato scientists. "Sweet potatoes are like turkeys," said Scheuerman. "Most people eat them only at Thanksgiving, Christmas and Easter. They're available year-round, rich in Vitamin A and can be prepared in a variety of ways. You can bake, fry, boil, steam, pan-roast and charcoal-broil sweet potatoes, make cakes, cookies, casseroles, soufflés, croquettes, stuffing, salads, breads, waffles, biscuits, pies and puddings out of sweet potatoes. French-fried sweet potatoes and sweet potato chips are delicious. There is even a sweet potato punch."

People in the Southern states, and African-Americans around the country, eat more sweet potatoes than any other Americans. "Blacks and Southerners are raised on sweet potatoes. They love sweet potato pie. During the Civil War, there were over a million acres in the South in sweet potatoes. The Civil War was fought by the South on a diet of sweet potatoes," Scheurerman noted.

On his quarter-acre experimental plot in Livingston, Scheuerman tests a dozen different varieties of sweet potatoes. "Over the years I've tested more than 50 different varieties. I'm always trying to come up with a better sweet potato, better-looking, better tasting, insect and disease-resistant sweet potato," he explained.

Sweet potatoes do exceptionally well in the Livingston area because of the sandy soil and because the plants are irrigated. Water is pumped into ditch groves next to the plants and goes directly to the lower roots, without getting the sweet potatoes wet. Sweet potatoes grow on mounds higher than the irrigation ditches. "Because California sweet potatoes are not rained on to the extent they are in other states, the California sweet potato does not develop deep eyes, bumps, become misshapen or rot, problems caused by heavy precipitation elsewhere, added Scheurerman.

Sweet potato harvest time in California is mid-September through October. After sweet potatoes are picked, they are sent to market or kept in storage bins in sheds with controlled temperatures for sale over the next six to eight months.

TWENTY-FIVE

MODOC COUNTY

END OF A 10,000-YEAR-OLD CIVILIZATION

As WARS GO, it was a faint blip in the annals of human experience—89 killed, a few hundred wounded. Yet, the six-month Modoc War waged in Modoc County in the northeast corner of California from November 1872 to June 1873, virtually ended the 10,000-year-old Modoc civilization, one of the oldest cultures in North America, as documented by archeologists.

Numerous descendants of the Indians, soldiers and settlers who were combatants in the war met for three days at Lava Beds National Monument on the battlefield strewn with jumbled boulders, lava flows, deep crevices, craters and caves. The meeting led to emotional and philosophical encounters. The National Park Service Symposium on the Modoc War in March 1988 attracted more than 250 men and women from across America—descendants, historians and others fascinated with the little-known episode of history.

"Descendants of Modocs, of soldiers and early settlers who lost their lives in the war or who fought and lived through it, identify themselves to me from time to time when visiting Lava Beds," said Doris I. Omundson, superintendent of the national monument. She noted that the symposium was inspired by her realization that many of the descendants had never met one another. She recruited Klamath Falls historian Francis (Val) Landrum to chair the event. Other historians familiar with the war agreed to address the group.

It was a war of five major battles and several skirmishes. The 52 warriors of the Modoc fighting force stood off an army of 1,000 soldiers during a six-month siege in which they defended a natural lava fortress called the Stronghold, a network of caves linked by natural trenches. The Indians smuggled some supplies past the surrounding U.S. soldiers, but eventually ran low on water and food and were forced to surrender.

Only six Indians were killed in the fighting while 53 federal troopers lost their lives including General E.R.S. Canby. Also killed by the Modocs were 17 civilians, two members of the Oregon militia and two government Indian scouts. Four Modocs were killed by a lynch mob after they had been taken prisoner, one warrior committed suicide rather than surrender and four Indian leaders—Captain Jack, Schonchin John, Boston Charley and Black Jim—were sent to the gallows Oct. 3, 1873, four months after the war ended.

During the symposium, a plaque listing the names of everyone killed in the war was dedicated. The monument superintendent observed, "They were all doing their jobs, the soldiers, most of them new immigrants from Europe to America, the 60 officers, several graduates of West Point, the Indians who loved their tribal lands. Each one wanted the best for themselves and their families. We remember all of them who participated in the anguish of the tragedy that was the Modoc War." Killings by both Indians and settlers occurred from time to time over a 20-year period leading up to the war.

Author Richard Dillon, 65, former head librarian of San Francisco's Sutro Library and author of "Burnt-Out Fires," a 1973 book about the Modoc War, keynoted the event, saying the real heroes were those who tried, unsuccessfully, to prevent war.

Cheewa James, 48, great granddaughter of Shacknasty Jim, a prominent Modoc warrior, was at the gathering. James is a former Klamath Falls television anchorwoman who was working in public relations for the Sacramento schools. "We need to be very careful of the way we interpret history," she cautioned. "We need to understand the implications. My great grandfather and his people were called savages. They weren't savages. They were human beings with their own unique language and culture living in peace and harmony generation after generation for centuries until the settlers entered the picture and pushed them aside. They were fighting for their survival.

"What kind of men were these Modoc warriors? Were they, as history records, renegades who murdered without thought? I think not. One has to be careful making judgments." James noted that 150 to 200 Modocs were holed up in the rock fortress those six months, the 52 warriors plus their extended families. Among those born during the siege was James' grandfather. "On top of that, my great grandfather's two brothers, Shacknasty Frank and Ellen's Man George, were killed in the fighting," she continued. "Can you imagine the condition of those Modocs, half-starved, physically and psychologically torn up fighting against overwhelming odds?" Many other descendants of the Modocs, seated side-by-side at the symposium with the grandchildren and great grandchildren of soldiers and settlers, aired strong feelings about the war.

"It wasn't my people's war. They were reacting to the years of provocations by the white settlers who stole the Modoc land and killed our people...as happened in 1854 when 41 Modocs out of 68 were ambushed, shot and killed for no logical reason," said Lynn Schonchin, 41, a Chiloquin, Oregon, high school teacher and great grandson of Schonchin John, one of the four Modoc leaders who were hanged.

Next to Schonchin sat Melissa Meacham Stewart, 52, of Portland, Oregon, great granddaughter of Alfred B. Meacham, superintendent of Indian Affairs for the Modocs and a member of a peace commission that attempted to stop the fighting. "I grew up on stories my mother and grandmother told about the Modoc War," said Stewart.

The peace commission, which also included General Canby, was attacked by Modocs and Canby was killed. Meacham was shot four times and partly scalped by Schonchin's great grandfather, but survived. The Modoc War was the only war in which a general of the army was killed by Indians. George A. Custer was a lieutenant colonel at the battle of Little Big Horn in Montana.

Orthopedic surgeon Dan Halferty, 65, came down from his home in Portland for the conference. His grandfather was Capt. Oliver Cromwell Applegate of the Oregon Militia. "I lived with my grandfather for a year when I was 10 and he was 87 in 1932. I would sit around and listen to his stories about the Modoc Wear," Halferty recalled. "He was 27 when he fought in the Modoc War. My grandson is 27, flying helicopters for the Navy. I'm trying to put all that in perspective."

The descendants of the Indians, soldiers and settlers walked together for miles exchanging stories as they crossed the desolate battlefield. They paused and reflected at what happened at Captain Jack's Stronghold, at the cross marking the site where General Canby was killed, at Guillem's Graveyard where a historical marker noted: "Here, during the Modoc War of 1872-73, soldiers killed in action were buried. The bodies were later moved to the National Cemetery in Washington, D.C. in the early 1890s."

Don Colwell, 75, was among those walking through the battlegrounds. The war started at his grandfather's ranch when Indians stole butchered beef hanging out to cure for the soldiers and burned the ranch house. Margaret Powell, 66, was another descendant of a settler family. Her grandparents' home was converted into a fort during the war.

After the war, 301 members of Captain Jack's small Indian band were exiled by train to Quapaw Indian Agency in Oklahoma. Other Modocs were sent to Chiloquin, Oregon, to live on a reservation with the Klamath tribe. The U.S. government issued an edict "banning the Modocs from California forever."

Seldom Kirk, Captain Jack's grandson, was interviewed by the author in 1968. Kirk, 84 at the time, had lived his entire life in Oregon only 60 miles from the California border. He prided himself on never stepping over the line into the state where his people "lived 10,000 years and then were banned forever from entering again. In time that edict was forgotten. But I never forgot," insisted Kirk who was born 11 years after the Modocs were banned from California and exiled to Oklahoma and Oregon.

"I have never seen the old battlegrounds, and I never want to see them." he declared. "It stirs me up inside to think about it. Soldiers and settlers molested my people," he continued. "They slaughtered Modocs, just as Modocs are accused of massacring soldiers and settlers. But that part's always forgotten. Why should I go to the place where the government tried to wipe out my people?"

"They called Modocs uncivilized. Huh!" snorted Kirk. "When Modocs said their names, early settlers and officials couldn't spell them. So, they gave Indians a batch of ridiculous white man's names." He was referring to names given to the Modocs like Scarfaced Charley, Steamboat Frank, Shacknasty Jim, Boston Charley.

Joe Ball, tribal leader of the Modocs in 1968 was present during the interview with Seldom Kirk. He echoed Kirk's sentiments, "History has not been kind to my people. Our forefathers were not warlike people. Just the reverse. They were not aggressors. It was resistance to aggression. Our people lived in what is now the northeastern corner of California for thousands of years. They were minding their own business on traditional tribal grounds. Do you think white settlers were minding their business when they came in and ordered the Indians to leave so they could take over their land? I think not."

Today there are nearly 1,000 Modoc descendants, most of them in the Klamath Falls area and some still in Oklahoma. But there are no full-blood Modocs left. Their bloodlines are mixed with the Klamath, Snake, Sioux and other tribes and with other races and nationalities. When the Modocs were exiled, the government insisted that they no longer speak the Modoc language or practice their culture, religion or other Indian ways.

"By the time my father was born in Oklahoma in 1900, the dominant culture succeeded in blowing the old Modoc civilization to the winds," said Cheewa James. "They say the Modoc culture is dead, that they took the life and spirit out of the Modocs during the Modoc War," spoke up Tom Ball, 39, a Modoc from Portland, his voice choking with emotion. "I go to the Modoc Cemetery at the old Klamath Indian Agency. I clean off the graves. I can feel their spirits. My people often hear the drums still beating out here on the Lava Beds, the sacred land of the Modocs at the foot of snow-covered Mount Shasta, our sacred mountain. As long as the spirits are here our culture will never be lost."

TWENTY-SIX

MONO COUNTY

BODIE: A TOWN FROZEN IN TIME

"*Good-bye God, I'm going to Bodie*"—From 1881 diary of little girl moving with her parents to the "wickedest town in the West."

Howling winds bellowed down the mountain into town, flapping shingles on weathered homes and stores, tugging at walls and windows with fierce force, hurling dust through empty streets. Nobody was home. Nobody but a park ranger is ever home in Bodie, abandoned since the 1930s.

A riotous gold camp, Bodie is best remembered for its reputation as the "wickedest town in the West" during its heyday in the 1870s to the 1890s. It was then that most of its 170 surviving structures were erected, and the town boasted a population of more than 10,000—the biggest place between Sacramento and Salt Lake City.

Bodie had 65 saloons. It was the home of gunslingers like Three Finger Jack and Johnny Behind the Rocks. Killings, robberies, stage holdups and street fights were part of daily life. The red-light district along Virgin Alley and Maiden Lane and a huge Chinatown were part of the local scene. The Rev. F.M. Warrington wrote in 1881: "Bodie is a sea of sin, lashed by tempests of lust and passion." More than $500 million (today's value) worth of gold and silver were gouged out of its diggings. By World War I, only a handful of people were left in the "top of the world" mining town, so called because of its 8,300-foot elevation.

The Cain family were among the last to leave. They had been there ever since J.S. (Jim) Cain, then 25, and his wife, Lile, moved to Bodie in 1879. Jim Cain brought electricity to the town over the world's first long-distance power line—13 miles from a hydroelectric plant. He made a fortune building a huge cyanide plant, one of the first of its kind, extracting gold from the Bodie tailings with it. He wound up owning the town and the 550 acres of Bodie's diggings when mining ceased and everyone left.

To his dying day, Jim Cain told his children and grandchildren never to sell Bodie Bluff and 9,000-foot-high Standard Hill overlooking the town because "there's a lot more gold in the mountain waiting to be found." This admonition and a love for Bodie became the Cain family legacy.

You can hear it in the reflections of Jim Cain's 71-year-old grandson, Walter, as he talks about the old one-room Bodie school. "My desk with my name carved in it is still there," he said, going on to describe the last days of Bodie. "It was a three-or-four-day wagon trip to the nearest railhead. Miners and their families carried only small items out with them when they left. It was cheaper to buy all new things than to pay the freight to haul their possessions out."

All through the 1920s, 30s and early 40s, towns like Bodie stood vacant, abandoned and ignored all over the West—ghost towns. But that quickly changed after World War II when scavengers discovered that there was money to be made on Old West relics. They descended on the old mining camps and carted away everything of value, ripping entire buildings out for timber. "It started happening in Bodie. My family hired watchmen to prevent the looting," Walter Cain recalled. "We realized Bodie was a special place and ought to be preserved as a historic monument. We spent years trying to get the state to set it aside as a park."

Finally, in 1962, the state paid the Cains $65,000, one-fifth of the appraised value at the time, for the town, the huge mill where ore was crushed, mining equipment, all the buildings and everything in the buildings. Bodie became a state historic park. "Nothing here has been restored or faked. Everything is as it was when people walked away from Bodie," explained Jack Shipley, long time Bodie State Park ranger.

"Ever since the state acquired Bodie, we have fought hard to preserve the haunting feeling experienced at Bodie, this unique look into the past," noted Don Murphy, president of the California State Park Rangers Association, an organization that works to preserve the integrity of state parks. "There is absolutely no place like Bodie on the face of the Earth. It's not just the mining. It's the whole human experience at Bodie, the hopes, dreams, desires of people, their way of life. This is what got California rolling in the first place. That heritage, all those things are important to preserve."

To reach this remote ghost town, tucked away in a hard-to-get-to corner of sparsely populated Mono County, requires driving over 11 miles of extremely rough dirt road, left deliberately unpaved, to serve as a reminder of what it was like to go to and from Bodie when it was booming in the late 19th-Century.

Visitors stroll the streets of this time warp in the mountains, viewing the 170 buildings that remain preserved in a state of arrested decay. Shelves of the Boone Store are filled with dust-covered products of the 1920s. Spider webs hang from the ceiling. Across the street in an old hotel a 19th-Century pool table sits in the lobby with an inch of dust waiting for players that never show. Like the Leaning Tower of Pisa, the "swaying" Swazey Hotel looks like it will fall over any moment. Coffins covered with dust and spider webs stand open and ready in the windows of the local undertaker.

The Bodie Cemetery is filled with tombstones etched with poignant epitaphs that capture the sorrow of Bodie, the children that perished from disease, men shot to death in barroom brawls, those killed in mining mishaps. The grave of Evelyn Myers, a child accidentally killed by a miner on April 5, 1897, is marked with a tombstone depicting the little girl, head bowed, with angel wings on her back.

HIGH ALTITUDE RESEARCH STATION

JUST IMAGINE—harbor seals plucked from the Pacific Ocean living on top of Mono County's 14,246-foot White Mountain, California's third highest peak. Also living on the mountain top were: chickens wearing sunglasses; seven hundred pampered rats; deer mice jogging on tread mills; hibernating yellow-belly marmots and golden-mantle ground squirrels; a herd of 36 pregnant sheep; monkeys, turkeys, guinea pigs...

Hundreds of scientists from throughout the world, astronomers, geologists, archaeologists, specialists from a wide variety of disciplines, even including a team of Russian cosmonauts, come to the University of California's White Mountain Research Station, the highest scientific base in America, to study insects, plants, animals and birds, to measure rocks, or embark on astronomical "fishing trips" as they scan the universe. Geologist Forrest Wilkerson from the University of North Carolina, for example, is studying the rates of movement in the formation of rocks on the peak. A student from UC Davis studies butterflies living in the upper reaches of White Mountain.

Scientists from Scripps Institution of Oceanography brought the harbor seals to the mountain top to see what effect high altitude has on deep-sea diving mammals. Researchers from Loma Linda University spent the summers of 1993, 1994 and 1995 studying the effects of high altitude on 36 pregnant sheep and their fetuses. Some 135 chickens wore sunglasses in tests by U.C. Berkeley scientists to measure the intensity of ultra-violet rays while living for months on the peak. The bespectacled chickens shared quarters with 700 pampered rats, the dozen deer mice on tread mills, and hibernating yellow-belly marmots and golden-mantle ground squirrels.

Rats brought to the mountain top live a third longer. Hearts of the animals one generation to the next are larger. They increase in size. They have more red blood cells, than lowlanders, larger lungs. They are less susceptible to disease. The deer mice on treadmills proved that animals at high altitudes tire twice as fast as do their cousins living at sea levels.

Hibernation studies were conducted for America's space program. The thought is that future space ships may carry crews that take turns working and hibernating on long-distance flights in order to conserve energy, food, oxygen and time. It is known that animals that sleep much of the year live considerably longer than related non-hibernating animals. Perhaps, said U.C. physiologist Raymond J. Hock, man some day may unlock the mysteries of hibernation and apply them to his own life to solve mysteries of outer space.

During the author's visit to the mountain, Dr. Hock lifted a sleeping marmot from its cage. The animal never as much as flicked a hair. Its pulse was imperceptible. "Awake, these animals are vicious—they chew their way out of heavy galvanized cages here in the lab," explained Dr. Hock, as he lifted the marmot's mouth to show its chisel-like teeth. He held up its sharp fierce claws.

The scientists do their work at three facilities on White Mountain, the Summit Station, a stone structure on the very top of the mountain at 14,246 foot elevation, a 450-square-foot research laboratory that can house four people; Barcroft Laboratory, a two-story Quonset hut at the 12,470-foot-level, and Crooked Creek Station at 10,150 feet.

In the summer of 1994, two log buildings were purchased by the University of California and transported to Crooked Creek from downtown Los Angeles, 300 miles north to White Mountain. One was the Starlight Room Bar and the Grand Burger hamburger stand, the other housed a ticket sales office, a travel agency and security firm. Now the log structures serve as a dormitory that can sleep 36 researchers, a large dining room and a kitchen.

Prior to 1980 when the scientific stations were operated year round, White Mountain was the highest place of year-round human habitation in America. But weather conditions were so extreme and the cost to maintain the laboratories so expensive that when the power lines were destroyed in a 1980 storm winter operations ceased. In recent years the research facilities on the mountain top operate from May through October.

The author visited the research stations on two different occasions when they were operated year-round, both times in winter. It took photographer Frank Brown and me five hours to make the rugged 35-mile trip from Bishop to Barcroft Lab, the last 17 miles by "weasel" across deep snow. Emergency log cabins stocked with provisions and firewood were located at strategic spots along the way.

The second winter visit was accomplished in a Sno-Cat that lumbered up the steep slopes, creeping over 15-to-20 foot snowdrifts. Photographer Rick Meyer and I accompanied Dan Cutshall to Barcroft Lab for astronomical observations. At 9:30 p.m. Cutshall trudged through the deep snow to begin his long night's work on the mountain top. The lights of Bishop twinkled 9,000 feet below. Cutshall turned his flashlight on and off, signaling friends in the town below as he did each night. It was a cloudless night. The temperature was zero. A 10-knot wind howled over the rocky ridge, making the wind chill factor 22 below. Thousands of stars flickered brightly in the crisp clear sky. The quarter moon was inching through Orion.

The bearded Cutshall opened a box protecting an 8-foot telescope from the elements, lifted the bulky, but light (35 pound) telescope out of the box, secured it in a mount for this particular night's series of photographs, then attached a camera. He scrunched down, peering through the lens to line up the telescope with Polaris, the North Star. At precisely 10 p.m.—and then again at midnight, 2 a.m. and 4 a.m.—he tripped the camera shutter for a 10-minute time exposure, capturing the wiggly track of the pole star. He repeated this procedure at another site, a half mile east and 15 minutes away by Sno-Cat.

The nightly photography sessions was part of a year-long survey of the sky to determine the feasibility of placing a major observatory at about the 13,000-foot level on the peak. "The study," explained David Cudaback, UC director of astronomy on the mountain, "is to demonstrate that the clear skies and low water vapor in the air on White Mountain make it perhaps the best possible place in the United States to locate a major observatory." Although a Caltech 18-foot-diameter astronomic dome equipped with a 62-inch telescope has been part of the Barcroft station for years, a major observatory has yet to be erected due to the cost and severe winter weather.

But for one year Cutshall and Will Crljenko conducted the daily survey of the sky, alternating week-long, all-night photography stints on the mountain. Each man was on the mountain top 10 days, then had four days off. Between shootings of the sky, the man on the mountain took cover from blasting winds, bitter cold and sometimes blizzard conditions inside a 4-foot-high, 5-foot-wide steel cubicle anchored with heavy cable—his protective shelter containing a propane heater and candles for light. One of the cubicles was blown away when no one was in it, despite the cable anchors.

The night we spent with Cutshall as he surveyed the sky with his telescope and camera, his beard and mustache iced up from his breathing. "It's weird what the cold and wind do. Some nights my eyes water up and ice forms around the rims of my eyeballs," said the rugged 6-foot, 175-pound mountain man. "The corners of my eyes freeze shut and I have a helluva time seeing to focus. Sometimes the wind screams across the ridge as much as 130 miles per hour. Man, it's grueling. But I love it. I'm a quasi-hermit. I like the solitude. And the beauty of the nights sitting on top of this mountain are unbeatable."

Astronomer Cudaback talked about the "tremendous survival capabilities Cutshall and Crljenko have. It takes special stamina to work at these elevations, even more so to work in howling hurricane-like winds, in temperatures that drop to 20 and 30 degrees below zero with wind chill factors 70 and 80 below zero."

A half mile down the hill from where Cutshall and Crljenko lived and worked was the main lab at Barcroft. Hal Scharnhorst, 66, a life-long bachelor and the old man of the mountain at the time, was spending his eighth year as a maintenance worker at the high altitude research station. "Scientists who come here tell me living in a high place adds years to a person's life. I hope to be going strong when I hit 100," Scharnhorst said. "Lonely? I've never been lonely on this mountain. Even at times when I have been the only one at the station for as long as seven to 10 days in the winter. Scared, yes, when the wind kicks up more than 100 miles per hour and it seems like the whole works is about to blow away."

Some who come here to work leave the same day, unable to cope with the thin air. They get altitude sickness, which effects include deterioration of memory, judgment and ability to perform motor

tasks. Symptoms vary from person to person and are sometimes con-
tradictory--sleepiness, insomnia, lassitude, restlessness, irritability,
euphoria. Scharnhorst continued, "You don't have the stamina you
have in lower elevations. My first two nights back on the mountain
after four days off, I inhale a dozen good swallows of oxygen from a
tank before retiring. Then I sleep like a baby. If I don't take the oxygen I get a humdinger of a headache and toss and turn all night."

A base station supporting the high altitude complex is three miles
east of Bishop. Dave Trydahl, manager of the station, noted that the
three scientific research stations on White Mountain, owned and
operated by the University of California since 1950, are available to
researchers worldwide. Educational groups, from elementary to post
doctorate also have access to the facilities and to summer field camps.

TWENTY-SEVEN

MONTEREY COUNTY

CALIFORNIA'S FIRST THEATER

THE FIRST PAID THEATRICAL PERFORMANCE in California is believed to have taken place at Jack Swan's lodging house and saloon for sailors in 1847. And the show goes on to this day in the same adobe building in Monterey. However, the plots haven't changed much in 150 years—California's First Theatre features 19th-Century melodramas four nights a week during summer and on weekends the rest of the year.

Among the first productions when Swan opened the theater were "Nan, the Good for Nothing" and "Putnam, the Iron Son of '76." Plays in the late 1990s included the British farce, "Prince of Liars," the Western melodrama, "The Hand of the Law," and the 19th-Century Temperance play, "Ten Nights in a Barroom." Heroes are cheered. Villains hissed. Just as in Jack Swan's day.

Swan was an English sailor of Scottish ancestry, who sailed the seven seas until 1843, when, at the age of 31, he settled in Monterey and became a pieman. He was so proud of being a pioneer Californian that he always appeared on the street wearing a hat with a wide band inscribed "Pioneer of '43." His next venture was the adobe boardinghouse and saloon for sailors he built in 1846. It was members of two companies of Col. Jonathan D. Stevenson's New York volunteers assigned to Monterey who suggested Swan use his boarding house to stage plays. Life had become dull for Stevenson's men.

Sailors who stayed at Swan's boarding house became the actors at Swan's theater, taking the roles of both men and women, wearing scarves and projecting high voices when playing female parts. The theater remained open for two seasons, 1847 and 1848. Seats went for $5 each performance and the house reportedly was always packed.

In 1848 Swan and his cast brought down the curtain for the final time. They joined the rush for gold in California's Mother Lode. Swan struck it moderately rich in the gold fields. He returned to Monterey and converted the lodging house-theater into one of Monterey's finest homes where he lived for many years. He wrote a book recalling his mining experiences called *A Trip To The Gold Mines of California in 1848,* which sold well and to this day is an important reference volume of that era. He later moved to Jolon where he died in 1896 at the age of 84.

By 1906 Jack Swan's old theater and home was falling apart. Residents of Monterey realizing the historic value of the property, banded together that year, raised money to buy it and deeded it to the state. Since 1937, melodramas like those produced by Jack Swan, have been staged continuously in California's First Theatre at Scott and Pacific Avenues, a few blocks up the hill from the Old Customs House Plaza. "We claim to be the longest continuous theatrical group in the same theater in the United States," said Laverne Seeman, who leases the theater from the state and is director of The Troupers of the Gold Coast. Seeman began working at the theater as an usher in 1952, was soon acting in the melodramas and in 1967 became the troupe's director.

None of the performers or anyone connected with the theater is paid. "For all of us it is a labor of love," noted Barbara Souza, the theater's piano player, box office attendant and intermission bartender during the 1990s. Many, like Laverne Seeman, have been volunteers at the theatre for years. Richard Boone of Paladin-fame got his start here.

Bobs Watson typifies how many actors feel about the First Theatre, "For me, performing at Jack Swan's mid 19th-century theater has been one of the highlights of my life. It's always a lot of fun. I have many friends in Monterey because of that theater and I keep going back every chance I get."

Watson was a soldier, a private at Fort Ord in 1952 during the Korean War, when he appeared in his first performance at the theater, playing both Dr. Jekyll and Mr. Hyde. He appeared in three other plays, "Ten Nights In a Barroom," "Wages of Sin," and "Fatal Wedding," performing more than 100 times when he was off duty during the two years he was stationed at the Army base. In Hollywood, Watson appeared in 160 movies and scores of television. As a child actor, age 7, he was Pee Wee in "Boys Town." When Spencer Tracy received an Oscar for his role in the film, he wired Watson saying, "Bobby half this statue belongs to you." It was signed "Uncle Spencer."

Bobs Watson was 8 in 1939 when he played the heart-wrenching role of Pud, starring with Lionel Barrymore in "On Borrowed Time." He is one of the six Watson brothers, along with Coy, Billy, Gary, Delmar, and Harry, who have appeared in scores of movies as child actors and continuing on in films throughout their adult lives. All of the Watson brothers have also worked for years as news photographers for Los Angeles newspapers and Southern California TV stations. In Bobs' multi-faceted career, he has also been a popular United Methodist minister for 30 years.

Ever since the 1950s, whenever Bobs Watson is in the Monterey area, he takes in a performance at California's First Theatre. And he's always called up out of the audience to the stage to do "The Face on the Barroom Floor" as part of the melodrama's olio. In the summer of 1995, as happens every time, his rendition of Hugh D'Arcy's famed 1877 monologue brought down the house.

By California state law, only melodramas written before the year

1900 may be produced at the theater. The simple hero falls into the clutches of evil, but virtue always triumphs. During the melodrama there is always an olio. And every evening at California's First Theatre ends with the audience singing along with songs played by Barbara Souza, old favorites like "Ain't She Sweet?" "Bicycle Built For Two," and "Take Me Out to the Ball Game." Jack Swan, the Scottish sailor who jumped ship in Monterey, would feel at home watching a show in the theater he founded in 1847. He would be delighted the theater 150 years later is still using his old format, the 19th-century melodrama.

CHRISTMAS IN THE ADOBES

THE CALENDAR is turned back to the 1840s and 1850s in old Monterey as a touch of history is added to Christmas in this seaport town. Hundreds of men, women and children stroll along a pathway marked with flickering *luminarias*—candles anchored in sand in lunch-size paper sacks—leading to 15 of the oldest adobes in town. Inside the mud-walled buildings, each illuminated by candlelight, "Christmas in the Adobes" is celebrated as it had been when Monterey served as California's capital under the Mexican flag and in California's first years as a U.S. territory.

"Our ancestors, the founding fathers of Monterey and the state of California would be very pleased if they could pop in on us today and see their adobes furnished and maintained as they had them," beamed Martha Cooper Lang, a volunteer hostess in the 1823 Cooper-Molera adobe. Her great-grandfather, New England sea captain John Rogers Cooper, built the house when he married Encarnacion Vallejo, sister of General Mariano Vallejo, founder of the city that now bears his name.

Inside each adobe a different Christmas theme is presented. At Cooper-Molera it was a Victorian Christmas, with Captain Cooper's painting of the Queen of England looking down from one of the walls. Hot cider, gingerbread and pound cake were served.

At nearby Casa Gutierrez, erected by Joaquin Guitierrez in 1849, a humble adobe where Joaquin and his wife Josefa raised their 15 children, taquitos and enchiladas were cooked over a roaring fire in a barbecue pit and served with tamales to the celebrants. Several hundred Californians today trace their ancestry to Joaquin and Josefa. Many of the people of Monterey, population 28,000, are distantly related to that early California couple.

In Casa de los Cuatro Vientos (House of the Four Winds), vintage 1830, Rebecca Hinckley 7, dressed as an elf, distributed popcorn balls to each child who entered. The all-women Monterey Civic Club saved the House of the Four Winds from demolition in the early 1920s, launching a drive that spared Monterey's historic district from the bulldozer. The house, adorned with period Christmas decorations, continues to be owned and preserved by the club.

All the other adobes in the open-house festivities make up the seven-acre Monterey State Historic Park. Each year since 1983, the Old Monterey Preservation Society and other organizations sponsor "Christmas in the Adobes." In each adobe guides explain the history of the building and point out fascinating features. Admission is charged and proceeds go to the Monterey Preservation Society for the maintenance and upkeep of the historic structures.

TWENTY-EIGHT

NAPA COUNTY

ROBERT LOUIS STEVENSON SLEPT HERE

THE RETIRED PRESIDENT of one of the nation's largest companies had such an intense interest in Robert Louis Stevenson that he sold his New York home and moved as close as he could to where the famed author spent his honeymoon. To commemorate the Scottish writer's "California episode," Norman H. Strouse then established a Stevenson museum in St. Helena, a tiny Napa County town 60 miles north of San Francisco.

Strouse, retired president and chairman of the board of the world's largest advertising agency, the J. Walter Thompson Company, had been a lifelong admirer of the author of *Treasure Island, Kidnapped,* and *Dr. Jekyll and Mr. Hyde.* He collected everything of Stevenson's he could lay his hands on; and his collection, housed in the Silverado Museum, is valued by experts to be worth in excess of $1 million.

In 1968 Strouse and his wife, Charlotte, sold their New York home and moved to St. Helena "because this is Stevenson country and this will be our final home," vowed Strouse. "We established the Silverado Museum in this lovely California valley instead of New York or some other place, because this is where a Robert Louis Stevenson Museum rightfully should be," Strouse explained to the author. "It was here, on the slopes of Mt. St. Helena that the most romantic episode in Stevenson's life occurred, his honeymoon, the subject of one of his finest prose works, *The Silverado Squatters.*"

Having met Fanny Van de Grift Osbourne in France, where she went to study art as an escape from the philandering of her San Francisco court reporter husband, Stevenson followed her to America. Fanny divorced her husband, and she and Stevenson were married in Oakland in the spring of 1880. Strouse noted that Stevenson's marriage scandalized his affluent parents in Scotland, Fanny being a 40-year-old, divorced woman, 11 years his senior. His parents cut off his allowance, leaving him penniless. "They took up residence at the abandoned Silverado Mine high on the shoulders of Mt. St. Helena," related Strouse, "and lived in an old bunkhouse through the summer."

Stevenson roamed the mountainside, visited characters throughout Napa Valley and researched the history of the abandoned silver mine. "His many notes of the enchanting, almost primitive scenery surrounding Silverado later provided descriptive detail for not only *The Silverado Squatters,* but for *Treasure Island* and many of his other works," noted Strouse. Stevenson's impressions and copious notes that spring and summer and during his earlier weeks in Monterey and San Francisco were reflected in his writings the rest of his life.

Strouse was filled with little-known observations about the famous author: "Robert Louis Stevenson followed the pattern so often seen today among children of the affluent. He sponged off his father's generosity. He became an agnostic rebelling against his parents' Scottish Presbyterianism. He became a hippie, who wore long hair, a velveteen jacket, dirty clothes and went barefoot. He shook the foundations of the Stevenson household in Scotland.

"His marriage came as a shock. But Fanny proved to be his salvation. She nursed him back to health, encouraged his writings. After four years of marriage, he would write: 'She is everything to me; wife, sister, brother, daughter and dear companion; and I would not change to get a goddess or a saint.'"

Strouse set up an endowment and established the Vailima Foundation, named after Stevenson's plantation home in Apia, Western Samoa, to provide for the establishment and operation of the Silverado Museum. In 1969 the Museum opened in an old chicken hatchery in St. Helena, a building that was a prime example of the stonemason's art in 19th-Century California. In 1979 the museum moved to its own new building adjacent to the St. Helena Public Library. On exhibit are more than 9,000 Stevenson items, one of the largest private collections in existence, including: First editions of all of the author's works during his brief life span--ailing all his life with catarrhal consumption, Stevenson died of a brain hemorrhage at the age of 44 on his Samoa plantation. Over 100 books from Stevenson's personal library are here; along with the last part of a manuscript Stevenson wrote the day he died; original manuscripts and scores of Stevenson's letters and more than 80 letters written by Fanny Stevenson to the author's mother; three copies of the famed filippic "Father Damien" (only 25 were printed); Stevenson's first book written at age 16, the "Pentland Rising" and a first edition of a "Child's Garden of Verses" inscribed by the author to his wife.

There are original portraits and sculptures of Stevenson, portfolios containing more than 1,000 Stevenson family photographs and memorabilia such as the author's lead soldiers, wedding ring and writing desk he used in Samoa.

Strouse began collecting books while in high school in Olympia, Washington. His collection of books is one of the finest private collections of its kind. For years he had been one of the leading bibliophiles in America. He wrote extensively on book collecting, his titles including: *How to Build a Poor Man's Morgan Library, The Lengthened Shadow,* and *The Passionate Pirate.* He also wrote *The Silverado Episode,* the story of Stevenson's year in California.

For 40 years before moving to St. Helena, Strouse came to Napa Valley every chance because of his insatiable interest in the Stevenson episode. He repeatedly hiked the mile long trail near the summit of

Highway 29 north of St. Helena to the Stevenson honeymoon site, now the Robert Louis Stevenson State Park.

Stevenson and his bride lived for three months in the bunkhouse "to live out of doors with the woman a man loves is of all lives the most complete and free," wrote Stevenson. The bunkhouse is gone. All that remains is a simple tablet in the quietude of the forest, a tablet placed by the Women's Club of Napa County in 1911, inscribed: *"Doomed to know not Winter only Spring, / a being Trod the flower / April blithely for awhile, / Took his fill of music, / joy of thought and seeing, / Came and stayed and went, / nor ever ceased to smile."*

"No poet could have described the spirit of Stevenson more fittingly or memorably than he himself when he wrote those lines," observed Strouse, who could not have opened his museum at a more appropriate time, the 75th anniversary of Stevenson's death, the 90th anniversary of the summer on the mountain. Strouse died in 1992 at the age of 85, active until the day he died in his quest to learn everything he could about Robert Louis Stevenson, still collecting letters, original manuscripts, personal possessions.

"The interest in Robert Louis Stevenson continues worldwide as much as ever," noted Edmond Reynolds, museum manager. "Four of his 150 books *Treasure Island, Kidnapped, A Child's Garden of Verses, and Dr. Jekyll* and *Mr. Hyde* have never been out of print since he wrote them. Western Samoa released a new issue of Stevenson stamps in 1994 the same year the Bank of Scotland issued a pound note with Stevenson's portrait."

Liz Baer, one of the trustees, noted that the museum continues to purchase new Stevenson material and periodically receives gifts such as the recent donation from the author's step grandson of a painting of a horse that belonged to Stevenson. Roger G. Swearingen of Santa Rosa is another trustee. Swearingen has been an English literature professor at Yale, the University of North Carolina and UC Davis, and is the author of the authoritative guide to the writing and publication of Stevenson's many prose works, *The Prose Writings of Robert Louis Stevenson: A Guide*. With his wife, Sarah, he also edited for publication the complete, original manuscript of *The Amateur Emigrant*, Stevenson's own account of his trip in 1879 across the Atlantic and across the continent to California. Faber and Faber Publishers, London, are publishers of Swearingen's new biography, *Robert Louis Stevenson: Spirit of Adventure.*

"For anyone writing about Robert Louis Stevenson, the Silverado Museum is one of the places where you have to go. Norman Strouse was *the* Stevenson collector for nearly a half century and the museum has an abundance of material about the author's life," said Swearingen.

Writers doing articles and books about Stevenson have come to Silverado Museum from throughout the United States, from as far away as Russia, Italy, Spain, England and Scotland. The Japanese, in particular, have had a great interest in Stevenson, with several writers coming from Japan to do research in St. Helena. The Museum is open without charge daily except Mondays and holidays from noon to 4 p.m.

CALISTOGA WILL MAKE YOU A MUDDER

I T WAS SAM BRANNAN who started the Gold Rush in 1848 when he stepped ashore in San Francisco wildly waving a vial of gold and shouting: "Gold! Gold! Gold from the American River!"

He started another stampede 10 years later when he stood in the dusty streets of Calistoga 70 miles north of San Francisco and bellowed: "Mud! Mud! Bathe in the therapeutic volcanic ash mud from the slopes of Mt. St. Helena!" And people have been wallowing in the mud of Calistoga ever since. There are six mud emporiums in town, including Sam Brannan's old spot, now called Indian Springs. Leland Stanford of railroad and university fame bought out Brannan and later sold to Jacques Pacheteau. Jack Lambrecht bought out the Pacheteau family interests in 1954 and operated the baths called Pacheteau's Hot Springs until 1984. John and Pat Merchant have been running the place since 1988.

"A mud bath is one of nature's oldest therapies," insisted Lambrecht. "The thick mud mixed with hot mineral water bubbling from beneath the surface leaves a person refreshed, like a newborn. Immersion in a tub of hot mud relaxes nerves, opens pores, loosens tight muscles and stimulates circulation. It also makes you sweat."

Every year about 100,000 people come to Calistoga at the foot of

Mt. St. Helena, a dormant volcano, to take mud baths. The mud dug from surface pits behind the baths is volcanic ash saturated with mineral water bubbling up from the hot springs.

Workers at the baths shovel the mud into wheelbarrows and fill 3-foot by 6-foot, 2-foot deep tubs. Bathers lie on their backs up to their necks in hot mud for 10 minutes. They shower. They sit in a tub filled with mineral water for 10 minutes, then sit in a steam room for 10 minutes and finally they spend a half hour on a bed under a heavy blanket. "It's the world's greatest heat treatment. Everyone sweats profusely while taking a mud bath. That's what it's all about," said John Merchant. "Mud baths date back to Roman times."

The 100,000 people who come to Calistoga every year must find it worthwhile, especially since they pay between $40 and $50 for the one hour treatment. People have been dunking, wallowing and sweating in the mud baths of Calistoga ever since 1858, and keep coming back.

TWENTY NINE

NEVADA COUNTY

E CLAMPUS VITUS

IT IS WITHOUT A DOUBT one of the oddest fraternal organizations or historical societies in the United States. The stamp of the tongue-in-cheek "Ancient and Honorable Order of E Clampus Vitus" is everywhere in the old gold rush towns of California and Nevada.

More than 500 historical sites, crumbling ruins and existing structures in the Mother Lode country are marked by monuments and descriptive plaques erected by E Clampus Vitus. Old courthouses, barbershops, livery stables, saloons, churches, brothels, mines, schools, homes of well-known historical characters, railroad depots, breweries, newspaper offices, cemeteries and such are all duly memorialized. There are E Clampus Vitus plaques to "the real native sons of California" (the Indians), and to the Chinese and Black miners who played important roles in the development of the West. Kenneth J.

Fryer of the Fresno chapter called it "memorializing places and persons that civilization and history may otherwise have forgotten."

E Clampus Vitus is a carry-over from the days of the riotous old mining camps. The Clampers, as members of the organization call themselves, lightened the cares of gold rush days and made the old frontier ring with laughter.

"E Clampus Vitus was a spoof and satire of the solemn and mysterious fraternal orders and lodges so widespread in the old gold rush towns," explained Bill Byars, Vice Sublime Noble Grand Humbug of the Grand Council of E Clampus Vitus, at the time the author interviewed him. Byars, a Nevada County carpenter who lives in Grass Valley, was the second highest ranking officer in the organization.

"It was an outgrowth of the ordinary miner not being accepted socially by the early-day merchants and town leaders in their lodges," Byars said. "So, the miners organized their own fraternal order—E Clampus Vitus. Every man who gained membership immediately became an officer of equal indignity—which is still true today. It's a fun-loving, hell-raising organization that perpetuates history as a serious sideline."

There are Clampers throughout California and Nevada, with the heaviest concentrations in the old gold rush towns. No parade, celebration or event in the Mother Lode is ever without Clamper activity—marching Clampers in black pants, red flannel shirts and black top hats, Clamper bands, Clampers riding old fire engines.

The 32 E Clampus Vitus chapters in California, three in Nevada and one in Utah are named after historic characters, extinct gold mining camps and old railroads: The Virginia City chapter carries the name Julia C. Bulette, Nevada's most celebrated madam of the gold rush days and "gentle companion to the miners." Auburn's chapter is called Lord Sholto Douglas in honor of an English actor of no fame whatsoever who was hooted and howled out of mining camps all over the West. Mountain Charlie is the name of the San Jose chapter and the Reno chapter is called Snow Shoe Thompson, both famous early-day mountain men.

To join, a man must be sponsored by a Clamper, be at least 21 and "be breathing." Members are from all walks of life. California and

Nevada governors have been Clampers. The membership application asks such penetrating questions as: "Would you give a sucker an even break? Will you ever use the blunderbuss to protect the widow and orphan?"

In the beginning, when the first chapter was organized in 1849 in Mokelumne Hill by a miner named Joe Zumwalt out of Pike County, Missouri, the stated purpose was good fellowship and promoting the welfare of widows and orphans of miners. "Zumwalt gave the Clampers their costume," reported Clamper historian Bob Wyckoff. "He wore black pants, a faded red flannel shirt and a high black silk hat." The initiation ceremony takes the PBC (Poor Blind Candidate) into the "chasm of terror and despair in high hopes of reaching the safe haven of Clamperdom." It's a takeoff on initiation ceremonies of a number of fraternal orders and lodges.

What does E Clampus Vitus stand for? "Nothing that we've been able to figure out," reported Vice Sublime Noble Grand Humbug Byars. "We're not sure where the name came from, but you have to admit it sounds good."

WRIGHT BROTHERS, JOHNNYS-COME-LATELY

VISITORS TO GRASS VALLEY in Nevada County are told the Wright Brothers were Johnnys-come-lately. Townspeople here insist the first man to fly was not Orville Wright. They claim it was their own red-bearded, red-headed, locks-down-to-the-waist, unabashed eccentric Lyman Gilmore.

Grass Valley telephone books and Chamber of Commerce brochures proclaim unequivocally: "On May 15, 1902, Lyman Gilmore, seated in a 32-foot-span monoplane powered by a 20-horse-power steam engine and flash boiler, was launched down a chute 100 yards long into the air, then continued in flight for some distance on its own power. There is conclusive evidence Gilmore built and flew his craft 19 months before the Wright brothers made their first flight Dec. 17, 1903, at Kitty Hawk. Lyman Gilmore was robbed of his place in history by the remoteness of this place and by his own secretiveness."

Postcards in local stores show photographs of Gilmore and his early airplanes. A mural covering the entire front wall of the Lyman Gilmore Intermediate School (grades five through eight) on a high hill overlooking Grass Valley salutes the aviation pioneer. The mural shows Gilmore standing amid a cloud leaning on a drawing board, his goggles pushed back on his forehead. His bright yellow monoplane, reproduced from plans he drew in 1898, is shown in flight. "I believe Lyman Gilmore was the first man to fly because I want to believe it," said Carol Hughes, secretary of the school.

Hjalmer E. Berg, retired San Francisco State University American history professor, past president of the local historical society and owner of a Grass Valley bookstore, insisted: "I'm sure Lyman flew an airplane before the Wright brothers. He recorded that fact in his log. Unfortunately, there is no verification for his claim." In his log Gilmore wrote that in 1902 he made more than 20 successful flights in the steam-powered monoplane, some as short as 100 yards, some as long as a mile.

Born in 1874, Gilmore wrote that he flew a glider in the hills of Grass Valley in 1891 when he was 17. In 1898 he wrote the War Department urging this country to "harness the air and make use of it as a means of transportation. America must build a fleet of air ships." He signed his letter Lyman Gilmore, "The Aerial Fulton." (Robert Fulton designed the first commercial steamboat.) Although his claim that he was the first to fly an airplane has been universally ignored, except here in Grass Valley, Gilmore is generally credited with the establishment of the first commercial air field in the United States on March 15, 1907—It was on the 50-acre air field, now the site of the school named in his honor, that he built his hangar and early airplanes.

In the late 1920s, a certificate from the Daniel Guggenheim Fund for the Promotion of Aviation was sent to Gilmore applauding his "contributions to the establishment of a nationwide system of transportation." It was signed by Guggenheim and Charles A. Lindbergh.

"Lyman vowed in 1908 that he would never shave or get a haircut until William Jennings Bryan was elected President," recalled Arletta M. Douglass, member of the Nevada County Historical Landmarks Commission. "Bryan was never elected. And Lyman stuck to his guns." She also believed Gilmore got his airplane off the ground before the Wright brothers. "But I don't think Lyman flew the plane. I believe he did it by remote control." Gilmore died in 1951. Many old-timers in Grass Valley like Douglass, retired dentist Harry Stewart and hardware store owner Downey Clinch knew him.

"When I was a kid I would ride my bike out to Gilmore Field and listen to Lyman tell his flying stories. I would stand in his hangar with my mouth wide open and look at his old airplanes," Stewart remembered. The hangar and three of the monoplanes he built in 1908-10 were destroyed in a fire in 1935. Stewart said men who are now dead told him when he was young that Gilmore flew before the Wright brothers. "But they said he was so afraid someone would steal his flying machine inventions that he would fly his airplane in secret."

Clinch, a lifelong aviation buff who also knew Gilmore, said Gilmore was 25 years ahead of his time. "He built passenger airplanes with aluminum wings and fuselages long before anybody else did. He was probably first to have retractable landing gears on his airplanes," Clinch insisted.

All the students at Lyman Gilmore School have stories to tell about their hero. "They named our school after him because he flew before the Wright brothers. He never took a bath and even though he stunk they still named our school after him," declared Kam Chandler, 11, a sixth grader.

THE GREAT REPUBLIC OF ROUGH AND READY

I N 1850 a tiny Nevada County hamlet declared itself the Great Republic of Rough and Ready. The nation lasted just 12 weeks, but the town with the long and colorful name has been celebrating the historic event ever since. Secession Days are celebrated each summer in Rough and Ready.

Tradition has it that the Gold Rush camp declared itself independent from California and the United States in reaction to a mining tax that incensed local citizens. At a mass protest meeting reportedly held April 7, 1850, Col. E. F. Brundage supposedly delivered a manifesto creating a new nation. The republic enacted its own laws, elected its own officers, including Brundage as president. But the 3,000 miners and others who lived in Rough and Ready soon tired of being an independent republic and after 12 weeks threw in the towel. They rejoined the union on the Fourth of July.

These sparse details of the Great Republic are duly recorded on an historical plaque in the center of town and in brochures about the community's history. Local history books make passing mentions of the tiny, short-lived nation, the earliest-known reference in a book published in 1862.

A History of Nevada County published in 1880, for example, reports that "It was during the uncertainty of the 1850s, that Col. E.F. Brundage conceived the idea of a separate and independent government. He issued a high-sounding manifesto and called a mass meeting. The whole affair was severely ridiculed and soon The State of Rough and Ready vanished like the mist."

Constance Bear, the town's historian and a reporter for a local newspaper, told of spending years "searching libraries, writing letters to the Library of Congress and the U.S. Archives trying to get information about the Great Republic of Rough and Ready, to no avail. There are the references in some early histories but no documentation, no newspaper accounts, no letters from those who were here describing what went on. My hope is someone, someday will find letters about the affair tucked away in an attic or an old trunk." Regardless of more substantiating evidence, the early history books are good enough for the people of the sleepy little town, population 4,000, some 60 miles northeast of Sacramento. Secession Days are the biggest celebration each year.

Retired cowboy and stagecoach maker Jim West, endowed with a great flowing white beard, has led caravans of covered wagons and men and women on horseback three nights and four days along the old Immigrant Trail from Rough and Ready 30 miles to Wheatland as part of the Secession Days festivities, which includes a parade of cars, a children's parade, a chili cook-off, a peddler's fair and several other events. It culminates in the staging of a festival highlighted by the traditional outdoor performance of the play "The Saga of the Great Republic of Rough and Ready."

The town came by its unusual name in 1849 when Captain A.A. Townsend and a party of 25 gold miners who came West from Wisconsin founded the place. Townsend served in the Army under Zachary "Rough and Ready" Taylor, America's 12th President, and named the town after his hero. Today, Rough and Ready retains many vestiges of its past, from William Fippin's 1850s blacksmith's shop to the 1854 Grange Hall and the quaint clapboard Rough and Ready School that served five generations of the town's children until it closed in 1953.

THIRTY

ORANGE COUNTY

A COUPLE OF WALTS: FIRST, MR. KNOTT

THIS IS A STORY ABOUT TWO MEN who brought world-wide attention to Orange County and Southern California, Walter Knott with Knott's Berry Farm and Walt Disney, with Disneyland, two of the nation's best known and most popular amusement parks.

Walter Knott's berry patch, planted in 1920 in Buena Park, became an institution that has thrived as one of America's great show places. Knott was 70 years old when I interviewed him in 1960. At the time he was still living in the same modest two-story frame house that stood behind his original berry stand.

That house 40 years later was now behind the Chicken Kitchen, hardly noticed by visitors to Knott's Berry Farm. But for Cordelia and Walter, then as busy as ever, the house was most convenient, 10 steps out the back door to the kitchen Mrs. Knott actively supervised each day and another 10 steps to Walter's office. "My wife never took time to join clubs. I never learned to play golf. Cordie's interests are in the kitchen. Her friends are the people she works with in the kitchen. I'm busy running the 'Farm'," Knott explained.

Knott and his family were as typically American as buckwheat pancakes, homemade pickles, jams and jellies, fried chicken, hot biscuits and berry pie—his stock in trade. The story of Walter Knott is the story of a man who pulled himself up by his bootstraps, who transformed adversities and failures into storybook success. "My hard times were blessings in disguise," said the silver-haired proprietor of Knott's Berry Farm. "Hard times are almost vital along life's path. I feel sorry for a fella who makes a success right off the bat."

His life was anything but a success "right off the bat." His father, a La Verne minister and citrus grower died when Knott was 6. "My mother worked in a laundry to support the family. My brother and I helped, too, even though we were barely of school age. We planted vegetables in vacant lots in Pomona where we grew up, and peddled them all over town. By the time I was a sophomore in Pomona High School, I thought I was pretty smart, that all I had to do was give the world a little shake and all the apples would fall in my lap," Knott related. He told how he quit school and discovered that very few of the apples fell in his lap for several years.

Knott married his childhood sweetheart, Cordelia Hornaday, on June 3, 1911. Two years later the young couple homesteaded on the Mojave Desert, five miles north of Newberry. He recalled, "I built an adobe home. I dug a well. We spent three and one-half years on the desert. And all we had to show for it was a family of kids. For we went flat broke, lost everything homesteading. Cordie and I finally packed up what few possessions we had and drove two old horses and a wagon to San Luis Obispo, where we went to work as sharecroppers."

In 1920 the Knott family moved again, this time to 20 acres of barren land in Buena Park. They struck out on their own—rented the property and planted it in berries. "I put up a roadside stand. We sold berries from it and also peddled them all over the Los Angeles area. We grew a number of different varieties. I heard about a new berry that Rudolph Boysen, park superintendent at Anaheim, developed. Boysen mixed pollen from a number of different berries," Knott related. "But he did not commercially promote or give a name to his berry. I tried them. They did well. Soon we became known all over the countryside for the new berry. I decided to call them boysenberries." Rudolph Boysen, whose berries were made famous by Walter Knott, died in 1950.

For years Knott had the biggest boysenberry patch in the world. He sold plants to berry growers across the nation and in many foreign countries. In 1960 Knott stepped out of the picture as a boysenberry producer. But Knott's Berry Farm ever since has been the world's biggest boysenberry *buyer,* purchasing the berries from growers in the San Joaquin Valley and Oregon.

It was hard times during the Great Depression that "drove" Knott into the restaurant business. "Just before the crash we bought 10 acres of the land we were renting. Things got so slow we were unable to make payments. My wife got the idea to sell chicken dinners. That was in 1934. The first day Cordelia cooked and served eight dinners, at 65 cents each. That's how this phase of our business began. Today the restaurant will seat 1,000 diners at any given time and serves 2 million chicken dinners a year." said Knott during the 1960 interview.

By 1940 the Knotts owned the original 20 acres they first rented 20 years earlier. As Knott put it, "Mrs. Knott and I were both 50 in 1940. We had managed to make a little money over and above what it cost to live. We took time to take stock and look back. We had achieved our success through hard work during 10 years of the Great Depression and Mr. Roosevelt's New Deal. We had no notion originally to do Ghost Town. It all started with the covered wagon diorama out in an asparagus field on our property. But once we got started there was no stopping. We're still working on Ghost Town. I doubt whether I'll ever finish with it."

Through the years, Knott's Berry Farm, America's first "theme" amusement park has kept growing little by little until today it is 150 acres filled with more than 165 rides, shows and unique attractions. There are three roller coasters, including the Corkscrew, the world's first 360-degree roller coaster. An 1881 narrow-gauge train and a genuine Overland stagecoach take visitors on a tour through the park. There's the Ghost Town, Camp Snoopy a six-acre park within the park designed especially for kids under 12, Fiesta Village, an Indian encampment with Indians telling the stories of their tribes, a wild water wilderness with California's longest, man-made, white-water river, the Kingdom of Dinosaurs, a 20-story parachute fall and so much more.

And all through the years Knott's unique enterprise has been a family-owned and operated venture. Twelve family members are on the board of directors. Children, grandchildren and great grandchildren of Walter and Cordelia Knott have all worked at the park and continue to do so. "My kids have learned how to work, to believe in work and to enjoy work, and so have their children," Knott said. Cordelia died at the age of 84 on April 23, 1974 and Walter died a week before his 92nd birthday, December 3, 1981.

VISITING WITH MR. DISNEY

I WORKED WITH WALT DISNEY numerous times at Disneyland doing feature stories for The Los Angeles Times, from the time the amusement park opened in 1955 until his death December 15, 1966. One time I flew with him in his private jet from Burbank to San Diego to sail on the largest square-rigged sailing ship under the American flag, the Coast Guard three-masted, 295-foot training barque Eagle. From San Diego we sailed overnight to Los Angeles under full sail. Walt was like a little kid in a candy factory. He was all over the ship filming "home movies" with his camera. On the bridge. In the rigging. He loved every minute.

Disney, like Walter Knott, spent time on a farm. He was born in Chicago December 5, 1901, the fourth son of Elias Disney a farmer and carpenter. His mother, Flora Call Disney, was a school teacher. Disney knew what it was like to be poor. Discipline was strong in his home. His father had a paper route in Kansas City and the Disney boys were up before dawn helping their father deliver papers. They lived on a farm near Marceline, Missouri, a typical midwest town that is said to be the inspiration and model for his "Main Street U.S.A." in Disneyland.

Disney was a cartoonist for his McKinley High School newspaper in Chicago. He drove a Red Cross truck in France and Germany in World War I. He began his animated film work in Kansas City, then came to Los Angeles. His cartoon Steamboat Willie was a success in 1928. He was on his way. Mickey, Minnie, Donald Duck, Pluto, Goofy and his cast of characters led to unbelievable success. "Snow White and the Seven Dwarfs," his first full length feature film came out in 1935. Disneyland opened in 1955, Disney World in 1966. Whatever our age, we all grew up with Walt Disney. To all of us he is like a member of the family.

No matter who a person is, rich, poor, prime minister, president, king, queen, laborer, we're all equals on a visit to Disneyland. Everyone reacts in a similar way to this enchanted kingdom. And Disney himself frequently played host to world leaders at Disneyland. As a reporter covering these special visitors I was lucky to be at Walt's side on his personally guided tours. For example:

Prime Minister Jawaharlal Nehru and his daughter, Indira Gandhi, who also became prime minister of India, were Walt's guests. Dwight and Mamie Eisenhower and their family were visitors. Accompanying both groups, I watched them completely enjoy themselves throughout their stay. Fifth and sixth graders from Anaheim and Santa Ana schools sang "Happy Birthday" to Nehru, who was turning 72. He and his daughter took a trip to the moon, sailed beneath the Seven Seas in a submarine, and drove down Main Street in a replica of a 1903 electric car. "I've had a wonderful time," Nehru enthused to Disney.

Former President Eisenhower and his family spent the day after Christmas in 1961 at Disneyland. The famous Eisenhower grin never ceased during his entire visit. "I suppose you might say I'm enjoying this as much as the grandchildren. No! More!" Eisenhower declared with unabashed glee, as the family went around the park on a freight train from the Old West. Crowds waved and yelled, "Hi Ike!"

Eisenhower then took the wheel of the Yangtze Lotus on the jungle ride. At the Disneyland Fire Department he hopped behind the driver's seat of an antique fire truck, donned a fire chief's hat and blasted the siren. "I never dreamed it would be this much fun," he said to Disney, quickly adding, "Walt, we loved every minute, and promise to be back soon."

THIRTY-ONE

PLACER COUNTY

WINDOWS OF DEATH

F OR YEARS, pastors of a modest white-frame church in Lincoln, a small town in Placer County, have been trying to solve the stained-glass window mystery—but to no avail.

The windows in his church memorialize preachers who were murdered, killed by a locomotive, or died on their knees. Some of their last words were: "Don't give up." "Blessed Jesus." "Nearing heaven. At the gate. Entering paradise." There are 24 of these windows in the United Methodist Church.

"I know the windows came with the church when it was erected in 1890," said the pastor, the Rev. Alf Christensen during the author's visit there in 1970. "But the reason for the windows has everyone in our denomination stumped. We cannot find out how they came to be installed."

Each of the 20 by 80-inch windows memorializes a camp meeting preacher who migrated West from southern states to minister to the spiritual needs of gold miners in California's Mother Lode country. None of the preachers ever served the Lincoln Methodist Church at the base of the Sierra Nevada foothills in Placer County 25 miles northeast of Sacramento.

Inlaid in lead, the richly colored yellow, gold, blue, red and black windows are mounted in vestibule doors surrounding the sanctuary. Each window is decorated at the top with typical Christian symbols—crosses, doves, sheaves of wheat, clasped hands, lilies, angels and anchors. But the inscriptions are far from typical: Rev. John Calvin Stewart—murdered by a traitor; Rev. George W. Wood—Died in his buggy on the way to duty; Rev. Drury K. Bond—died in California, Sept. 12, 1861, saying "Don't Give Up;" Rev. James M. Fulton—Died on his knees in California; Rev. G.W. Humphrey—Died saying "Glory. Glory;" Rev. Solomon W. Davies—Missionary to California, killed by a locomotive; Rev. John F. Campbell—Ascended Oct. 10, 1878; Rev. J.K. Price—Bold and humble, entered rest April 27, 1888; Rev. Lewis Featherstun—died in triumph; Rev. J. T. Cox—Remarkable preacher. "I'm sure the founders of the church were dead serious about them," Rev. Christensen said. "There was nothing camp about it in 1890. I'll have to admit they sound corny in this day and age."

Will P. Ralph, archivist, Pacific School of Religion, Berkeley, has attempted with others to solve the mystery. "I wrote many letters to retired ministers who served the church in earlier years and widows of ministers," said Ralph. "But no one seems to know the story behind the windows."

Historical background on the ministers memorialized in the windows is contained in the book *The History of Southern Methodism on the Pacific Coast,* published in 1886 by the Rev. J. C. Simmons, a book that may have been the inspiration for the windows. Consider some of the following descriptions: Of the Rev. J.T. Cox, remembered on a window as "a remarkable preacher," Rev. Simmons wrote, "The early part of his life was spent in sin. When he was converted he served God as faithfully as he had Satan. Rev. Cox weighed 300 pounds. He preached with power and pathos. As an exhorter he was almost without rival. Amid some of his perorations you could almost hear the thunders of Sinai and feel the crack of doom."

And the Rev. Featherstun must, indeed, have died in triumph, if Rev. Simmons' account of his death is correct. The Rev. Featherstun said on his death bed: 'I feel I am going to die; but it is all right with me. I am ready." Minutes later Rev. Featherstun reportedly uttered these final words: "Nearing Heaven. At the gate. Entering Paradise! Glory! Glory!" he is said to have shouted. "The angels. The angels. Good-bye. Good-bye. Farewell. Farewell." The Rev. Simmons concluded, "Thus in one breath he bade farewell to Earth and greeted Heaven."

The Rev. Stewart was killed by a companion, "The traitor," in Chihuahua, Mexico. The murder occurred during the Civil War as Rev. Stewart, whose sympathy lay with the South, was attempting to return to his home in Alabama from California by traveling across northern Mexico on horseback. The traitor allegedly "blew Rev. Stewart's brains out with a gun, then stole Rev. Stewart's saddlebags, his Bible and hymnbook." As for the Rev. Wood who died in a buggy, Rev. Simmons wrote: "He always said he wanted to die with the harness on. God gave him the desire of his heart, for on Sept. 14, 1871, on his way to his last appointment, while seated in his buggy, angels swept down the sky and bore the old soldier to his home in Paradise."

In 1970 the Rev. Christensen urged that the church be set aside as a state or national monument. In the late 1990s, the Rev. Bill Alexander, was still attempting to get the church designated as a historic site because of the highly unusual stain-glass windows. "There's at least another 100 years of life left in the old building. And the stained-glass windows are priceless," commented the minister, who was a policeman in San Jose, Santa Clara and Milipitas before he became a preacher.

"When anyone walks into our church, they are fascinated by the windows. They want to know more about the ministers memorialized," related Rev. Alexander. "People ask us for information about the preachers depicted in the windows and why the windows were placed in the church. I sure wish we could tell them and wish we could find out the full story behind the windows."

THE VOLUNTEER FIREMEN OF AUBURN

THE FIRE ALARM sounded in the 19th-century Shanghai Bar in Auburn, a small Mother Lode town. Harry Yue, proprietor of the saloon, stopped pouring drinks. He grabbed his fire-fighting jacket and helmet and declared: "Down 'em boys. I've got to run." Yue was assistant chief of the Auburn Hook and Ladder Company, oldest continuously active volunteer fire department in the West, first organized in 1852. Yue had been a volunteer fireman with the outfit for 59 years in 1995 when he was 78 years old. He was still going to fires where he cheered his colleagues on but no longer did the grunt work handling the hoses.

Townspeople in Auburn have always considered their Hook and Ladder Company one of the finest small town fire departments in the nation. It's no idle boast. The Auburn Fire Department has one of the best fire ratings possible, much better than many paid professional fire departments. A San Francisco fire chief once said he would gladly swap two of his men for every one man in the Auburn Hook and Ladder Company. Auburn, 34 miles northeast of Sacramento and seat of Placer County, has a population of 11,300. The town's fire department has had as many as 75 volunteers in recent years.

Henry Gietzer was 87 when he retired as fire chief in 1990. He was the oldest and in office longer then any other fire chief in California at the time. A retired banker he had been on the department 68 years and chief for 43 years. He had never been paid a penny for the thousands of hours spent working with the fire department. Nor had any other member been paid a salary until 1992 when Howard Leal became chief, and was the first to receive a salary. By 1995 the department had six paid firemen, including the chief, and the rest volunteers.

When the siren goes off in Auburn volunteer firemen come running from everywhere. Teachers leave their classes. Merchants close their stores. Plumbers, barbers, bartenders, service station attendants head for one of the town's three fire houses. "Tradition is a big part of it, 140 years in Auburn, from 1852 to 1992, never any paid firemen, always volunteers, always the highest caliber of dedicated men," said fire chief Leal.

In the heart of Auburn stands the Old Fire House, a narrow, red and white, sharp-towered frame structure built in 1891. When members of the Auburn Hook and Ladder Company put up the Old Fire House (it was the New Fire House then), it was the tallest building in town. It was used until 1954. Townspeople say the Old Fire House will stand as a historic monument as long as there is an Auburn.

In 1995 Boy Scouts from Auburn completely restored the Old Fire

House, including putting a new roof on it and painting it. In that same year, Disney Studios were in town to film the movie "Phenomenon" starring John Travolta and Robert Duvall. Longtime volunteer fireman Harry Yue's Shanghai Bar and Auburn's Old Fire House are featured prominently in the film.

Logs of Auburn's Fire Department going back to the beginning are still intact. At first it was hardly more than a bucket brigade. By 1854 the first Fireman's Ball was held—to raise money to buy axes, ropes, buckets and a shed to keep them in. The Ball has been celebrated ever since, one of the biggest events of the year in Auburn.

In 1855 Auburn was nearly destroyed by fire. The town was quickly rebuilt using more stone and bricks. And all places of business were ordered to keep barrels of water ready in case of fire. In the early days the whole town turned out to help the volunteers man the buckets and the two wheeled horse-drawn wagons.

When Henry Gietzen was fire chief he talked about the savings to the town each year in salaries that would normally be paid to firemen:

"The Auburn Hook and Ladder Company represents a tremendous savings for the taxpayers. The department has a long waiting list of able-bodied men of the community just itching to get on the department in the worse way. It's always been like that. The men take great pride in the department. We're very selective about new members coming aboard. We're training all the time." Said Harry Yue whose great-grandfather came to Auburn from China in the 1850s to prospect for gold: "In this town it's a real privilege to be a fireman."

THIRTY-TWO

PLUMAS COUNTY

"WELCOME PEGGERS!"

WORDS like *muggins, fifteen-two, his heels, his nobs* and *two-spotter* echoed through the fairgrounds pavilion at Quincy in Plumas County as opponents faced each other across long tables. The action consisted of moving small wooden pegs along rows of holes in wooden boards. The name of the game was cribbage and this mountain town with a population of 6,000 fancies itself as the cribbage capital of the world. Signs all over town proclaimed: "Welcome Peggers!" Every first weekend in May since 1972 upwards of 350 of the top cribbage players in America vie for the title of "World Championship Cribbage Player."

We were on hand when Jesse Jarrell, of Pittsburg, California, defeated Mike Taborski of Quincy after 13-hours of tournament play. Jarrell won two of three games in the final match. "This is the greatest thrill of my life," exclaimed Jarrell as he clutched the perpetual trophy in one hand and his $1,500 cash prize in the other.

It was a disappointing loss for Taborski. "We not only host the world championship cribbage tournament but we believe the best cribbage players in the world live in Quincy," said Taborski. By 1995 Quincy residents had won 10 of the 24 world championship single tournaments. Nick Ayoob of Quincy and Bernard Rubin of San Mateo are the only three time winners of the competition. Double's matches are also played.

Cribbage players descend on the logging town each May by private plane, bus, car, camper and motor home. Quincy, the county seat of Plumas County, is 170 miles northeast of San Francisco. The year we were there bearded prospector Larry Johnson hiked in from his diggings. Four nurses drove up from San Francisco. Nick Pond, a TV sportscaster, flew in from Raleigh, N.C. Sugar grower Bob Herkes came from Hawaii. The oldest player that year was Roy Carmichael, 87, who drove up from his Vina, Calif. ranch. Youngest player so far was 9-year-old John McNair who flew to California alone from Boston. His uncle, Roger Ryan met him at the San Francisco Airport and drove him to Quincy. Players come from as far away as Alaska and Maine.

Ev Bey, publisher emeritus of Quincy's weekly Feather River Bulletin, explained how his small town happens to sponsor the oldest and biggest annual cribbage tournament in America. "In winter there's not a helluva lot to do in Quincy. The logging is shut down. We're snowed in half the time up here in the mountains. So, we play cribbage. Quincy grade school teachers use cribbage to teach our kids math. Cribbage boards are made by students in high school shop classes. When peggers think of Quincy, they think of cribbage. The town is nuts about the game."

Bey and the local Chamber of Commerce manager, Bob Moon, were playing cribbage one night in 1971 when they came up with the idea of having a countywide cribbage tournament. Moon suggested that it be statewide. Bey said: "Hell, there ain't a world tournament. Let's make it worldwide." And, that's how the tiny mountain town became the cribbage capital of the world. Bey, by the way, won the world championship in 1992. He is president of the American Cribbage Congress, sanctioning body of the game.

Tournament players have included Joe Wergin of Madison Wisconsin, "the Grand Old Man of cribbage," former president of the American Cribbage Congress, retired postmaster of McFarland, Wisconsin, and author of *How to Win at Cribbage*. He said 15 million Americans play the game. "Cribbage was invented by the British poet Sir John Suckling in 1635," Wergin noted. "Before his invention Suckling was best known for his song that began: 'Why so pale and wan, fond lover?'" Now, no one even knows the second line, but cribbage lives on.

OLD PAT IS FINALLY LAID TO REST

IT WAS JUNE 22, and after a particularly severe winter in the mountains of Plumas County, the winter snows finally melted in Howland Flat, a mile-high, deserted mining town. So, they were finally able to bury old Patrick J. O'Kean.

O'Kean, lifelong prospector and gold miner, died at age 81, six months earlier in Quincy, 40 miles to the north. But it was impossible to drive over the twisting rocky dirt mountain road into the snowbound ghost town. Five years earlier the miner and his friends trucked a large boulder into the ghost town graveyard. O'Kean selected a spot for the big stone and declared: "When I die, boys, this is where I want my bones laid to rest."

O'Kean's remains were kept in Anderson's Mortuary in Quincy six months. When it was finally possible to get to Howland Flat, 125 of O'Kean's friends followed a cloud of dust left by the hearse as it wound up and down steep mountain slopes to the ghost town cemetery. Before traveling the last 11 miles, the funeral possession stopped at Reilly's Saloon in LaPorte for one final round of Old Bushmills Irish whiskey—Pat's favorite.

Father John Moloney, who drove more than 100 miles to officiate at the service for his old friend, took along an empty bottle of Miller's High Life from Reilly's Saloon. The priest filled the beer bottle with water from O'Kean's favorite creek, blessed it and later sprinkled the holy water on the flag-draped coffin. Many of the miner's cronies were on hand: Frank "High Grade" Reilly, 80; Dick O'Rourke, 80; Marie "Ma" Sandberg, 88; Roy Post, 83; "Whiskey Creek Joe" Malouin, 60; and Austin "Last Pocket" Stirratt, 65.

"Whiskey Creek Joe" walked six miles over the mountains from his claim. "Ma" Sandberg allowed how she first met Pat at the Bunker Hill mine in '32. "He had a coat on one shoulder and his pick, shovel and pan on the other," she recalled. Mel Ponta, a friend of Pat's for 40 years, fell into the freshly dug grave as he placed the marker at the head of the hole before the coffin was lowered. Ponta wasn't hurt. He was helped out of the grave by several members of E Clampus Vitus, preservers of old mining camps.

Howland Flat, once a riotous gold camp, is but a memory of the past—a collection of a few abandoned old clapboard buildings propped up with timbers, and several more structures collapsed into piles of rubble. O'Kean, a lifelong bachelor with no known kin, was born in County Mayo in Ireland. The lure of gold brought him to California's Mother Lode.

"He was a fine, fine mon," said Dick O'Rourke, wiping away a tear. The rarefied air of the mile-high ghost town was pungent with the scent of Irish whiskey. Toasts were drunk to Pat at graveside. "A mon of integrity and honesty. That was Patrick O'Kean," continued O'Rourke. "Pat once said: 'We don't have much in the world. A man who cannot keep his word has nothing.'"

"He was one of the last of the old-time miners," eulogized Father Moloney. "His heart was in these parts. What little fortune he amassed in his digging he shared with his fellow man. He had deep faith in God."

THE TAYLORSVILLE QUILTERS

*B*lessed are the quilters for they shall be called peacemakers.
                                    —Saying posted in the Taylorsville Church

The quilters in Taylorsville, a Sierre Nevada town tucked away in a lonely corner of Plumas County, are the backbone of the community. They help down-and-out families pay rent and utility bills and keep them in groceries. When a house was destroyed in a fire it was the quilters who came to the rescue and provided food, clothing and shelter. They restored the only church in town. They dug a well in the local cemetery so grass and flowers would grow on graves. Their list of good deeds goes on and on.

"It could get pretty boring being stuck in a house in below freezing weather and snow all over these mountains if you didn't have something to do," said Margaret Cooke, who was 82 in 1995 and founded the Taylorsville Ladies Coffee and Sewing Circle in 1957. "Five of us started quilting in 1957 to raise money to keep the church from falling down. It was a wreck," recalled Lucille Stead, who was 76 in

1995 and like Cooke still quilting as much as ever.

The women of Taylorsville (population 250) spend most of their spare time from Labor Day to the first of May quilting. They quilt together at the church on Tuesdays and Fridays with potlucks for lunch. They quilt the rest of the time at home.

Every year the women of Taylorsville hold their annual May Quilt Show in the picturesque white frame 1875 Taylorsville Community United Methodist Church, a church built with square nails. Inside the church is a plush red carpet and red cushions on the 1875 original hand-hewn wooden pews. The carpet and cushions were paid for by the quilters.

Quilters from up and down the Pacific Coast come here each May to display old and new quilts in the church sanctuary and the social hall behind it. On the first Saturday in October the Taylorsville quilters present their annual fall festival in the church selling the quilts they create throughout the year. The quilters keep none of the proceeds. The sales exceed $5,000 with half going to the support of the church, the other half for a community project.

"Many of us are not members of the church. But everyone in town uses the church for weddings, receptions, parties and funerals," explained Marion Kunz, 86, a quilter since 1966. The quilters range from as young as 30 to Etta Lewis who quilted until she lost her eyesight when she was 90. When she could no longer see she continued to come to the quilting bees to lend moral support. She died in her late 90s.

"I never met a group of women that make outsiders so welcome," said Maxine Buzzell, who moved to Taylorsville from Sun Valley in 1977 when her husband Del (Buzz) Buzzell retired as a Los Angeles city fireman. "We came to Taylorsville as strangers. I never quilted before, but I'm a quilter now," laughed Maxine.

On a wall in the church social hall where the quilters gather is a bit of prose by Ann Lohn, entitled "Creation": *"God sewed a patchwork quilt at creation. She called the blue and white squares sky. The rich browns, yellows, blacks, reds and tans she called Earth. The cool green and deep murky blues she called oceans. God quilted in patterns of tall mountains and deep valleys. She knotted her thread and took the quilt off the frame. Then she flung it into space…"*

THIRTY-THREE

RIVERSIDE COUNTY

THE VALHALLA OF TROLLEYS

AIR BRAKES HISSED. Wheels squealed as a string of old streetcars rounded a curve. And the streetcar buffs cheered. It was a typical weekend day at Perris, 65 miles southeast of Los Angeles, home of the Valhalla of trolleys. On the tracks are streetcars from Ireland, Canada, Japan and cities across the United States—Toonerville trolleys, double-deck coaches, streetcars with stained-glass windows and carpeting, streetcars operated before the turn of the century.

Streetcar enthusiasts from all over California, other states, and several foreign countries descend on the small Riverside County town to restore old trolleys at the 62-acre Orange Empire Railway Museum. There are 1,200 members of the museum founded in 1956. All kinds of people are streetcar buffs—ministers, doctors, dentists, scientists, lawyers, insurance agents, cops, firemen, teachers, students, shopkeepers, housewives and sailors. They come on weekends and vacations, some who are retired are here every day to restore the weather-beaten, dilapidated streetcars to the shape they were in when they rolled off assembly lines 50 to 100 years ago. They spend their own money for supplies needed in refurbishing their trolley, as well as lay tracks, and put up trolley wires.

Joe Webber, a longtime member of the Railway Museum, was 73 when we caught up with him. A self-styled "railroad and streetcar nut" since he was a teen-ager, Webber is a retired Hughes Aircraft engineer. He and his wife, Norma, fell in love with a quaint 1900 Bakersfield and Kern Electric Railway streetcar that operated in Bakersfield until 1941 when the trolley company went out of business. The old car was among scores of streetcars and railroad cars in various stages of decay awaiting restoration at the museum. "It was in terrible shape, rotting away on a museum siding," Webber said. "We took pieces of the streetcar home and sorted them out in our living room. That was the beginning of our restoration project."

The Webbers became so involved with their retirement hobby that they sold their home in Gardena and moved to Perris to be near the museum, where they could work in one of four huge galvanized steel railway barns. "We have blueprints and photographs of the turn-of-the-century trolley when it was brand-new," Webber related. "We had to remake nearly all the wood and metal pieces. It was exasperating at times, but we persevered. All that's left now is to electrify it."

The Webbers spent 10 years restoring the bright yellow streetcar to what it was like when it first rolled down the streets of Bakersfield in 1900. When it is electrified it will operate weekends on the six miles of track at the museum where the Webbers are conductors. "We have three daughters, 10 grandchildren and seven great grandchildren," said Norma Webber. "We had a ball putting the old streetcar back together and get a big kick out of running restored streetcars on the museum tracks. Our grandchildren are forever amazed that grandpa and grandma are streetcar conductors."

One of the operating streetcars, Kyoto No. 19, is made of wood and was shipped in pieces from America to Japan in 1890. It operated until 1961, when one of the museum's members was able to buy it and bring it to Perris.

One of the most unusual streetcars being brought back to life, called the Descanso, carried hundreds of the newly departed from 10 mortuaries in downtown Los Angeles to cemeteries on the outskirts of the city from 1909 to 1924. "As far as we know, this is the only streetcar of its kind left in America," said David Kelly, who is working on the project with four other men. Only a handful of cities operated funeral streetcars during the late 1800s and early 20th century. The casket was placed in front and mourners rode in seats behind the casket. The funeral trolley, with 36 stained glass windows, was used because dirt roads were extremely rough and often impassable. Kelly and the four men working on the funeral car spent nearly two years working on a two-decker Hill of Howth streetcar used in Dublin from 1923 to 1959.

When Bruce Thain of Brooklyn was a sailor stationed aboard the USS Point Defiance home ported in San Diego, he spent two years working on the Hill of Howth, on every liberty he had off the ship. It was Jim Walker, an insurance agent and secretary of the Trolley Museum, who saw a photograph of the double deck trolley in an Irish magazine described as the last of its kind. So, Walker wrote to Ireland, and the museum bought the car by mail for $85 and paid $2,500 to have it shipped to Perris.

"This is an escape," said Joel Marsh, co-owner of a fire alarm business and vice president of collections at the museum. "I enjoy working on this stuff." The museum is open every day, with rides on the restored historic streetcars and two trains, one diesel and the other steam, available on weekends.

SAVING AN ECOSYSTEM, AND ITS LIZARD

A 13,000-ACRE STRETCH OF DESERT 15 miles east of Palm Springs was purchased for $25 million to save, preserve and protect a rare, elusive lizard—along with its habitat, a delicate ecosystem containing diverse flora and fauna. The world's only home of the Coachella Valley fringe-toed lizard is within the dunes of the Coachella Valley Preserve.

Those who come to the preserve expecting to see the 8-to-10-inch-long, sand-colored, black-mottled lizard, an endangered species, are almost always disappointed. Since the dedication of the preserve in 1986 only a handful of visitors have seen one. The others had to settle for photographs and descriptions at the Thousand Palms Oasis Visitors Center.

The fringe-toed isn't a leaping lizard. But it's a real speedster, able to bury itself in the sand almost in the flick of an eyelid. With its shovel-shaped snout, the lizard digs several inches into the dune and disappears in seconds. It gets its name from fringe-like scales on its toes that provide traction, like snowshoes, on the sand. A heat sensor on top of its head that looks like an eye warns the lizard when the temperature is too hot, and it's time to duck beneath the sand.

Superbly adapted to being a dune dweller, the fringe-toed lizard's snout has a trapdoor that prevents sand from entering its nose and lungs. Its double set of eyelids, one horizontal, the other vertical, also keep out sand. Beetles, crickets and other insects provide the main diet for the lizards, which hibernate beneath the sand surface from November through March.

"Years ago, fringe-toed lizards were found on sand dunes scattered throughout 200 square miles of Coachella Valley. Today several thousand exist only on a mile square of sand dunes in the preserve," noted Cameron Barrows, Nature Conservancy's Southern California manager.

Areas where the lizards once thrived are now desert communities, golf course, mobile-home parks. With the habitat shrinking and further development looming, the Nature Conservancy, the U.S. Bureau of Land Management, the California Department of Parks and Recreation, the U.S. Fish and Wildlife Service, and the California Department of Fish and Game joined forces to purchase the preserve land and manage it as wild desert.

"In 1980, when the federal government listed the Coachella Valley fringe-toed lizard as threatened, the action initiated a series of events that culminated in the establishment of the preserve," explained Barrows. He added, "Off-road vehicles were running amok on the sand dunes, killing the fringe-toed lizards in wholesale fashion. The dunes where the lizard lives are replenished with sand washing down an alluvial fan from the Indio Hills and blown into dune areas by strong winds." To preserve the lizard's habitat, it was necessary to protect the area generating the sand as well as the dunes. By setting aside 13,000 acres, an entire ecosystem of flora and fauna once common through-out much of Coachella Valley is being preserved, Barrows said.

Within the preserve are a dozen oases containing the largest groves of desert fan palms in California. There are palm-boring beetles, cockroach-es, Jerusalem crickets, giant red velvet mites and a round-tailed ground squirrel that, like the fringe-toed lizard, are found nowhere else on Earth.

Paul Wilhelm is probably better acquainted with fringe-toed lizards than anyone. "I've grown up with the lizards. I've seen them all my life," said the nature writer and former resident caretaker of the preserve's Thousand Palms Oasis. "I have seen fringe-toed lizards swimming under the sand many, many times. When they bury themselves in the dunes you can see them moving rapidly under the surface, disturbing the sand on top."

Wilhelm's father bought the 80-acre Thousand Palms Oasis in 1906 from prospector Albert (Alkali) L. Thornburg for two mules and a wagon. The oasis is a lush grove of huge 60-to-70-foot-tall, 100-to-250-year-old fan palms surrounding a spring-fed pond. In 1932, when he was 20, Wilhelm built a home there out of palm logs. His pump house now serves as the preserve's visitors center.

Wilhelm, a lifelong bachelor, sold the oasis to the Nature Conser-vancy in 1984 with the provision he would live out his life in a cabin he built near the palm log house. "For me, seeing the oasis and the desert surrounding it set aside forever as a nature preserve is a dream come true," Wilhelm said. He pointed to a thicket of mesquite bush-es growing on the summit of a nearby mountain. "Cahuilla Indians for centuries have cremated their dead and buried their ashes in that mesquite grove. I have heard them sing their funeral dirges from the mountain top since I was a little boy. The fringe-toed lizards, the oasis, the Indian burial grounds. There are many sacred things saved and protected in this unique nature preserve," said the old man.

GIANT FIGURES ON THE DESERT FLOOR

ARCHAEOLOGIST BOMA JOHNSON gazed at the 154-foot figure of a man etched on the desert floor. "When I am alone on the sites of these giant prehistoric effigies, the hair on my arms prickles," he said. "I get goose bumps when I think of the things that took place here centuries ago. It's a spiritual experience. I have an awareness of the spirits guarding these very special places." Johnson was the U.S. Bureau of Land Management's specialist on the mysterious figures along the Colorado River from Bullhead City 300 miles to the Gulf of California.

More than 200 of the giant figures have been discovered. They were made by ancient people who scraped away huge areas of stone laid down during the Ice Age on mesas overlooking the river. There are figures of men and women, serpents, horses, mountain lions, lizards, and spiders. Also, geometric designs, and mazes of prehistoric dance patterns with ancient trails leading from one to another.

Beginning in 1975, Johnson recorded the effigies, called intaglios, geoglyphs, gravel pictographs, or gravel petroglyphs. Some of the figures are believed to have been made as recently as 150 years ago. Others appear to be possibly 10,000 years old.

To the Indians of the Lower Colorado, the Quechan, Mojave and Cocopah, the giant figures are religious shrines. "For my people the giant figures are not something of the past," said Weldon Johnson, a Mojave Indian, who is assistant director of the Colorado River Indian Tribes Museum at Parker, Arizona. The spiritual life of the Colorado Indians revolves around this legacy of giants. "They are our sacred objects, held with the same respect as the giant Buddha statues in the Orient or statues in the Catholic Church," related Johnson.

Little has been published about these remnants of prehistoric civilizations. "We are just beginning to scratch the surface. Most of the discoveries have been made since the 1970s," noted Jay Von Werlhof, senior archaeologist at Imperial Valley College in El Centro. Brawley pilot Harry Casey working with Von Werlhof logged 600 hours flying his Piper Cub low over the desert in search of relics of the prehistoric culture. Casey has found 150 previously unrecorded sites with figures and rock alignments as far as 100 miles east and west of the Colorado River and equally far south along the western coast of the Mexican mainland.

Some of the rock alignments recorded by scientists are a quarter of a mile long. They were pushed together to form patterns by ancient man. Von Werlhof believes the rocks, like the giant figures, were religious symbols to the prehistoric Indians. "I believe the rock alignments were spiritual signs created by ancient man as he prayed to his gods asking for the restoration of a lost paradise," he said. He theorizes that some of these alignments are 10,000 years old because tools that old have been found at the sites.

There are brief mentions of the giant figures in diaries of the first Spanish explorers in Southern Arizona and California and in the writings of pioneers and early military groups. Pilots from Blythe, Needles and Yuma spotted some of the giant figures from the air in the 1930s. In 1943 Generals George C. Marshall and Hap Arnold flew over the figures with civilian pilot George Palmer. Marshall wrote at the time: "These crude pictures of man and animal outlined in rocky soil, visible only to the gods and passing birds, are so grandiose in scale as to take one's breath away."

Johnson has spent considerable time over the years talking to Colorado River Indians to learn what he can about the giant figures. "Many of the figures represent the creation story and the perpetual struggle of good and evil," he explained. "There are 14 pairs of giant figures of man along the river with one man depicted in all cases with full body and the other always missing its head and one of its limbs."

Johnson accompanied the author and photographer Jose Galvez to a 27-foot-long, 12-foot-high horse, drawn on the stony desert pavement near an Indian trail used by Spanish explorer Juan Bautista de Anza in 1774-76. At the site, the archaeologist noted, "We believe the horse was made by Indians about the time of the de Anza overland expedition, because it would have been the first time Indians of the area ever saw a horse."

As more people take offroad vehicles to the undeveloped mesas overlooking the Colorado River where the giant figures are found, the possibility of damage to this legacy increases. Fences have been erected by the Bureau of Land Management and by concerned groups in Blythe to protect a few of the figures.

THIRTY-FOUR

SACRAMENTO COUNTY

LICENSE PLATE FACTORY

I T WAS PRESS DAY at the license plate factory. "Don't wear blue denims. The guards won't let you in if you do," reporters were warned by Sid Smith, Department of Motor Vehicles public relations man. "That's so you won't get mixed up with the inmates who always wear denim—so none of the prisoners will try to escape masquerading as newsmen."

California's license plate factory is in Folsom Prison in Sacramento County. The DMV and Folsom Prison held the first press day in history at the maximum-security prison to call attention to California's new seven-character personalized license plates. Until then the personalized plates had been limited to six characters.

Of the prison's 3,600 inmates in 1996, about 200 worked in "LPF" as the cons affectionately call the license plate factory. The prisoners insist its the best place to work behind bars. The pay is better than that for other jobs, an average of 35 cents an hour or $38 a month to spend for "candy, soft drinks and cigarettes." They work four days a week, 10 hours a day. There is a long waiting list for the job. It takes about two years on the list to be accepted. A con has to be an honor prisoner to work in LPF, where 4.5 million license plates were manufactured in 1996. Production was running about 20,000 plates a day.

"LPF is the place to work in this joint," said Frank (Yellow Hammer) Hampton, who was 90 and the oldest inmate at Folsom when press day was held in 1978. Hampton had been turning out license plates for eight years and had spent 54 of his 90 years behind bars. "I've never used dope, never robbed or raped anyone," confided Yellow Hammer. Then why are you here, the old man was asked. "Murder!" said Yellow Hammer. "I killed 19 people." (Prison guards verified Yellow Hammer's boast.)

The license factory howls with noise from the 500-ton hydraulic presses, operated by inmates who hand-set letters and numbers for each plate. Once in awhile, messages secreted by the prisoners between the plates and paper coverings are detected. "Help. I'm being held prisoner in a license plate factory," is one of the more popular ones. Now and then the prisoners stamp out obscene or humorous plates that are almost always detected and destroyed. It takes two hours and 15 minutes from the time the 6 inch by 12 inch aluminum plates are cut, pressed, painted and packed for shipment.

The factory is inside 20-foot high, 2-foot-thick stone walls surrounding the 1890 Old Folsom Prison, 25 miles east of Sacramento. California license plates have been made exclusively at Folsom since 1947. Before that they were made by a private firm in Los Angeles.

Since personal plates were first made available in 1970 more than $310 million in revenue has been made on the sale of the vanity plates with more than $33 million in revenues in the most recent year reported. Revenue earned from the sale of the personalized plates is made available to environmental projects such as the purchase of ecological reserves, protection of rare and endangered animal species, bird sanctuaries and for such things as abatement of air pollution caused by motor vehicles.

"Working in LPF is better than walking the yard all day," said one prisoner, who pressed two plates with a personal message: "OUT SOON" "I HOPE"

STATE LIBRARY: A GOLD MINE OF BOOKS

As ONE OF ITS EARLIEST ACTS, the California Legislature created a library on January 24, 1850. It started as a bookcase in the State Senate.

Today, with more than 8 million books, photographs, manuscripts, documents and other historical material, the California State Library is one of the West's leading libraries, with more than 1.5 million volumes on its shelves. Yet, many Californians do not know it exists. The library is to the Legislature and state offices what the Library of Congress is to the U.S. Senate and House of Representatives.

"The California State Library is a sleeping dinosaur, an incredible treasure. We hold in trust a remarkable mass of material, a real breadth of California history," said Gary E. Strong, state librarian from 1980 to 1994.

The library remained in the Capitol until 1929, when it moved across the street to its present home, the stately five-story granite structure called the Library and Courts Building, which it shares with the Supreme Court and 3rd District Court of Appeal.

In 1994 a portion of the State Library collections and several of its operations were moved to a new structure, Library and Courts Building Two connected by a tunnel under N Street to Library and Courts Building One.

Every day state employees on official business borrow hundreds of books and documents from the library. The library's rich resources are also available to the public for research purposes, and it is a gold mine for historians, scholars and writers. Take maps, for example: James Marshall's original hand-drawn map of his discovery that triggered the Gold Rush of 1849 is here. So are maps for mines, cities and assorted places throughout the state from the earliest days.

Through the years the library has acquired practically every book written about California. It has diaries and journals by Spanish explorers, early settlers and the forty-niners. More than 125,000 photographs are in its archives, dating to the mining camps of the 1850s. There are thousands of photographs of Los Angeles, San Francisco, Yosemite National Park, Sacramento and other points of interest from the 1860s through the 1890s.

The library is also the repository of all state legislation, state Supreme Court briefs and publications from every state department. For example, among the documents are all 28 volumes of records and briefs before the courts and various land commissions in Mexican and Spanish land-grant confirmation cases. So are budgets and publications from all 58 counties and the cities and towns of California.

Collections include papers of prominent Californians from the earliest days of the state, including those of such pioneers as John Sutter, John Bidwell, P.B. Reading, William Peace Davis and James Wilson Marshall. There are papers of California religious movements, political groups and unions. The State Library operates the Talking Book Library for the blind with 11,000 users in Northern California, and the prestigious Adolph Sutro Library in San Francisco, boasting a renowned collection of rare manuscripts and books and one of the finest genealogy resources on the West Coast.

Noted author and historian Kevin Starr who was born in 1940 is the seventh state librarian since 1900. He was appointed by Gov. Pete Wilson with the approval of the State Senate. Starr frequently appears before the Legislature as advocate for all 172 library jurisdictions in California. The jurisdictions, numbering about 1,000 libraries, are as small as the City of Vernon with a library that consists of a couple of shelves behind the City Clerk's desk, to the city of Los Angeles with 96 branch libraries. Among Starr's duties is that of administrator of state and federal funding for the libraries of California. The 1995 budget, for example, was $51,620,000, of that, $34,209,000 was distributed to libraries all over the state.

As California's Librarian, Starr spends half his time visiting libraries. He officiates at ground breaking and dedication ceremonies for new libraries. He is the visible advocate for libraries throughout the state. And, being a popular speaker, he is in constant demand to make public appearances. "Although California is not one of the oldest states, it has one of the oldest state libraries in America," noted Cameron Robertson, assistant state librarian. "And, Kevin Starr is the spiritual leader of California's libraryland."

THIRTY-FIVE

SAN BENITO COUNTY

PINNACLES NATIONAL MONUMENT

Two National Park Service rangers stood beneath the gigantic 20-foot-high, 25-foot-wide boulder wedged between two walls of the cave. They were checking it for any movement. "What a time for an earthquake," joked Steve Debenedetti, park resources manager for Pinnacles National Monument. The rangers were using a highly accurate measuring device called a tape extensometer to monitor any movement in a network of boulders that form the roof of two caves in the national monument.

Quarter-mile-long Bear Gulch Cave and 300-foot-long Balconies Cave were formed over the centuries by an aggregation of differently shaped boulders sliding down narrow canyon walls and wedging against each other near the canyon bottom. When a boulder about six feet in diameter fell from the ceiling of Balconies Cave in March, 1983, the Park Service sealed the caves with iron gates. It was the first time since the establishment of the monument by President Theodore Roosevelt in 1908 that part of a roof of one of the caves had collapsed. No one was hurt.

The huge rock was jarred loose during a three-day storm. Seven inches of rain pelted the park, and streams meandering through the caves became rushing torrents. The caves were closed for nine months. Authorities feared that other rocks and boulders might fall, particularly since the caves sit on top of a particularly active segment of the San Andreas Fault, and earthquakes occur here frequently.

"We seriously considered sealing the caves permanently," said Edward R. Carlson, the chief ranger at the time. "But the caves are the highlight of the national monument. The caves are what bring people here. We received hundreds of complaints about the closure." About 50,000 visitors to the monument each year use the trails in the caves, some sections of which have to be crawled through. Other parts of the caves open into large rooms.

After the decision was made to reopen the caves, a seismograph was installed at the park visitors' center. If seismic activity of 2.0 or greater on the Richter scale is noted, all the critical points in the cave are immediately measured. If significant rock movement is detected or high water conditions exist, the caves are closed until conditions are stable. So far, seismic activity has not forced closure of either of the two caves, but from time to time the caves have been closed for short periods from high runoff water during heavy rain.

Pinnacles National Monument is a hikers' park. The main entrance is 35 miles south of Hollister and 35 miles north of Kings City in San Benito County. The monument has 16,000 acres of precipitous volcanic bluffs, spires and crags, and is bisected from north to south by a 1,000-foot-high ridge.

FAY AND CECILIA, TWO TREASURES OF PINNACLES

To RANGERS at Pinnacles National Monument two women, Fay Kennedy and Cecilia Bjornerud, are "real treasures." Fay was 93 in 1988 when I met the silver-haired, 5-foot, artist with a pixy smile. She was the answer to the rangers' prayers.

Every year in late February and March a multitude of wildflowers start popping out in a blaze of brilliant colors amid the towering spires and crags and all over the green rolling hills of Pinnacles National Monument. "It's the beginning of our busy season as people from miles around head this way to walk the trails to discover and enjoy the beauty and diversity of the wild spring flowers," said monument Supt. Jim Sleznick Jr. Spring comes early each year to this Central California park.

Chief ranger Ed Carlson said visitors ask him and other rangers time and time again throughout the day to help identify the various wildflowers. That was the year Sleznick had a brainstorm, "Let's hang a bunch of Fay Kennedy's watercolors on the walls of the Bear Gulch Visitors Center and let the visitors have the fun of finding and identifying the wildflowers on their own," said the superintendent. So, an exhibit of 40 watercolors of the most common wildflowers in the park painted by Fay Kennedy was officially unveiled to the public followed by coffee, juice, cookies and cake served by the rangers. Fay was guest of honor. Her latest painting, a bouquet of purple thistles, yellow mule ears, wild iris, lavender Chinese houses, California poppies, baby blue eyes and blue penstemon, the keystone of the exhibit, was completed a week earlier.

The artist was 13 when Teddy Roosevelt established Pinnacles National Monument in 1908. "I have lived close by the national monument all my life," noted Fay. "I love this place." She had been painting flowers since she was in grammar school, and had painted more than 300 different kinds of local wildflowers and at least 1,000 paintings of garden flowers. She lived in Hollister where she was still teaching an art class in her dining room three hours every Tuesday morning, charging $5 a lesson.

She painted in her studio every day in the home she lived in since 1930, and lived there alone after her husband, Cecil, a prune and apricot grower, died in 1968. "I have to keep painting because I have enough back orders to keep me busy for months. I can't slow up. But I don't care. I love to paint. I always have," she confided with a twinkle in her bright eyes. She said the most she ever charged for a painting was $200. A saying posted on her studio wall read: "I paint for love, not for money." The spring of 1988 was the one and only time her watercolors of the Pinnacles National Monument wildflowers were on public exhibit. Fay Kennedy died a year later, never filling all her back orders.

Cecilia Bjornerud is the other "treasure" of Pinnacles. She spent 8 years, from 1980 to 1988 when she was 68 to 76 years old, in the mountainous park cataloguing plants, shrubs, rushes, sedges and trees. A volunteer botanist, she dedicated all her time, talent and effort, living in the park year round in a motor home doing an inventory that had never been done since the creation of the park.

Every day, the hearty great-grandmother trudged 10 to 15 miles up and down mountains, along creek bottoms and in dense brush looking for new species she had yet to encounter. By the time she finished, she had catalogued more than 700 different species of plant life in the national monument, more than 400 that were known to exist there. "The other day I found eight new species along the creek bed," she noted excitedly when we spent one November day with her out searching for new things.

She was living in her 1967 mobile home beneath the jagged spectacular Pinnacles carved by rain, wind, heat and frost that gave the monument its name. Cecilia had no electricity or running water in her tiny home on wheels. She cooked with propane, read by kerosene lantern. "My needs are simple," she allowed. "I'm living like I did when I was a child growing up on a farm in Wisconsin. I love this. I'm doing exactly what I want to be doing."

Her mobile home was filled with botany books, including the $140 set of Abrams Illustrated Plants published by Stanford University, a gift from national park colleagues. There were shelves lined with notebooks, her day by day record of her work. A striking painting of a blue oak tree hung from a wall, a gift from ranger Clyde Stonaker who painted it for the botanist when she was studying oak trees in the park.

She was a first and second grade teacher in rural Wisconsin elementary schools and worked as a nurse for 10 years in San Francisco. Her lifelong avocation was botany. "My father was a self-taught naturalist. He knew all the trees in Wisconsin," she said explaining her penchant for plants.

She was never alone as she hiked through the monument from one end to the other constantly searching. The park was alive with wildlife—deer, raccoon, fox, bobcat, wild pigs, rabbits, rodents, bats, woodpeckers, quail, vultures, badgers and snakes. "I carry a stick to protect myself from the rattlesnakes," Cecilia related. "I have no intention of doing the snakes any harm. They always get out of my way. I say 'Excuse me' when I shoo them." She said she never tired of her long walks. "You know how it is with Norwegians. A Norwegian mile is seven miles long. My health is good. It's healthy to live in the woods. Look at the history of botanists. Many of their life spans are exceedingly long because of this kind of life style." When she wasn't searching for new species, she gave nature talks to campers.

"Cecilia Bjornerud's pressings and descriptions represent an important part of the Pinnacles National Monument archives at park headquarters. We use her information every day of the year," commented the monument's chief ranger Bill Lester during a 1995 interview. "Cecilia is a Pinnacles treasure, really some kind of a woman. And most amazing of all is that she completed this entire body of work as a volunteer, without getting paid." The botanist now lives in San Luis Obispo but still visits the monument from time to time.

Her favorite plant in the monument? A dry-land orchid she was surprised to find here. "When I dried and pressed the orchid I discovered it had more than 90 tiny exquisite green flowers on the stalk. It was incredible," she observed, adding, "You know, cataloguing the plant life in Pinnacles National Monument was the most exciting thing I ever did in my life. I was out searching for new species from sunup to sundown. I never tired of it. For me it wasn't work. It was absolutely fun."

THIRTY-SIX

SAN BERNARDINO COUNTY

THE LINCOLN SHRINE IN REDLANDS

N O OTHER TOWN IN THE WEST marks Abraham Lincoln's birthday with as much pageantry and fervor as Redlands. Each February 12, upwards of 1,500 Boy Scouts, Girl Scouts, Cub Scouts and Camp Fire Girls march through town. Bands in the Lincoln Day Parade play Civil War songs, and each year outstanding Lincoln scholars deliver a Lincoln Day speech.

In the center of Redlands, population 43,000, some 70 miles east of Los Angeles, is an impressive octagonal marble shrine to the 16th President filled with original Lincoln letters, as well as personal belongings of President of Mr. and Mrs. Lincoln. On exhibit in the shrine is crepe material from the coffin of the assassinated President, a well-worn cane belonging to Lincoln, his favorite set of cuff links. All photographs known to have ever been taken of the President and nearly every book written about Lincoln are in the library as well as numerous books, manuscripts, documents and newspapers of the Lincoln era.

Why does Redlands go all out each year in its remembrance of the Civil War President who never even saw California? What is a shrine to him doing in a town that's half a continent away from Lincoln's birthplace in Kentucky, and from Illinois where he made his mark before going to Washington?

It's all because of a penniless British youth named Robert Watchorn who was born in Alfreton, Derbyshire, England in 1858. He toiled in the coal mines of his native land from the time he was 11 until he left at the age of 22 to come to America to work in the coal mines of Pennsylvania, where in the grand rags-to-riches tradition, he became a millionaire. By 1890 he had become the first secretary of the United Mine Workers of America. Later he became U.S. Commissioner of Immigration. In 1916 he founded his own gas and oil company. And, in 1931, at the age of 73, he took $100,000 of his fortune and built a shrine to his hero, Abraham Lincoln, who had long fascinated and inspired him. People who visit the shrine always ask, "Why Redlands?"

It is because Watchorn, who lived in New York, had a vacation home in Redlands, a popular winter resort in the late 1800s and early 1900s for wealthy Easterners. At the dedication of the shrine in 1932, Watchorn said he had built the shrine and endowed it " because it will stand for other generations to be inspired by kind-hearted, pure-minded Abraham Lincoln, America's greatest hero, who turned the currents of freedom into the souls of millions of his fellow men."

Watchorn spent his life collecting Lincoln material. He filled the Lincoln Memorial Shrine with it and left an endowment, now valued at $250,000, to support the shrine. In 1912 he commissioned famed sculptor George Grey Barnard to do the massive head of Lincoln, the centerpiece of the shrine. Barnard also did a Lincoln statue that stands in Manchester, England, and Lincoln statues in Cincinnati and Louisville. Elmer Grey, architect for the Beverly Hills Hotel and Pasadena Playhouse, designed the shrine. And artist Dean Cornwell did the colorful and richly symbolic murals under the shrine's dome ceiling.

Watchorn, who died in 1944 at age 86, had been a friend of national leaders and persuaded many of them, including Presidents

Herbert Hoover, Calvin Coolidge, Franklin D. Roosevelt and Theodore Roosevelt; Vice Presidents Charles Curtis and Charles G. Dawes, Chief Justice Charles Evans Hughes, and Secretaries of State Henry L. Stimson and Frank B. Kellogg, to donate material to the shrine. Norman Rockwell, another friend, donated his painting "Thoughts on Peace on Lincoln's Birthday," which appeared on the cover of the Saturday Evening Post on February 12, 1945.

On the evening of the dedication, Watchorn was host to the first of the annual Redlands' Lincoln dinners. Each year an outstanding Lincoln scholar discusses some aspect of the President's life. Paul M. Zall, author of *Abe Lincoln Laughing,* spoke about Lincoln's masterful use of humor, and historian Don Fehrenbacher talked about the death of Lincoln. James M. McPherson, author of the Pulitzer Prize-winning Civil War book *Battle Cry of Freedom* was one of the speakers.

Lincoln scholars and researchers come to the shrine from throughout the nation and from many foreign countries to use its resources: more than 5,000 books, many rare 19th-Century volumes; a collection of 4,000 pamphlets, both pro and con, many published when Lincoln was alive, and Civil War newspapers from both North and South. The museum has one of the most complete Lincoln stamp collections in existence.

The children of Redlands are probably better informed about Lincoln than the children of any town in America. Each elementary school class visits the shrine at least once a year. School children studying American history are bussed to the shrine daily from around Southern California. Redlands, a small city in southwestern San Bernardino County, is hardly what most people would think of as the "Land of Lincoln." Yet, the nation's 16th President would likely feel at home here.

MYSTERIOUS MUSIC OF GIANT DUNES

JACK HEREFORD slowly made his way up the steep, seemingly razor-sharp ridge of the giant sand dune in Devils Playground in San Bernardino County. Each step of the way, he sank deep into the sand. He was climbing to the summit of one of the highest sand piles in America to hear it "boom" and "sing." Such eerie sounds are emitted by only a few high dunes in the deserts of the world, and

Hereford has been tracking them for years.

Why some dunes boom and sing remains a mystery. Their shape is clearly a factor. The dunes that have been found to produce the phenomenon are constantly blown on one side by winds that pile the sand higher and higher, causing the slope on the opposite or protected side to become quite steep and creating what is called a "slip face." The higher the dune, the louder the booms and other strange sounds. But, as British physicist Ralph A. Bagnold, a leading authority on dunes, has written: "There is yet no real explanation of the mechanism by which the sounds are produced."

In the vast, uninhabited Mojave Desert 50 miles southeast of Baker, Hereford was a lonely, ant-like figure as he made his way up 700-foot high Kelso Dune. It took the prospector-mining engineer two hours to reach the summit, at the southeast end of a 25-mile sweep of sand piles called Devils Playground. Reaching a 32-degree slip face on the lee side of the dune just beneath its peak, Hereford fell to his hands and knees and began triggering slides. "The steepness of the slip face must be 32 degrees or awfully close to it for the phenomenon to work," he noted.

The desert stillness was shattered by strange sounds. Low-throated booms echoed repeatedly as a wide section of sand slid down the slope. Loud, tuba-like "umpahs" filled the air. Vibrations from the shock waves shook the peak. Other sounds rising from beneath the surface of the dune were vaguely similar to barking seals.

"Marco Polo described a booming dune in his journal," said Hereford. Members of Charles Darwin's party heard the phenomenon in the desert on the west coast of Chile in 1835. "Lord Curzon of Kedleston collected age-old myths from the Middle East about singing dunes," related Hereford, who heard the booming for the first time when he climbed Kelso Dune prospecting for magnetite in 1964. "Union Pacific Railroad tracks lie to the north of the dune. I thought it was a train going by. But there was no train," he recalled.

Bagnold, in a book he has written, tells of hearing the phenomenon in Egypt, 300 miles from the nearest habitation. He describes "a vibrant booming so loud I had to shout to be heard by my companion. Soon other sources, set going by the disturbance, joined their music to the first, with so close a note that a slow beat was clearly recognized. This weird chorus went on for more than five minutes continuously before silence returned and the ground ceased to tremble."

Bagnold has theorized that the booming and singing could be a piezo-electrical effect—the generation of electricity in the quartz crystals of sand due to mechanical stress. Hereford has recorded the orchestration of the dune. He plans to return after dark to see if it is possible to detect electrical luminescence when the pile of sand vocalizes. He has spent the greater part of his life living in and studying the marvels of the desert. "I have learned how sand moves, how high it flies—usually 10 to 14 inches off the ground, never more than 30 inches high in the biggest blows," he related. "There is no end to the mysteries out here," he mused, surveying a sea of ripples etching the smooth, velvet-like texture of a beautifully rounded shoulder of sand. "Ripples start forming with winds of 10 to 13 miles per hour. When the winds go beyond 50 miles per hour, ripples no longer form."

After a couple of hours on the peak of the strange tower of sand, it was time to leave. Jack Hereford ran down the steep slip face, playing a symphony of booms, wailing sighs, shrieks and squeals all the way to the bottom.

THIRTY-SEVEN

SAN DIEGO COUNTY

THE STAR OF INDIA

" WINDSHIPS LIKE THE STAR OF INDIA *opened up the globe, and in doing so, they brought our modern world into being.*
—Craig Arnold, librarian, San Diego Maritime Museum

The 1863 windjammer, Star of India, one of the earliest of the iron ships and the one of the oldest ships in the world that still actively sails, is the symbol of San Diego. The 205-foot, 19-sail, square-rigger sits proudly on San Diego's waterfront in all her restored glory. She has put out to sea nine times under full sail over the last 20 years.

The Star of India reeks with memories of lusty days of sail: She's seen mutiny, survived fire, been dismasted off Trincomalee, run aground off Kahului. Ice carried her almost to her doom north of the Arctic Circle. Beneath her bowsprit, nailed to the fo'c'sle, is the

Victorian-style figurehead of Euterpe, Greek goddess of music. Euterpe was the bark's name from time of christening in 1863 to 1906 when she became the Star of India.

Her first master, Capt. William J. Storry, perished on board from remittent fever contacted in Calcutta on her second sailing from London to India. He was buried at sea. From 1871 to 1896 she carried thousands of emigrants from England, Ireland and Scotland to New Zealand and Australia. Single women were quartered in dismal bunks aft, single men up forward. Separating the two were married couples and families. Several women who gave birth while sailing from the British Isles to Australia and New Zealand named their babies Euterpe, after the ship. The emigrants lived on a diet of hardtack and salt beef and pork during their weeks at sea. The ship often battled terrifying storms, "labouring and rolling in a most distressing manner," according to the ship's log.

In 1902 the windjammer began 21 years of sailing to the Bering Sea from San Francisco each spring loaded with fishermen and cannery hands and returning each fall with a cargo of canned salmon.

The booby hatch, affording a breath of fresh air for emigrants on the long, hard voyages, is still intact. So is nearly everything else the Star of India was outfitted with by Manx shipwrights nearly a century and a half ago. Twenty-one times the old windjammer sailed around the world.

The Star of India, a ship that never had an engine, slid down launching ways at Ramsey on the Isle of Man, November 14, 1863, five days before Lincoln delivered his Gettysburg address. She sailed the Seven Seas for 60 years until her owners finally laid her up in San Francisco in 1923. She was headed for the scrap heap. But as luck would have it she was spared.

Through the efforts of San Diego newspaper reporter Jerry MacMullen and J.W. (Sunny Jim) Coffroth, owner of Tijuana's Agua Caliente Racetrack, the Star of India was towed to San Diego in 1927. Sunny Jim put up $9,000 to buy the ship, and presented the bark as a gift to San Diego's Zoological Society. Once in San Diego the windjammer was tied up at the foot of a dirt road in the backwash of the city's skidrow. There she remained for years, rusting, all but forgotten.

At one point during the 1920s, police discovered a flourishing bordello on the old square rigger, much to the embarrassment of the Zoological Society.

In the late 1950s, Captain Alan Villiers, noted author and square rigger veteran, visiting San Diego from his home at Windrush, Oxford, England chastised the city for neglecting the rare relic of sailing days. "It was ships like this that opened up trade routes of the world, that made all the great discoveries, that fought most of the decisive sea battles," declared Villiers. "The Star of India is the doyen of them all. Yet, she sits on your waterfront rotting before your eyes. And no one seems to care." His words jarred San Diegans into action.

The Maritime Museum Association of San Diego was formed. The Zoological Society, concerned about animals, not ancient vessels, tired of its white elephant, gave the windjammer to the group, and for the first time in nearly 40 years the ship went into dry-dock for a survey to determine if she was worth saving.

Ken Reynard, a founding member of the Maritime Museum was at sea at the time, as he had been since a boy of 15. He was owner-skipper of a refrigerator ship, the Westgate, and for years had been fascinated with the Star of India. Learning her hull was in nowhere near the bad shape feared, Reynard sold the Westgate and in 1961 signed on as skipper of the Star of India, a ship that hadn't sailed since 1923. "I came on this thing to fix her up," explained the veteran sea captain to the author in 1973, "to do the best I could do for her. She was a derelict. An eyesore. But she was worth saving." More than $500,000 was spent restoring and maintaining the old windjammer.

"We've finally reached the point where we're ready to hoist the 18 sails, unfurl the 23,000 square yards of canvas I made myself, and take her out to sea," said Captain Reynard. "We're going to prove her seaworthiness after all these years. A ship is never finished until she's sunk," said the windjammer's skipper, "and this old gal has plenty of life left in her."

Reynard dreamed of the day when he would sail the Star of India up and down the coast off San Diego under full sail. But he didn't live to see the day. Another veteran of the sea, Captain Carl Bowman, who retired from the Coast Guard in 1960 after 31 years as a sailor and an aviator, succeeded Ken Reynard as master of the Star of India.

Bowman was commander of the San Diego Coast Guard Air Station when the Japanese bombed Pearl Harbor. At one time he was captain of the Coast Guard training bark, Eagle. He was deputy superintendent of the California Maritime Academy 1960-1971 and captain of the academy's training ship Golden Bear.

On July 4, 1976, Captain Bowman was in command when the Star of India spread her sails for the first time in a half century. He had the feel of the iron bark with a good blow filling the 18 sails from the flying jib to the mizzen tops'l as she sailed off the coast of San Diego. More than 500,000 people turned out to see the Star of India go to sea for a day, crowding the city's shores and sailing along with the windjammer aboard hundreds of small craft. It was the largest peacetime event in San Diego's history, the city's main activity as part of America's Bicentennial celebration.

Bowman was at the helm again in 1984, 1986, 1989 and 1993 on one-day sailings under full sail of the Star of India. Walter Cronkite was honorary helmsman on the 1989 sailing and Charlton Heston, honorary helmsman on the 1993 sailing. The Star of India had three sailings in August 1996 for the Republican National Convention in San Diego.

In 1995 the Maritime Museum Association purchased the Star of India's 19th sail, a mizzen topmast staysail for $9,000. That same year "The Euterpe Waltz" a concerto for piano, which was the rage in New Zealand in 1899, was performed for the first time in America by organist Robert Plimpton in a Balboa Park concert. Visitors are welcome aboard the Star of India for guided tours of the 1863 windjammer.

PRESIDIO HILL: SITE OF A FAMILY REUNION

PORTUGUESE NAVIGATOR JUAN RODRIGUEZ CABRILLO, sailing under the flag of Spain, was the Columbus of the West. In 1542, fifty years after Columbus discovered America, he landed at Point Loma and claimed California for the Spanish crown.

But it wasn't until 1769 that Gaspar de Portola, Franciscan Friar Junipero Serra and a group of Spanish settlers established the first settlement in San Diego on what is now Presidio Hill, site of the original California mission and fort in Old Town. Father Serra founded the first of the 21 California missions at Presidio Hill on July 16, 1769. The mission remained there for five years, then relocated to its present site six miles inland.

It was George White Marston, owner of San Diego's Marston Department Store, who gave the 40-acre Presidio site to the city of San Diego for a park and $400,000 to construct the Junipero Serra Museum located there. Ever since 1965 an ongoing archaeological dig by the San Diego Historical Society has been taking place on Presidio Hill unearthing thousands of artifacts from San Diego's birthplace.

Foundations of California's first church (the first mission), storehouses, a chapel, the commandant of the military fort's home, the 20-foot-high adobe wall surrounding the 300-yard by 300-yard settlement, the entrance, guard house and jail have been found. Also, the remains of 50 men, women and children, buried in California's first non-Indian cemetery have been discovered.

Bancroft's *History of California* reports that one of the last burials on Presidio Hill was that of Henry Delano Fitch in 1849. Of the 50 skeletal remains found, only six have been identified, Fitch, his four-year-old daughter, Natalia, a sea captain named Snook, a blacksmith named Jose Aurora, killed by Indians, and two children of another blacksmith named Romero. The latter three burials occurred in the late 1700s. Histories of San Diego mentioned a cemetery on the spacious bluff overlooking the city and sea, but none provided a clue as to the exact whereabouts of the graveyard. The cemetery was apparently abandoned and forgotten shortly after Fitch's burial.

The discovery of the Fitch grave generated a reunion of families in two nations whose members had been out of touch for more than a century. The two branches of Fitch's family—one scattered throughout Mexico, the other across the United States—were strangers until his grave was found. Since the discovery, scores of descendants of the early Californian have come from both sides of the border to visit the site, and to meet their distant cousins.

Identification of Henry Fitch was made by the discovery of a fairly well-preserved wooden coffin wrapped in an elaborate leather cover-

174

ing. On top of the coffin were the large letters HDF, a cross and two hearts etched out with copper-headed nails. Inside the 1849 coffin were the remains of a man Fitch's age and height, more than 6 feet tall. Next to the coffin was another containing the remains of a small girl. It is known that the only other member of Fitch's family buried on the hill was his daughter Natalia.

Fitch was a dashing Nantucket sea captain who sailed around the Horn, landed in San Diego in 1826 and fell in love with a beautiful señorita, Josefa Carrillo. He was Protestant and American; she a Catholic and Mexican. Josefa's family tried to discourage the romance. Even after Fitch converted to Catholicism and renounced his American citizenship to become Mexican, the church still would not marry the young lovers. So, they eloped, sailing to Valparaiso, Chile, where at last a priest married them. Then they returned to San Diego, where Fitch became a prominent attorney, merchant, cattleman, land owner, surveyor and ship owner. Some of Henry and Josefa's 11 children moved to various places in Mexico. The others became Americans when San Diego became part of the United States. The two branches of the family lost contact.

A few descendants of both sides of the border learned of the discovery of Fitch's grave. By word of mouth and by letter information of the find was passed along relative to relative throughout Mexico and across the United States, to places as far away as New England and Florida. More than 200 descendants have come to visit Presidio Hill and to later become acquainted with long lost relatives on both sides of the border. Lists of all known descendants have been circulated to members of the Mexican and American branches of the family by the San Diego Historical Society.

Descendants come from many walks of life, some are poor, some middle class, others rich. Some have presented family memorabilia to the Serra Museum: Dr. Benjamin Ely Grant III, a Bandon, Oregon, dentist and great-great-grandson of Josefa and Henry Fitch, gave the museum the early Californian's family Bible, published in 1770. Four-month-old Tara Wilson of San Bernardino, great-great-great-great granddaughter of the historic couple, is the youngest descendant to visit the gravesite on Presidio Hill.

Archaeologist Jack Williams, 13 when he made his first dig at Presidio Hill, is now the lead scientist for the San Diego Historical Society at the "Birthplace of California" site. To help support the Society's work there is a public archaeology program at Presidio Hill Thursdays through Sundays with the public invited to join the dig for a donation of $50. There is no telling what will be found at archaeological digs—the reunion of two branches of a family scattered across two nations has come about because people dug a few feet further into the ground.

THIRTY EIGHT

SAN FRANCISCO COUNTY

MECHANICS' INSTITUTE

AFTER WRITING SEVERAL LETTERS to the *San Francisco Examiner,* none of which was published, Mary Margaret Jones finally received a response. Arthur L. Price, who edited the letters to the editor page, wrote her: "You express yourself well enough but you need to be better informed. I suggest you join Mechanics' Institute." "I accepted Mr. Price's advice. He sponsored me as a member of the Mechanics'. I've been a member of the Mechanics' now for 40 years," said Mrs. Jones.

Mechanics' Institute, at 57 Post Street, in the heart of the city's financial district, has been a San Francisco tradition since 1854. The institute was destroyed in the earthquake and fire of 1906. The present nine-story institute building was completed in 1909, and houses one of the finest private libraries in California (about 200,000 volumes) as well as the oldest chess club in continuous operation in America. Novelist Kathleen Norris was a librarian here. Mark Twain, Robert Louis Stevenson, Jack London and Horace Greeley were members.

In 1854 when the Mechanics' Institute was founded, no school in California made provisions for the technical education of the laboring class. The founders were a machinist, a mechanic, a stonemason, a foundryman and a carpenter. Its purpose was to provide a library, lectures, debates and technical classes for workers. The institute spurred initial interest in the industrial development of California and promoted industry by staging 32 trade fairs in San Francisco through the year 1899. When Presidents Harrison, McKinley and Theodore Roosevelt visited the West Coast, they delivered speeches at the Institute.

Technical classes were not conducted at the Mechanics' Institute after the 1920s. The library and chess club came to be its most important functions. There are more than 6,000 members today—men and women from the working class, but also authors, scholars, students, professional people and members of the business community. It's one of the least expensive private clubs in San Francisco, costing but $10 to join with dues of $60 a year. Membership is open to any person of "good character."

Why would someone join Mechanics' when he or she could go to the nearest public library? "Mechanics' has a marvelous selection of books. Many books you will not find in the public libraries," explained Kathleen Pabst, library director since 1974. "Members can check out some really great old books as well as thousands of new issues each year. There are huge collections of foreign language books. Books on every imaginable subject. Mechanics' Institute subscribes to 500 periodicals and 41 newspapers. Members have a very possessive feeling about Mechanics'. They feel it is their own private library."

The library occupies three floors and shares the fourth floor with the chess club. Other floors are rented out for office space. Memberships pay $1/3$ of the cost of operation, with the other $2/3$ coming from investments and rentals.

Many members, especially retired men and women, come every day to sit in the beautifully appointed library, spending hours reading out-of-town newspapers, books, magazines and visiting with friends. About 1,000 members play chess, and among them are some of the

178

country's better chess players. Many of the great chess masters, such as Capablanca, Euwe, Alekhine, Lasker, Marshall and Bobby Fischer have given exhibitions at the club. "There are regulars here every day from the time the chess club opens until it closes ," said Max Wilkerson, chess club director.

ACADEMY OF SCIENCES—A BIT OF EVERYTHING

"A LITTLE BIT OF EVERYTHING UNDER THE SUN" is how many describe the California Academy of Sciences, the West's oldest scientific institution, established in 1853; others call it the Smithsonian of the West. It's a fascinating place to visit— the Steinhart Aquarium, Morrison Planetarium and Natural History Museum exhibits are all under one roof. But it isn't the public displays that attract scientists from throughout the world. It's what's tucked away in scores of laboratories, basements and storage areas— an array of millions of specimens and artifacts.

The academy attracts hundreds of scientists each year, who come from far-flung places around the globe to spend days, weeks and months doing research. For those scientists who need rock samples, insects, fish, fossils, reptiles, amphibians, birds, animals or plants for study and are unable to make the trip to San Francisco, the academy loans material to them. Also, members of the academy itself, supported mainly by private funds, embark on scientific expeditions to various parts of the world each year.

The academy has a gymnasium-sized ichthyology department that houses more than 2 million specimens of fish preserved in bottles filled with alcohol and stacked on shelves from floor to ceiling. There are "pickled" fish here from oceans, lakes and rivers throughout the world, from all the continents, from all the seas. It is one of the most comprehensive collections in the world, and some of the specimens date from the 1800s. Most of the world's approximately 300 research ichthyologists have visited the scientific lab at one time or another, coming from as far away as Russia, China, India and Australia. They come to take fish in bottles off shelves, much as a scholar would withdraw books from the library for a research project.

Often, ichthyologists write to the California Academy of Sciences applying for the loan of a single fish, or several fish, sometimes for as many as 100 fish. "Most of the loans are short-term, for six months to two years, but some of our fish have been on loan for as long as 35 years," said William N. Eschmeyer, curator of the department of ichthyology. "Ichthyologists are a tight-knit family. We pretty much know what everyone is studying. Sometimes when an ichthyologist requests certain fish on loan, members of the department will deliver one or more fish to that ichthyologist at a scientific meeting. We hand -carry these fish in plastic bags in our luggage." The academy will send as many as 5,000 fish through the mails in a year to scientists around the world. Eschmeyer is the leading authority on stonefish, which have the capability of killing a human. He has discovered and identified several new species of venomous fish.

Prize fish in the collection are two of about 200 coelacanth ever caught. The fish was believed to have been extinct for more than 65 million years until one was brought in by a fisherman in 1938. The coelacanth, from the waters of the Comoro Islands off the east coast of Africa, resembles a huge bass with unusually long flippers.It is an unexpected survivor of the time when sea creatures first crawled on land. So rare is the fish that its brains, heart and stomach have been sent separately through the mail by the academy to scientists in distant places for study.

"We mail plant specimens to botanists who borrow them sometimes for only a day, sometimes for several weeks, even several years," explained Dr. Elizabeth McClintock, curator of botany. The botany department has over 500,000 plants preserved and mounted on paper. "The importance of all our material is that it is used by the larger scientific community," said Dr. McClintock. "We don't want it stored away and forgotten in file cabinets."

Here, too, is found one of the largest herpetology collections in existence—230,000 snakes, frogs, salamanders, crocodiles, lizards and turtles. The academy boasts 8 million insects stored in 8,500 drawers. The department of entomology serves as the bureau of standards for 10,000 different types of insects.

Many of the world's experts in various scientific fields are on the staff of the academy. One I interviewed for a story in 1972 was Dr.

Edward L. Kessel, who was 67 at the time and the reigning authority for 40 years on flat-footed flies. From 1800 until the time I interviewed Dr. Kessel, there had been only four authorities on flat-footed flies. When dipterists—scientists specializing in flies—happen to catch flat-footed flies, they mailed them to Dr. Kessel.

Dr. Kessel pursued flat-footed flies all over the world. Most flies have rounded feet. "If you spent all your time catching flies, you might not catch a flat-footed fly in your lifetime," he related. "They're rare. You have to know where to look." He knew where. He had thousands of the tiny platypezidae, flat-footed flies, mounted on pins in file cases in his office at the California Academy of Sciences. There are 175 species of flat-footed flies. Like all flies, flat-footed flies have six feet. Kessel was the first person in history to observe and describe the mating of flat-footed flies. He did this by digging a hole under a mushroom, laying on the ground with his head in the hole and looking up. "Someone spotted me and came dashing over to see if I had a heart attack," he laughed.

The department of ornithology and mammalogy at the academy has 95,000 birds, 23,000 mammals. The geology department boasts 45,000 fossils, 14,000 rock specimens. Two Russians flew to the academy from Moscow to examine fossils and teeth of tiny, as yet unidentified creatures, found on mountaintops in their country.

Paleontologist Jean Firby is studying teeth and shells from tiny triangular "things" that thrived millions of years ago where the High Sierra is now. "We think they may be a squidlike beast," said Dr. Firby. "Teeth of these strange creatures contain 36% titanium. So far as is known, no organism (other than the triangular 'things') has this element in its body structure."

SAN FRANCISCO'S ROWING CLUBS

ON THE SAN FRANCISCO WATERFRONT across from Ghiradelli Square, side by side, stand the two staid San Francisco rowing clubs. Names and founding dates are inscribed on entrances: South End Rowing Club, 1873; Dolphin Swimming and Boating Club, 1877.

Until 1978 there were three old frame rowing clubhouses side by side. But the San Francisco or old Ariel Rowing Club merged that year with the Dolphin Club. And not long after that the San Francisco Rowing Clubhouse burned to the ground.

At sunup, noon and late afternoon each day scores of businessmen and women, policemen, firemen, politicians, waitresses, teachers, attorneys, judges, housewives and others come to the clubs. They enter with a key. Once inside they don swim suits, sweat suits for handball or gymnasium, shorts and shirts for rowing. It's a ritual going back to the 1870s.

They row in single and double boats hand-crafted in the early 1920s, in modern, state-of-the-art lightweight fiberglass sculls. A half dozen members of the Dolphin Club will hop into the 6-oar, 1887, John Wieland rowing barge, named after a famous San Francisco brewer and club founder. "Nothing is built today to compare with the old Wieland barge and the 1920s rowing boats," insists Phil Hunter, 82, a South-Ender for 65 years and club historian. Rowing has been a mainstay of the two rowing clubs since their beginnings. Many members row out to the Golden Gate and back, eight miles round trip, or around Alcatraz Island and back 3½ miles, every day for exercise and the sport.

As many are swimming enthusiasts as rowers. Members swim a mile to six miles in the cold, rough waters of San Francisco Bay, every day of the year. In winter, water temperatures drop as low as 40 degrees. "Believe me, when you hit that water your blood circulates," allowed Hector Stephen, 76, when I interviewed him. He was swimming at least a mile every day in the bay at the time.

Walt Schneebeli, 69, and historian of the Dolphin Club in 1995 when I interviewed him, had been a member of the club since 1948 and swimming in San Francisco Bay anywhere from a mile to six miles almost every day of the week for nearly a half century. Schneebeli collected fish for San Francisco's Steinhart Aquarium for 33 years before he retired. Frank Gibson, was 86 when I talked to him. He had been a South-Ender for 50 years and couldn't remember when he missed a day swimming in the frosty inlet. Many members are old timers in their 60s, 70s, 80s and even 90s.

The two clubhouses, built back to the 1890s, are filled with photographs, trophies and memorabilia dating from the 1870s. Each club has boasted several Pacific Coast and national rowing, swimming and handball champions over the years.

In 1938 all three rowing clubhouses were moved a quarter-mile down the beach in order that the Works Progress Administration might erect the present Maritime Museum Building. "The three clubhouses were deeded to the city. That was the only way it was possible to get WPA funds to move the old buildings by barge to the present locations," South-Ender historian Hunter explained. "The plan was to move the rowing clubs back next to the Maritime Museum when it was completed. That was in 1938 and we're still waiting for the clubhouses to be returned to their original locations. The water was calmer for launching boats in the old spot."

The South End Club had 550 members and the Dolphin Club had 850 members in 1995, about a third women. Membership in the clubs was exclusively male until 1976 when the gender gap was broken. Both clubs charge $100 initiation fees, $255 a year dues and $110 locker fees.

"For years women asked to join the clubs so they, too, could row and swim from a private club in San Francisco Bay. But they always received the cold shoulder from men. When a group of women tried buying one of the three existing clubs in 1976, they were finally admitted," recalled Laurey Greider who joined in 1983 and is a handball player and rower. She added, "Some of the men loved it when women joined. Some didn't. But it has worked out fine."

THIRTY-NINE

SAN JOAQUIN COUNTY

CALIFORNIA'S DELTA: A WORLD APART

THE "RUBE GOLDBERG" FERRY inched across the river from one island to another. Midstream, Bill "Muddy Bottom" Schelhase began the tedious task of hand-cranking the cables, lowering the apron to enable the lone truck to roll off the cumbersome craft. A huge ocean freighter reared incongruously above corn stalks in a nearby field. But this was no mirage—the freighter was sailing through miles and miles of open farmland in a narrow deepwater channel.

It was a typical scene in the watery wilderness of California's maze of inland islands—a world apart from the rest of the state. More than 50 of the Sacramento-San Joaquin River islands are fairly large, one to 20 square miles in size, dotting a 40-by-60-mile sector of the state stretching from Sacramento south to Stockton, westward to Carquinez Strait. Another 50 or so, called berms and reaches by islanders, are tiny isles smothered with tules and blackberry bramble, stranded in a web of rivers and sloughs.

This is California's bayou: shanty bars along rickety wharves; "Catfish Dinner" signs in tiny cafes; clouds of dust from cars on dirt roads crowning levees that rise 10 to 20 feet above below-sea-level island farms; cattle grazing on ranches; Basque sheepherders tending flocks; sagging dilapidated barns; little red schoolhouses; land alive with ducks, pheasant, beaver, muskrat, skunk, squirrel, fox and mink.

The Delta country is lush farmland gripped by dikes with fields of asparagus, potatoes, beets, corn, tomatoes, turnips, carrots and other vegetables. For thousands of years, tules, marsh plants, reeds and cattails decayed and tangled together to form islands of rich peat 40 to 60 feet deep.

The miles of placid island waterways have become the houseboat capital of the nation, and marinas and river resorts crowd the levees of Bethel and Andrus Islands. "Water's dirty, but safe to swim in," says Gordon Wells, who runs a tiny marina on Fabian Island, renting a dozen houseboats. "I'd like to be able to go back in time," he muses, "to when the Delta was one big monstrous swamp, miles and miles of tule jungle."

During the early 1800s the islands were one of the last refugees in the West for Indians to avoid contact with their conquerors. At about the same time the Hudson Bay Company penetrated deep into California in pursuit of pelts from small fur-bearing animals. Forty-niners sailed through island waterways to Mother Lode diggin's, and pirates hijacked gold-laden boats on the return trip. The pirates secured heavy anchor chains to trees on either side of channels and snagged the gold boats. It was Chinese gold miners who first laid aside picks and pans for spades and plows, to build the first levees and plant the first crops on rich island bogs.

In 1905, Benjamin "Uncle Ben" Holt came up with a piece of machinery that wouldn't sink as it moved across sponge-like peat. Uncle Ben invented the vehicle that laid its own portable track as it moved along. "It looks just like a great big caterpillar," shouted someone at the unveiling. Uncle Ben's garage on Roberts Island developed the caterpillar tractors that were converted into tanks by the British in World War I.

Many of the islands are populated with barge, boat, and riverside residents and with squatters who live in floating shanties. The latter have included such colorful characters as One-Eyed George, the Tule Queen, Louie the Lumpy, Old Pack, Gus of Hog Island, and Katfish Katy. In years gone by the islands crawled with these "river rats" living in shanties, ashore and floating, that have gone the way of the stern wheelers that once plied Delta waterways.

But there will always be river people. "We've been 20 years on the river," said Eric Ehrichs, 66, "living in the longest houseboat in the whole Delta." Ehrichs and his wife, Olga, mounted five rooms in sequence on an old San Francisco fire barge and anchored it at Turner Cut, a slough separating Roberts and McDonald Islands. "We had five soda fountains in San Francisco," Ehrichs said. "Wanted out. So we decided the hell with the city and came over here."

They were leasing 550 feet of frontage on the levee from a farmer. There wasn't another boat anchored anywhere near. "We love fish," said Olga. "We toss out a line, one night it will be a channel cat, the next, a nice striper or blue gill. We're only 12 miles from Stockton. It seems like 500."

The islands are populated by families dating back generations—Chinese, Mexican, Spanish, Irish, Jewish, English, Japanese, Polish, Italian. Some islands are owned by large corporations.

The Sam Huey family was growing potatoes on their 1,000-acre spread on Bacon Island. "Only a few Chinese families farming nowadays in islands," said Hong Huey. "In the old days there were Chinatowns all over the place. Chinese introduced farming to the islands, built the levees, drained the islands, burned the tule jungles. My grandfather was one of the pioneers."

Many Mexican, Japanese, and Filipino farm families live in tiny island settlements. These farm laborers haul potatoes, sugar beets, asparagus and other crops from fields to packing sheds in ancient flatbed trucks. Islanders commute island to island by single-lane drawbridges or by ferryboats.

When Muddy Bottom Schelhase wasn't sailing on one of his 10-minute, 800-foot voyages, he was in the bilge of the old boat knee-deep in ooze. "The damn thing leaks," he explained. "Mud pours in the bottom. I've got to keep shoveling it out in buckets to stay afloat." Hence his nickname.

Mandeville Island, six miles long, two miles wide, was one big farm. "Busiest time of the year for this old clunk," Schelhase said, "is 100 days from March through June when the asparagus is up." At the time nearly all asparagus canned in America was grown on California's inland islands. "When asparagus grows an inch a day, 150 men come out to the island to cut each plant, once every four days," Schelhase said. "When it grows two inches a day, they add another 150 men to cut it every three days; three inches a day, another 150 men to cut each plant every two days; five inches a day, another 150 men to cut each plant every day. That's 600 men at peak season, all riding this old ferryboat."

Those were indeed busy times when we rode over to Mandeville Island with Muddy Bottom on his Rube Goldberg ferry in California's Delta country.

FLOATING COPS LEND SECURITY TO LIFE ON DELTA

THE DISHEVELED, SCRAGGLY BEARDED RIVER RAT wearing an old wool turtleneck sweater and tattered trousers, his glasses glued together and encrusted with dirt, waved from the end of his pier to the "floating cops."

San Joaquin County Deputy Sheriff Barry Oaks and his partner John Pike returned the wave and headed their 22-foot boat for the rickety wharf protruding from a clump of bare willow trees. John Gordon, 79, was living with his sister, Bertie Smith, 69, on McDonald Island in an old shack embraced by the willows. The officers stopped to visit with Gordon, as Pike noted, "to see if all was well in his neck of the woods."

Oaks and Pike were among seven full-time, year-round San Joaquin County deputies assigned to patrol the islands and waterways of the Sacramento River Delta for the Sheriff Department's five-vessel Marine Service Division. In winter there are 3,000 boats on the 300 miles of water they patrol. In summer the number of occupied boats in the Delta jumps to as high as 8,000, and other deputies augment the Delta Patrol. Four other counties have Delta patrols—Sacramento, Yolo, Contra Costa and Solano—but the San Joaquin County sheriffs' unit is the largest. Among other duties, the deputies protect the barge, boat,and riverside residents who call themselves river rats. Among the river rats living on scores of tiny islands in the Delta are squatters, renters, homeowners and boat owners.

"I've lived the better part of my life in the Delta. I like it out here. Nobody bothers me. It's isolated, far away from traffic and crowds. I go fishing when I want," mused Gordon, a construction worker and farmer before becoming a river rat. The two deputies finished their visit with Gordon and then moved up the San Joaquin River. "We're involved with everything going on in the Delta," Pike said. "Many of the islands are inaccessible except by boat. We're like the Coast Guard. We work boating accidents, drownings, check boats for proper registration, proper equipment aboard, life jackets, fire extinguishers, etc. We arrest boat operators for drunk driving. We fill in for the Department of Fish and Game making sure people fishing have licenses and don't exceed the catch limit. We check for illegal hunting. We're firemen. We put out boat fires. It's never dull on the Delta Patrol."

The deputies tow disabled boats to marinas, and recover stolen boats. The Delta is a dumping ground for San Francisco Bay Area murder victims, and deputies from time to time fish bodies out of the rivers and sloughs with draglines. Oaks told about a $1 million marijuana bust. "We discovered a field of marijuana plants hidden by a levee and growing on one of the islands. We kept it under surveillance until the three marijuana farmers showed up and we arrested them."

A huge freighter flying the flag of Liberia sailed by in the Stockton Deep Water Channel, dwarfing the sheriff's boat. A sailor from one of the ocean-going ships had a stroke and was lowered over the side to the sheriff's boat for transfer to a hospital. This happened just a few days before we accompanied the officers on their patrol.

The patrol boat went by dozens of islands: Devil's, Bacon, Lower and Upper Jones, King, Mandeville, Union, Venice, Lost Isle (big enough only for a saloon and boat docks for its patrons) and Staten Island, yes, Staten Island, California. The islands are dotted with duck-hunting clubs, fancy yacht clubs and hundreds of weather-beaten boats languishing in back sloughs. The boats patrolled Middle, Old River, Calaveras, San Joaquin and Mokelumne Rivers and sloughs with names like Whiskey, Disappointment, Fourteen-Mile and Trapper. Sea lions frolicked in the water beside the patrol boat. Swans, ducks and coots floated lazily by.

"These guys working the Delta Patrol take care of all of our problems. They're our guardian angels," said Roger "Doc" Brown, who with Pat "Hamburger Patty" Ismaili, ran Herman and Helen's Floating Cafe tied up at Empire Island. "Nothing goes on that they don't know about," Ismaili said.

The Sheriff's patrol boat spotted the 16-foot outboard operated by the Delta mailman, Lou Sparrenberger, who had the only daily marine mail route in California. Lou delivered and picked up mail through the backwaters of the Delta. "Hi Lou!" shouted the officers as they pulled alongside the spare, sinewy mailman. "How long is your route?" I asked him. "Seventy miles. I cover three zip codes," Lou laughed.

He delivered mail to people living on islands, along the river bank, on top of levees, to mail boxes on front porches of houseboats. "The Delta is old-fashioned America," said the mailman. "It's California's Tom Sawyer country. Rich or poor, these river people are all genuine. God, when it's rainin' like hell, damn near ever one of 'em insists I walk up their pier into their place for a cup of coffee or a bowl of hot soup."

Such is life in California's Delta—a world apart.

FORTY

SAN LUIS OBISPO COUNTY

MORRO BAY, AFLUTTER WITH BIRDS

T HE SCREECHING and squawking grow more intense with each passing day. Fall migrations are picking up momentum. Soon the beaches, sand spit, mudflats and marshlands will be smothered with shorebirds settling in for winter. Morro Bay is one of the most important wintering grounds for shorebirds and waterfowl on the West Coast. And the bird watchers know it.

This bay, 230 miles north of Los Angeles, is a bird watchers' paradise. Individuals and groups from throughout the United States come here to see the shorebirds. To accommodate them, the state of California in 1963 erected one of the finest bird watching platforms and shorebird museums anywhere.

Morro Bay boasts one of the largest areas of marshland still in natural condition on the California coast. The 4^1/$_2$ miles long, three-eighths of a mile wide sand spit separates the 2-mile wide estuary from the sea. Spectacular 578-foot-high Morro Rock marks the entrance to the bay. The sand spit, Morro Rock, much of the shoreline and bay make up Morro Bay State Park.

Here, too, is a strand of towering eucalyptus fronting the shore—the only blue heron coastal rookery between San Francisco and the Mexican border. Upwards of 100 blue heron nests crown 120 to 150 foot high tree tops. Blue herons are 3^1/$_2$-foot-tall shorebirds. They may be seen here year-round, often standing motionless in the bay for a half hour or more, waiting to gulp the first fish that passes by.

To date nearly 400 different species of waterfowl and shorebird have been spotted in the bay by bird watchers. Sandpipers are forever piping the sand and mud for crabs and worms. Kingfishers, grebes, pelicans and cormorants drop out of the sky like divebombers. Hundreds of gulls, curlews, godwits, willets and sanderlings crisscross the sand with telltale footprints and rend the air with raucous calls.

Busy at the water's edge are avocets (shorebirds with upturned beaks), curlews (downward curling bills) and willets (straight beaks). Here you'll also see loons, scooters, egrets, white-faced ibis, pintails, widgeons, scaups, flycatchers and kittiwakes. Not to mention whimbrels, greater and lesser yellowlegs, guillemots, murrelets, puffins, bushtits, sapsuckers, pipits, shrikes, chats, and gnatcatchers...Morro Bay is for the birds.

HIAWATHA REVERED IN HALCYON

HIAWATHA, the 16th-century Iroquois Indian chief, is the object of considerable adoration in Halcyon, a small town in San Luis Obispo County, 175 miles northwest of Los Angeles. The community has a population of 125. It was founded in 1903 by a theosophical colony that came to California from Syracuse, New York, where three centuries earlier the confederation of the five Iroquois nations (Mohawks, Oneidas, Onandagas, Cayugas and Senecas) was formed by Hiawatha.

In the center of Halcyon, 20 miles south of San Luis Obispo, is a heart-shaped church, headquarters of the tiny religious sect, the Temple of the People, led by priestess Eleanor Shumway, the group's fifth Guardian-In-Chief, since its founding. "We are a worldwide organization, yet, we only have about 200 members, half here in Halcyon and the other half in Germany and England," explained Shumway. "The linchpin of our belief is abiding by the Golden Rule. We have religious services every day at noon, 365 days a year, a simple service where we stress following the Golden Rule and pray for the health and safety of everyone living on planet Earth."

Hanging from the walls of the Hiawatha Lodge, the social center of the Temple of the People are 22 oil paintings, each over four feet square, depicting scenes from the life of Hiawatha. A copy of Henry Wadsworth Longfellow's 1855 narrative poem "The Song of Hiawatha" lies open on a stand nearby. The paintings are the work of Harold Forgostein, Guardian-In-Chief of the Temple of the People from 1968 until he died at the age of 84 in 1990, when he was succeeded by the present spiritual leader of the group. Forgostein did the paintings over a 40 year period. None of the members of the sect is Indian. So, why Hiawatha?

The two founders of the Temple of the People, Francia LaDue and William H. Dower, were both active in causes relating to Native American rights for the Onondaga tribe in the Syracuse area. They were both initiated into the Turtle Clan of the tribe. Mrs. LaDue was the first Guardian-In-Chief of the sect, continuing as high priestess of the Temple of the People until her death in 1922. Dower served as the group's leader from 1922 until his death in 1937 when he was succeeded by Pearl Dower.

In the early 1930s Dower asked New York artist Forgostein to paint a picture of Hiawatha to be hung in Hiawatha Lodge in Halcyon because the Temple stressed the importance of the Indian chief and Hiawatha's contribution to the history of America's government. Forgostein became so taken by Hiawatha that he closed his art studio, moved to Halcyon, devoted his life to studying and painting Hiawatha, and eventually became head of the theosophical group.

When I interviewed him in the Temple of the People he explained that members of the sect revere the legendary Indian leader with the same regard that they do other masters such as Christ, Buddha, Diana, Isis, Joan of Arc, Confucius and Quetzalcoatl. "We believe Hiawatha is alive in the world today," insisted Forgostein, "physically working with all humanity, not just the American Indians. We believe Jesus, Buddha and all the other masters are alive in some form on Earth as surely as the sun shines.

"A master," he said, " is one who has conquered the limitations of matter. Masters are the higher self of humanity and watch over, protect and guide us. Masters have lived far more incarnations than we can understand. They are the spiritual mothers and fathers of all of us. A master is one who has entered the Eye of the Triangle in the Square Within Seven." He did not elaborate.

Forgostein took a copy of the *American Heritage Book of Indians* from a library shelf and opened it to the foreword written by the late President John F. Kennedy. Kennedy noted that "the League of the Iroquois organized by Hiawatha inspired Benjamin Franklin in his planning the federation of the American States."

"Hiawatha's principles in the formation of the League of the Iroquois were used as the model for the Constitution of the United States," continued Forgostein. "The American Indian was at his high point when Hiawatha lived. The religion of the Indian was as ethereal, as moral, as sacred and noble as any in history. Hiawatha employed miraculous powers to protect his people from evil forces of nature. He instructed the Iroquois in the arts of medicine, agriculture and navigation."

In his paintings, Forgostein depicts Hiawatha much as Christ is depicted in Christianity and Buddha in Buddhism. "The birth of Hiawatha is like that of Jesus and Buddha," he said. "Each mother was first visited by a great spirit from above."

One painting of Hiawatha shows the Indian chief being swallowed by a great fish much like Jonah's experience with the whale. Another shows Hiawatha slaying a fiery serpent. "His war lance is the flaming sun," related Forgostein. "His peace pipe is the silvery moon. His lance has as many points as the sands of the sea."

He told how the Temple of the People traces its beginnings to Madame Helena Blavatsky who founded the Theosophical Society in

1875 in New York. "Our teachings come directly from the masters through books dictated by the masters to Madame Blavatsky, books like *Isis Unveiled* and *Secret Doctrine.*

Many members of the Temple of the People are schoolteachers; Forgostein himself, a retired high school and junior college art teacher. The head priestess, Eleanor Shumway, taught 7th and 8th grade English and history classes in nearby Arroyo Grande for 24 years prior to becoming Guardian-In-Chief in 1990. Her parents moved to Halcyon and joined the theosophical group in 1942 when she was 8 years old. She never married.

"Halcyon is a quiet place," said Herb Lantz, retired management analyst for the Air Force. "Theosophy is such a deep study of religion, it demands so much of your time. That's why we have so few members. But once in, you cannot stop."

The Temple owns 30 of the 52 homes in the tiny town. The houses are rented by both members and nonmembers. There is a post office and a general store. The heart-shaped religious edifice in the center of Halcyon is called the Blue Star Memorial Temple in honor of Francia LaDue, the first Guardian-In-Chief, affectionately known to her followers as Blue Star. The backs and seats of the chairs in the temple are covered with blue fabric and the floor with gold carpet.

"Blue Star Memorial Temple is built on the lines of mathematical and geometrical symbolism similar to other sacred constructions such as Stonehenge, the pyramids of Egypt and the cathedrals of Europe," explained Eleanor Shumway. "The Golden Rule is the most significant thing about our teachings. It's no pretty slogan to embroider and hang in the parlor. It's like granite. It's a tremendous thing. If the world would only live by the Golden Rule, we could take all the locks off doors. All problems would be solved."

FORTY-ONE

SAN MATEO COUNTY

WHERE ELEPHANT SEALS COME ASHORE

S AN MATEO COUNTY is where elephant seals come ashore to mate, molt, and have babies. This is the only place on the mainland of America where people can walk to within a few feet of these monsters of the deep lying on the beach and listen to rangers provide information about the 14-to-16 foot long behemoths that weigh as much as 5,000 pounds and were at one time thought to be extinct. Elephant seals coming ashore on America's mainland is a recent phenomenon.

In 1965, elephant seals began coming ashore at Ano Nuevo State Reserve, 55 miles south of San Francisco,19 miles north of Santa Cruz. At first, just a few swam out of the ocean onto the beach. The first pup was born on the mainland in 1975. By 1995 more than 3,000 of the gigantic, funny-looking beasts with huge proboscis were spending several weeks on the mainland beach mating, molting and giving birth to over 800 pups, with 210,000 people from America and all over the world looking on in amazement.

Signs are posted all along a two-mile stretch of beach at the Reserve that caution: "WARNING! Elephant Seal Bulls Are Dangerous!" Elephant seal bulls mate with as many females as possible. The bulls set up harems on the beach and the cumbersome but extremely mobile bulls are constantly battling with one another for dominance among the females.

Their battles in the surf and on the sand, slashing one another with large canine teeth and inflicting severe wounds, are among the bloodiest battles of any animal species. At times the fights are fatal. Nearly all the bulls are badly scarred and bloodied from the encounters. While the violent courtship battles ensue, other females not involved are gathered together elsewhere on the sand, bearing their young within six days of coming ashore and nursing the pups for a month.

Females are much smaller than males, averaging 10 to 12 feet long, 1,200 to 2,000 pounds. Normally only one pup is born to each female. When they finish nursing they start mating.

All this frantic activity takes place in front of guided 2 hour, three-mile walking tours conducted daily from December 15 through March 31 each year by park rangers and 210 volunteers wearing state park volunteer uniforms. The seals cannot be seen except by taking the tour. The State Parks Department has set up rigid controls to keep anyone from getting too close, but does allow groups within 20 feet of the basking beasts. Tours are conducted when the giant seals are at their greatest numbers on the beach and when the mating, molting and birthing is taking place. During the rest of the year there are always a few elephant seals at Ano Nuevo. Visitors then are permitted to take self-guided tours along the sandy, unlevel trail.

"The volunteer rangers, who come from all walks of life, housewives, doctors, lawyers, police, secretaries, take a 12-week natural history course highlighting the biology of elephant seals," explained supervising ranger Gary Strachan. "It's comparable to a college course. It provides an educational opportunity for the public at no cost to the state."

It costs $4 to park a vehicle at the reserve and $4 per person to take the tour. Reservations are made up to eight weeks in advance. Weekends are almost always sold out weeks in advance. Weekday reservations are much easier to obtain. Special guided walks for school groups are held. Reservations for 9,500 students in school groups were sold out within 45 minutes in 1995. A maximum of 350 people a day see the elephant seals on the guided tours.

Gary Strachan had been a ranger at the reserve for 10 years in 1995, a state park ranger 21 years. "I grew up around here. When I was in my teens I would paddle out to Ano Nuevo Island. No elephant seals had ever been seen there at that time. This whole business with the gigantic elephant seals is incredible."

There are two species of elephant seals. The southern species thrives between Antarctica and the southern tip of South America, an estimated 300,000 in number. The northern species comes ashore two to three months a year on four Mexican islands off the coast of Baja California; on San Miguel, San Nicolas and Santa Barbara Islands off the coast of Southern California; on tiny Ano Nuevo Island off the Ano Nuevo State Reserve; in the Farallon Islands off San Francisco, and now on the mainland. In the last few years a few elephant seals have also been showing up at Piedras Blancas near San Simeon and Point Reyes north of San Francisco.

During the first half of the 19th-Century the giant seals were slaughtered along the coast of present day California for the oil rendered from their blubber. By the 1880s it was believed the northern species was extinct. In 1920 scientists discovered a small herd numbering less than 50 on Guadalupe Island off Baja California.

"When this happened the Mexican government immediately dispatched a garrison of soldiers to the island to protect the elephant seals from being shot by hunters. The Mexican government passed a law protecting elephant seals. The United States passed a similar law 10 years later," noted Strachan.

"The northern elephant seal species made one of the most fantastic comebacks of any animal in history," said Burney Le Boeuf, professor of biology at UC Santa Cruz and the leading authority on the huge marine mammal. He estimates the population of the northern seal at 130,000, all descendants of the less than 50 Guadalupe Island animals.

Ana Nuevo is a low, rocky, windswept point that juts out into the Pacific Ocean. Spanish explorer Sebastian Viscaino named it for the day on which he sighted it in 1603, Punta del Ano Nuevo, New Years Point.

The first elephant seals were seen on 13-acre Ano Nuevo Island, a half mile off Ano Nuevo State Reserve, in 1955. The first elephant seal pup was born on the island in 1961. In 1995 there were more than 1,000 elephant seals on the island. Elephant seals first made a landfall on the mainland across from the island in 1965. A single pup was born on the mainland in 1975. The following year seven pups were born on the mainland. In 1977 there were 16 elephant seal pups born on the Reserve beach, the following year the number increased to 86. In 1995 there were 800 births.

Le Boeuf has studied elephant seals at rookeries in North and South America. He and a number of assistants, including his wife, Joanne Reiter, also an expert on the marine mammal, have sprayed thousands of the beasts with names and numbers for identification using hair coloring and peroxide.

"It will be interesting to see what will happen to the population explosion of sea elephants along the California coast as time goes on," observed Le Boeuf during a 1979 interview at Ano Nuevo. "Where do they go from here? What happens when elephant seals begin showing up on public beaches in California? The first time a kid gets bitten by one or a person gets crushed by one, then what happens? Elephant seals could get very political in the next few years if they continue to make inroads along the California coast."

But as the numbers of the enormous ocean beasts who come ashore to mate, have babies and molt increased over the years, there have not been any serious contacts with humans, so far. A few have come up on the highway near Piedras Blancas. A few have appeared on public beaches. So far not many. When the giant seals show up in new places Burney Le Boeuf and Joanne Reiter are called upon for help on how to deal with the behemoths coming ashore.

The giant seals do not feed from the time they come ashore until they return to the sea many weeks later. When females come ashore to give birth they look like blimps. They spend 30 days nursing their pup. They begin mating 24 days after giving birth and mate for about a week with one or several bulls before leaving for their long swim with other females. Both males and females lose 40% of their weight when breeding. When females swim out to sea in search of food, they look like slimmed-down torpedoes.

Elephant seals live as long as 20 years. Females are able to give birth at age 3 but usually are 4 years old. Since the giant seal's gestation period is eight months, this delay means that the young will be born after the female reaches her breeding ground the following year. After nursing their babies and mating, the females are at sea for 70 days feeding and then return to molt. They are on land 2½ to 3 months of the year.

Pups are 3 to 4 feet long at birth and weigh an average of 80 pounds. After two months they weigh from 300 to 500 pounds. When the pups are 4 to 6 weeks old their original coat of black fur molts and is replaced by a shiny new silver coat. They learn to swim in the shallows off the beach. The pups remain on the beach another month or two after their mothers leave, then swim off. "About 60% of the elephant seals die before they are 3 years old. The giant seals , especially the young, are preyed upon by killer whales and sharks," said Joanne Reiter.

At sea, elephant seals feed on rays, skates, rat fish, squid, small sharks and other fish. Le Boeuf and his wife have mounted satellite tape and instruments on the backs of the marine mammals to track them. The giant seals tend to feed off the coast of Washington and Alaska when not ashore at Ano Nuevo and the California and Mexican islands. They are great swimmers that can stay under water as long as an hour at a time and dive to depths as deep as 3,000 feet, feeding and avoiding killer whales and large sharks.

Ano Nuevo State Reserve, 55 miles south of San Francisco, is the best place on Earth to see these mysterious denizens of the deep when they leave their ocean home and come ashore to mate, molt and, give birth.

FORTY-TWO

SANTA BARBARA COUNTY

LONE RANGER OF THE ISLANDS

B ETH FULSOM was the only human being on tiny, exotic Santa Barbara Island, 47 miles out to sea from Ventura. But she wasn't alone—she shared the one-square-mile, wind-swept, treeless island with 160,000 beady-eyed deer mice, thousands of sea gulls, pelicans and other sea birds and more than 1,000 sea lions.

Folsom, 33, has one of the most remote outposts of any ranger in the National Park Service. "I'm here by choice," the 12-year Park Service veterans said. "I love the island. Santa Barbara is the crown jewel of the five islands that make up Channel Islands National Park." She has been the sole ranger on the island for three years, and work shifts on the island of 10 days on and five off. During summer, seasonal rangers fill in for her. In winter, the ranger station is not staffed when she is off the island.

When she is here in winter, she sometimes spends her 10-day stints alone because few mariners risk fierce storms and treacherous seas to sail to Santa Barbara Island. "The sea gets so rough," Fulsom said. "Sometimes it breaks over the second pier of the dock, 25 feet out of water. There is no place for a boat to hide, no safe anchorage for boats to go to during winter storms." When the waters are calm, Fulsom makes the three-hour sea journey to Santa Barbara Island from Ventura aboard a National Park Service boat. When seas are too rough, she is flown to and from the island by helicopter.

Santa Barbara Island is another world from eastern Pennsylvania where Fulsom grew up. She graduated in 1982 from East Strouds-burg State College in the Poconos, where she majored in parks and recreation. Since graduating, she has been a ranger in five National Parks in Delaware, New York, Pernnsylvania and California. Her newest assignment, she insists, "is the best yet.

"One of my main reasons why I requested to be assigned to Santa Barbara Island is because of the outstanding diving here," Fulsom said. "Fish everywhere. Lobster. Diving with whales passing through and hanging around the island for a few days and with sea lions that swim up to your mask. Often I will put a line in the water and fish for dinner—sheepshead, opaleye, perch or calico bass, my favorite," she went on. "If I'm in the mood for lobster, I dive for one. Pretty good life, huh?"

Fulsom lives in a yellow stucco structure looming over the sea at Landing Cove. The building houses the ranger's four-room residence, a visitors center and a museum. She begins her workday by raising the flag and opening the visitors center. Then she radios park head-quarters in Ventura about weather and sea conditions, the number of boats in the anchorage, any citations issued and any unusual wildlife activity, "like pods of whales swimming by."

Fulsom wears many hats. She is a park ranger, a Santa Barbara County deputy sheriff, a California Fish and Game warden and an emergency medical technician who treats visitors who have minor injuries. If there is a serious accident, she radios for help. Because she is a law enforcement officer, she carries a .357 magnum. "I've never had to use it, but being alone in this out-of-the-way place, you never know what you might encounter," she explained. She patrols the water in a 60-horsepower inflatable boat. It takes her 20 minutes to circle the island.

The fewer than 3,500 visitors to the island each year are commercial fishermen who harvest lobsters, swordfish and sea urchins; pleasure boaters who anchor all along the east coast beneath the island's steep cliffs; and people who arrive aboard Island Packers concessionaire boats out of Ventura. Permits are issued by the Park Service for the eight island campsites, for a maximum of 30 campers at any given time. Visitors have to bring their own water and food, along with tents if they are staying overnight.

Beth Fulsom leads nature walks along the 5½ miles of trails that crisscross the saddle-shaped island, which rises 635 feet out of the water at Signal Peak, its high point, and 562 feet at North Peak. The island is covered with low-lying vegetation such as Australian saltbush, ice plant, prickly pear cactus, cholla and the giant coreopsis that resembles a dwarf tree, its thick woody stem growing as high as five feet. In spring, the hills of the island are ablaze with golden flowers blossoming on the coreopsis.

"Sometimes groups come out in good weather from schools up and down the coast from Santa Barbara to San Diego," she noted. "I lead them and all visitors on guided tours to sea lion rookeries, to view the small colony of spectacular sea elephants. I describe the flora and fauna, island history. We visit kitchen middens where prehistoric Indians camped." Kitchen middens are centuries-old Native American refuse dumps piled high with abalone and mussel shells.

Sea lions breed in December and pup in spring. Also in spring, island cliffs are alive with thousands of small, chubby, neckless Xantus murrelets, sea birds that instinctively tumble into the sea 48 hours after birth and then fly away. Santa Barbara Island is the largest known breeding colony of Xantus murrelets in the world.

The 160,000 endemic Santa Barbara Island deer mice add to the rough-and-tumble atmosphere. Before the new ranger station was completed in 1992, the island's lone ranger slept in a World War II Quonset hut. Deer mice often walked over the ranger's face and body during the night. So far, the new ranger house is mouse-proof, although the mice frequently chew through campers' tents in search of food. "One camper awakened to find three baby deer mice born during the night in one of his shoes," said Fulsom.

The animal life keeps things interesting, Fulsom continued. "There's never a dull moment," she related. "Mice sleep all day, and at night they crawl up and down the screens of my house chasing moths attracted by the lights. Sea lions at the bottom of the cliff outside my window bark all night long, but I'm used to it. The wind howls most of the time. The automated Coast Guard light passes over every 11 seconds. Barn owls let loose with raspy grackle calls. Yet, I sleep like a log." For exercise, she either runs 10 laps up and down the 300 steep steps leading from the landing to the top of the cliff or jogs four miles around the perimeter of the island.

"I never get lonely when I'm alone on the island," said Fulsom, who has electricity provided by solar panels mounted on the battery building next to the ranger station. "I have a television set but rarely turn it on. I'm a voracious reader with two or three novels going at the same time, and I love working crossword puzzles." When Fulsom goes to the mainland on her days off, she lives in Ojai and "moonlights" operating a boat for the Ventura Harbor Patrol. "I'm a working fool," she laughed.

At night on the island she sees the myriad of lights twinkling on the mainland. Palos Verdes Peninsula is the nearest landfall, 37 miles away. She also sees the lights on Catalina Island, 24 miles away. In the morning, Fulsom turns on her radio to hear the news and "to listen to the Sig Alerts as millions of people head off for work a few miles away in Los Angeles County, and here I am all alone, no cars, no roads, a world apart. I keep pinching myself to make sure this is really happening to me."

KIDS' CAMP AT THE ZOO

"WHEN YOU TALK TO THE ELEPHANTS do they know what you're saying?" 8-year-old Hayley Kenny of Irvine asked keeper Fred Marion at the Santa Barbara Zoo. Marion instructed the zoo's two Asian elephants, Suzi and Mac, to put their feet on the railing of an iron gate in the elephant compound.

The elephants complied. "They understand me," the keeper said. "See their big toenails. I keep them filed. In the wild, elephants wear out their toenails. They have five toes in front, four in back. Open your mouths," Marion commanded, and the elephants did.

Michelle Mangum, 7, of La Habra inquired about the weight of the elephants. "How much do you weigh?" Marion responded. Michelle said 40 pounds. "Suzi weighs 9,400 pounds. Mac weighs 9,200 pounds. It would take 235 little girls your size to weigh as much as Suzi," the keeper explained.

Bettina Brungsberg, 8, visiting the zoo with her sister, Beate, 7, from Essen, Germany, asked what the elephants eat. In a year's time, the keeper said, each elephant will drink 15,500 gallons of water, eat 100,000 pounds of oat hay, 12,000 pounds of alfalfa, 1,500 gallons of grain, 5,000 potatoes, cabbages, carrots and apples and 1,600 loaves of bread.

"Elephants like carrots," Marion told Bettina, handing her a piece of carrot. "Hold the carrot out in front of you. Suzi will take it from you with her trunk."

The keeper cut several carrots into small sections and the dozen boys and girls behind the gate walked up one at a time and stood in front of the two elephants. One at a time each elephant raised its trunk and accepted the snack from the child's hand.

The 7 and 8-year-olds were day campers at the Santa Barbara Zoo founded in 1962. The zoo has been acclaimed "a model of excellence among small zoos in America" by the American Association of Zoological Parks. Each summer 1,000 boys and girls from 3 to 11 years old are enrolled at the zoo's summer camp. Many of the 140 accredited zoos in America, including the Los Angeles Zoo, have modeled similar summer camper programs on the one held here since 1977. Some campers come only for a day, some for a week, but most sign up for a three-week session. The zoo runs three of the full three-week camper sessions. Cost is $20 a day, $90 a week, $200 for three weeks. Some children stay for the full nine weeks.

This was the third summer Bettina and Beate Brungsberg and their parents vacationed in Santa Barbara from their home in Germany. The two girls spend six weeks at the zoo camp each year.

"Our underlying philosophy and objective is to teach respect for the environment, for the animals and for themselves," explained Carolyn Strange, camp director. Campers learn about the animals of the world. Each day is dedicated to a particular subject, such as: Habitats, endangered species, animals of South America, Africa, Australia, animals of wetlands, deserts and rain forests, primates, reptiles, birds, mammals, misunderstood animals, animal communication and animal camouflage. One night every three weeks the campers bed down in sleeping bags at the zoo, after going on a safari around the 81-acre zoo to see how animals behave at night.

Santa Barbara Zoo is on a hilltop overlooking the Pacific Ocean and a lake that is a bird refuge with the Santa Ynez Mountains as a backdrop. It is both a zoo and a botanical garden. The more than 500 animals representing 120 different species, including several that are rare, vanishing and endangered, live in natural settings surrounded by vegetation typical of their habitat.

The zoo has 35 full-time employees, 60 part-timers in summer, 135 volunteers and 23 people running the camping program. Students from universities and colleges throughout the state are here on internships. It is a private, nonprofit zoo with a board of directors made up of civic, business and educational leaders of Santa Barbara, and operates on an annual budget of $2 million.

Zoo campers commune every day with elephants, giraffes, lions, monkeys, otters, pandas, lemurs, capybaras, giant anteaters, white handed gibbons, iguanas, alligators, spoonbills, flamingos and many other fascinating beasts and birds from the world of the wild. Every day, campers stand in front of a dozen flamingos, having contests emulating the dazzling pink and white birds to see who can stand on one leg the longest.

My wife and I have visited zoos all over North America, Mexico and South America, Europe, Japan, China, Australia and many other places. The Santa Barbara Zoo has always been one of our favorites. It's our four granddaughters' favorite zoo, too.

FORTY-THREE

SANTA CLARA COUNTY

THE WINCHESTER MYSTERY HOUSE

E VER SINCE **1923** people have been visiting the strange house in San Jose, probably the most bizarre private residence ever built, and left wondering what it was all about.

The old house has 160 rooms, 10,000 windows, 2,000 doors, 40 bedrooms, 13 bathrooms, 47 fireplaces, 40 staircases and 9 kitchens. And it has had only one resident, a 4 foot 10 inch, 95-pound widow—Sarah Pardee Winchester, heiress to the Winchester Arms fortune.

Workmen toiled around the clock to add to the sprawling house throughout the years that the mysterious recluse lived there, allegedly because she had been told by a spiritualist that she would live as long as work continued on the residence, but she died there anyway in 1922 at the age of 85, bringing an end to the sounds of saws and hammers of the 16 carpenters who had worked around the clock every day, including holidays, for 38 years.

It is said she spent $5.5 million of her $20 million inheritance building and furnishing the mansion, partially hidden behind towering trees and shrubs to keep the curious from looking in.

During a 1903 visit to San Jose, President Theodore Roosevelt drove by the house and expressed an interest in meeting the mistress of the mansion and see the wonders of her work. She refused, replying that her home was not open to strangers.

There are scores of fascinating balconies, turrets and towers. A stairway with seven turns and 44 steps that rises only nine feet. A spiral staircase with 42 steps, each step two inches high. Stairways that lead nowhere and melt into walls and ceilings. A linen closet as big as a three-room apartment and a cupboard next to it less than an inch deep. A magnificent grand ballroom with hand-carved walls and a ceiling made of 19 different rare woods imported from various parts of the world.

Why did she do it? A Boston spiritualist claimed she warned Mrs. Winchester that vengeful ghosts of thousands of men, women and children killed by her husband's guns would never leave her alone. The medium is supposed to have suggested that Mrs. Winchester would come to no harm if she built a haunted house for friendly ghosts who would ward off the unfriendly spirits. Mrs. Winchester kept no written records, no diaries or letters. Whatever her reasons for building the strange house she never confided to her large staff of employees.

Occult signs, however, are everywhere in evidence. The spider web pattern, Mrs. Winchester's favorite design, is seen throughout the house on doors, windows, ceilings, floors and walls. Most windows have 13 panes; nearly all walls 13 panels; chandeliers, 13 globes; stairs, 13 steps. There are 13 bathrooms.

One room is filled with trapdoors. There are secret passageways and a mysterious blue seance room supposedly entered only by the tiny widow.

Mrs. Winchester was an accomplished organist and often could be heard playing favorite melodies in the early hours of the morning. A bell in one of the towers was said to have been tolled by one of her servants each midnight to welcome incoming flights of good spirits and again at 2 a.m. as the ghosts returned to their sepulchers.

In her lifetime, Mrs. Winchester was an extremely generous person, contributing much of her inheritance to charitable groups. In 1911 she established the William Wirt Winchester Memorial Sanitarium for Tuberculosis in New Haven, Connecticutt, with a $1.2 million endowment in memory of her husband, who died of the disease in 1881 after the couple had been married 15 years. Their only child, a daughter, died at the age of one month.

The home was purchased by a San Jose family a year after Mrs. Winchester's death. It has been open for visitation ever since. A museum on the six-acre grounds next to the house includes a large display of various models of Winchester guns, an ironic addition, if, indeed, the mysterious widow constructed her bizarre home to ward off the spirits of those killed by guns bearing her name.

AT AGE 3,500, SHE'S ALL WRAPPED UP

FOR SEVEN YEARS, Thothmea, an ancient Egyptian priestess, called California home. The priestess, a 3,500-year-old mummy, "resided" at the Rosicrucian Egyptian Museum in San Jose from 1987 to 1994, when the Rosicrucians donated the ancient princess to a museum in Brazil. The Rosicrucian Museum, established in 1932, has the largest number of Egyptian mummies on display on the West Coast, seven when Thothmea was hanging out there, as well as one of the largest collections of ancient Egyptian artifacts in America. Before coming to California Thothmea languished in the attic of an upstate New York home for 50 years until the Rosicrucians found out and purchased her. Thothmea was not a major historical figure as mummies go. She was one of 39 mummies of royal and priestly figures found in 1881 in a tomb on the site of ancient Thebes. Hieroglyphic inscriptions on her coffin identified Thothmea as a priestess who dedicated her life to the service of Isis, one of the most important goddesses of ancient Egypt. She arrived in America in August 1888, as a gift to the U.S. Ambassador to Egypt from a high Egyptian official. The diplomat presented the 4-foot-2-inch mummy to a museum in Round Lake, New York.

"As the mummy was carried into the museum in its coffin an organist played a lively number," a newspaper account from the day reported. "Then a choir of 40 girls sang a hymn that began: "AWAKE! AWAKE!" and then the mummy was read poetry. After that glorious new beginning, Thothmea was acquired by a man in upstate New York. His daughter, Inez Sewell, does not know how her father obtained Thothmea. She knows only that she inherited the mummy and was trying to find a home for her when she learned about the Rosicrucian museum. She was the person who sold Thothmea to the museum.

Thothmea joined the other mummies in the museum collection, which also includes ornate mummy cases decorated in colorful paintings of the highlights from the person's life, as well as mummies and mummy cases of cats, lambs, falcons, a baboon and other birds and animals.

The Rosicrucians' interest in Egyptian artifacts has roots in the ancient Egyptian origins of its philosophy. The group, which claims 225,000 members and has its North American headquarters in San Jose, draws on mysticism, philosophy and science and generally believes that all things are permeated by a pantheistic "god spirit." A nonsectarian, philosophical fraternity, the Rosicrucians claim a 14th century BC Egyptian ruler, Ikhnaton, as their grand master. Ikhnaton advanced the doctrine of one god instead of many.

Rosicrucians (Latin for rosy cross, their symbol is a cross with a rose at the crossbars) trace many of their philosophical ideas to ancient Egypt, accounting for the group's outstanding collection of early Egyptian artifacts, amassed from several scientific excavations early this century, from purchases from other museums and from individuals primarily in the 1930s and 1940s.

The museum also contains exhibit cases filled with amulets and scarabs from ancient tombs as well as figurines, toys, jewelry and a reproduction of King Tutankhamen's coffin and the great pyramid of Cheops. There are also alabaster canopic jars containing various brains, hearts, intestines, stomachs, livers and gallbladders of the mummified dead.

Ancient Egyptians believed in immortality. Bodies were mummified to preserve them for resurrection and the vital organs were essential for the return to life. They were removed, put into jars filled with palm oil and placed next to the coffin holding the mummy inside the tomb.

Another treasure in the collection is a replica of the Great Rosetta stone inscribed in ancient Egyptian and ancient Greek. Found by an officer in Napoleon's army in 1799, the original stone was the key used to unlock the meaning of Egyptian hieroglyphics. The museum displays a full-size replica of the Egyptian tomb of a XII dynasty noble who lived in 2000 BC, surrounded by walls covered in hieroglyphics and paintings. In the center of the main chamber is a 3,000 pound sarcophagus lifted out of a shaft in the floor. A painting of the Goddess of the Night hovers over the stone coffin for protection. As in Egyptian tombs, the hieroglyphs portray episodes from the life of the nobleman.

While the Rosicrucian Museum has the largest number of Egyptian mummies on the West Coast, Chicago's Field Museum has perhaps the largest collection in the nation with 26. Adding to those collections is a difficult task today, largely because Egypt no longer permits any of its antiquities to leave the country

"I have about 200 entries so far and believe there are probably a total of about 300 Egyptian mummies in this country," said Art Aufderheide, professor of pathology at the University of Minnesota-Duluth Medical School who is establishing a registry of mummies in the United States. "Nearly all of them came here in the late 1800s and early 1900s during a period of Egyptomania when there was great public interest in mummies."

Rosicrucian Museum curator Dale H. Jordan, said that if anyone else has a mummy stored away in an attic, garage or basement, he would be most happy to know. "You never know where or when you might find a mummy," Jordan said. "We acquired Usermontu, a priest who died in 630 BC, by sheer fluke. We bought two sealed mummy coffins from, of all places, Nieman-Marcus in Texas in 1971 and, lo and behold, Usermontu was in one of the boxes. The museum paid $15,000 for both mummy cases. The mummy was a bonus."

The identify of Usermontu was authenticated by the British Museum. The old high priest's father, Basemut, lies mummified in the London museum. A headstone from Usermontu's tomb is on exhibit in the Louvre. Usermontu in excellent state of preservation, lies in a glass case in the San Jose museum with his tongue sticking out as though he were speaking.

The museum, erected in 1966 to replace the original structure, is built in the style of an Egyptian temple and features at its entrance a reproduction of the Thebes Avenue of Ram Sphinxes. Open from 9 a.m. to 5 p.m. seven days a week except for Thanksgiving, Christmas, New Year's Day and Good Friday. "A goodly number of Egyptian scholars come here from throughout the world each year to use the museum's resources for research. And bus loads of sixth graders from schools up and down California make field trips to the museum. The kids love this place," said Cynthia Stretch, Registrar.

FORTY-FOUR

SANTA CRUZ COUNTY

BEACH BOARDWALK AMUSEMENT PARK

SANTA CRUZ'S BEACH BOARDWALK is a time machine, a vintage warp. There are touches of another era in this amusement park that dates back to 1904. Take the Marini family at the Beach Candy Shops: Owner Joe Marini Sr., has been making saltwater taffy since 1921 in the same taffy machine at his shop on the boardwalk at Santa Cruz.

"My dad opened this candy shop in 1915. I came here five years later when I was 10. Dad bought the taffy machine new in 1921. I've been using it ever since," explained Marini, busy at work making taffy in his shop. He was 87 years old in the summer of 1997, the oldest active taffy maker in America, maybe in the world, using the same cotton candy machine since 1939. His candy showcases are filled with old favorites like red dollars, cola bottles, hot lips, juju fruit and jelly beans.

It's fitting that Joe Marini Sr., is part of the Santa Cruz Beach Board-walk scene, the oldest amusement park in California, described by its owners as the last of the West Coast's old-time amusement parks. Its two oldest rides, the 1911 merry-go-round and the 1924 Giant Dip-per wooden roller coaster are national and state historic landmarks. The park, too, has been designated an historic landmark. Side by side with the latest laser video machines in the arcade are penny machines, some more than a century old, that still take only a penny to operate.

This city became famous for its mile-long, wide-wide beach in 1865 when John Leibrandt built the first public beach bathhouse here and launched Santa Cruz as a seaside resort. In 1904, Fred Swanton opened the Santa Cruz Beach Boardwalk, patterned after Coney Island. It was destroyed by fire two years later, then rebuilt and reopened in 1907.

And for the last 90 years, people have been dancing up a storm in the colorful Moorish-style Coconut Grove Ballroom at the Beach Boardwalk. The ballroom, with its array of domes, arches and flying flags, is a Santa Cruz landmark. It was renovated in 1981 at a cost of $10 million. When dancers aren't tripping the light fantastic it is used for conventions, trade shows and meetings.

The Beach Boardwalk's merry-go-round is the work of famed Danish woodcarver Charles I.D. Looff, who carved 72 wooden horses and brought in a German-made, 342 pipe band organ in creating his Santa Cruz masterpiece. Looff also did the famous merry-go-round at Coney Island in 1875. Looff's horses with long, flowing manes, jewel-studded bridles, muscular legs and spirited expressions have been spinning in a circle ever since to the music of the antique organ. In 1924, Looff's son, Arthur, spent 47 days erecting the Giant Dipper at a cost of $50,000, one of 80 wooden roller coasters still running in the United States.

In 1987 the park spent $145,000 for a pair of new trains for the Giant Dipper, rated as one of the 10 most exciting roller coasters in the country. More than 45 million riders have screamed in sheer bliss sailing down the 70-foot drop at 55 m.p.h.

"It's still a thrill every time I ride the Giant Dipper," confessed Charles Canfield, president of the Santa Cruz Seaside Company, whose family has controlling interest in the private corporation that owns and operates the park. Canfield's father, Lawrence, joined the park's board of directors in 1928 and served as president from 1952 until his death at 79 in 1984. "I started working here running kiddy rides when I was 16," Canfield said.

The Boardwalk is open seven days a week from Memorial Day to Labor Day, weekends and holidays the rest of the year. It employs 1,300 during the summer, 500 to 600 part-time the rest of the year and has an annual payroll of $5.5 million. Nearly every kid in Santa Cruz has worked at the amusement park at one time while growing up in the beach city.

There are 28 rides at the Beach Boardwalk. In 1997 an all-day unlimited ride pass cost $18.95. The newest attractions were a virtual reality roller coaster and a laser tag arena, the latest in technology alongside the turn-of-the-century rides.

Each February there is a clam chowder cook-off with 90 booths featuring 90 different clam chowder recipes. And every summer there are two free concerts each week for 10 weeks. Upwards of 10,000 people turn out for a performance conducted on a bandstand on the beach with the audience sitting on the sand. Performers in 1997 included Chubby Checker, Jefferson Starship, The Kingsmen, and the Drifters.

In the 1980s in October there was an annual Brussels sprouts festival (90% of the nation's Brussels sprouts grow nearby) featuring such exotic dishes as Brussels sprout pizza and Brussels sprout ice cream. The Santa Cruz County Octagon Museum features a exhibit on the history of the Beach Boardwalk from time to time called "Never a Dull Moment."

Ever since 1904 Santa Cruz has had a love affair with its Beach Boardwalk. It's a special place for this California seaside town.

FORTY-FIVE

SHASTA COUNTY

THE TOWNS OF IGO AND ONO

T STARTED IN MINING CAMP DAYS. The Chinese gave in, then stayed put and the towns are still Igo and Ono. Igo is 15 miles southwest of Redding in Shasta County. Ono is five miles southwest of Igo. While a great deal of activity centered in the mining camps of Piety Hill and Horsetown in the 1850s, about 500 Chinese miners quietly worked nearby in the vicinity of present-day Igo.

"The white miners got to watching the Chinese," related Albert Rains when I first visited the two tiny towns in 1969. Rains, the last of the Wintun Indians in sparsely populated Shasta County's Clear Creek country, was 82 at the time. He continued, "Seeing the Orientals were doing pretty good, the white miners came along and ran the Chinese out. 'I go! I go!' the Chinese said as they left their diggins' and moved five miles southwest."

Another old-timer in Igo, Sydnie Jones, who was two years older than Albert Rains, said the same thing happened several weeks later when the Chinese hit a good streak of gold in the vicinity of present-day Ono. "Only this time the Chinese refused to budge," declared the widow Jones. "'Oh no! Oh no!' they shouted. They stayed put and that's how the towns got their names."

"We're the oldest of the old-timers in these parts," said Rains. "The story on how these two towns became known as Igo and Ono has always been the same. Sydnie and I should know the history of this place. We were born here."

"Anybody that's been around here any length of time at all knows about the Chinese," said Mrs. Jones. "When I was a little girl there were a few Chinese families still here. But they've all left. There was a storekeeper named Can, a saloonkeeper named Go Get and a Chinese lady named China Mary. There's a Chinese cemetery here. Every so often a few Chinese will come through here asking questions about the old days," noted Mrs. Jones, who had a photograph of one of the old Chinese merchants of Igo hanging on her living room wall.

NIAGARA OF THE WEST

TEDDY ROOSEVELT called it the eighth wonder of the world. It was one of Bing Crosby's favorite spots on Earth. People who live in Burney, a Northern California lumber town, call it the Niagara of the West.

In the heart of 565-acre McArthur-Burney Falls Memorial State Park, is one of the most spectacular waterfalls in America. Twin falls from Burney Creek and hundreds of plumes of water cascade over and through porous lava rock along the face of a 129-foot high, 250-foot wide cliff. A rock-hewn trail winds to the foot of the falls, then continues a quarter of a mile to a footbridge over the creek, and continues through a wilderness of ponderosa, incense cedar, Douglas fir, willows and aspen. A similar trail follows the creek above the falls.

Black swifts nest in lava niches behind the falls. An ocean shore-bird, the black swift normally nests in coastal bluffs. Spring-fed streamlets issue from porous volcanic rocks through an emerald green carpet of five-finger ferns, tiger lilies and moss, blanketing the cliff face. In winter, mist from the falls turns to delicate snow showers spraying nearby trees and bushes.

Jack Sanders, bearded and taciturn, had been the state park ranger at McArthur-Burney Falls 24 years when we encountered him. He repeatedly turned down promotions and transfers to stay by the falls. He had been in one park longer than any other ranger in the state park system. "It's the waterfalls that has kept me here. I have seen waterfalls all over America. Each one is different and unique in its own way. But Burney Falls is really something special," Sanders insisted.

The falls are off California 89 in Shasta County, halfway between Lassen Peak and Mt. Shasta. The 128 campsites in the park, all in close proximity to the waterfalls, are booked solid from Memorial Day to Labor Day.

Ranger Sanders talked about the pristine beauty of the forest surrounding the falls in autumn, when the leaves change color, and when the landscape embracing the falls is canopied with glistening snow in winter. "It is something to behold when the mist from the falls freezes and sticks to everything, and long icicles hang from the moss and ferns on the face of the cliff," Sanders mused.

He said his wife, Pat, and their three children shared his deep affection for Burney Falls, as did the Ilmawi, Ahjumawi and Ahtsugewi Indians who lived here for centuries and considered this a sacred place for visions and meditation. "Can you blame me for remaining just a common ordinary ranger in order to be able to spend the big part of my lifetime here?" he asked. "The soothing sounds of the rush of water over the falls alone is worth all the promotions I have turned down."

FORTY SIX

SIERRA COUNTY

DOWNIEVILLE'S GALLOWS

I T WAS HALLOWEEN and in Downieville, Sierra County's hamlet that serves as the county seat, a spotlight shined eerily on the only gallows on public display that was actually used in a California hanging. Glowing in the yellow light was a noose formed with 13 wraps of a rope dangling from a cross beam a sprung trap door, and the 13 steps leading to the platform of the gallows. "It's a piece of history, a slice of the Old West. Everybody has heard about a gallows but few have ever seen one," said Lee Adams, who at 32, was the youngest sheriff in the state at the time.

It was in Downieville that convicted murderer James O'Neal, 20, met his Maker, November 27, 1885. His name is spelled in historic documents in various ways—O'Neal, O'Neil, O'Neill. A newspaper of the day describing his execution carried the headline: "He Didn't

Seem To Care. James O'Neal Faces Death With A Cigarette In His Mouth And Indifference In His Heart." The story told how O'Neal "mounted the gallows cool and unconcerned with a firm step. He bid good-bye to spectators he recognized. He took his hat from his head and flung it into the crowd. Sheriff Samuel C. Stewart pulled the lever. The body shot downward six feet. The neck was broken by the fall." O'Neal was executed for killing his employer, John Woodward, a dairy farmer, with a pistol shot to his head in a dispute over $8 owed in wages.

The gallows, used only for the one hanging, stands next to the Sierra County sheriff's headquarters in the courthouse in the center of Downieville, population 350. Sierra is the second least populated county in the state, with 3,200 residents.

The restored gallows was officially dedicated as a California Registered Historical Landmark in 1988, "as a reminder of California's colorful criminal justice past." Sheriff Adams spearheaded the drive to restore the gallows, which was falling apart, and to have it set aside as a historical landmark.

The State Department of Parks and Recreation granted Sierra County $17,000 for the restoration project, the county provided an additional $1,000 and individuals donated $805. In addition to repairing and replacing some of the timbers, steps and platform boards on the 1885 gallows, a bench for rest and meditation was placed next to the structure, a retaining wall was built, and a display was mounted for documents pertaining to the hanging.

"The gallows was disassembled and placed in storage in the attic of the old 1854 courthouse after the hanging of O'Neal," said Sheriff Adams. "In 1927, Sheriff George Bynon re-erected the gallows as a public display on the courthouse square. Three years later Bynon's successor, Sheriff Charles Winstead, dismantled the gallows, claiming he didn't think it was conducive to happy thoughts. In 1933, the next sheriff, Dewey Johnson, put the gallows back up again next to the courthouse." The gallows was in bad shape, barely holding together and weathered and worn, when Adams generated interest in seeking a grant for the restoration.

"We have no fear of anyone getting on the platform, roped off from access, and accidentally hanging himself. The noose is engineered to fall free from the cross beam from as little as five pounds of weight," explained the sheriff. "And the trap door is locked in an open position."

HAL, SWEETIE PIE, & THE SIERRA BOOSTER

H AL WRIGHT AND HIS WIFE, SWEETIE PIE, were busy typing side by side getting out the latest edition of the fortnightly *Sierra Booster* in the tiny town of Loyalton. The year is 1997. Hal is 93, and his wife Allene, better known as Sweetie Pie, is 85. They've been publishing their newspaper together for 48 years. With a circulation of 3,500, mountain towns served by the paper include Hallelujah Junction, Portola, Camptonville, Loyalton, Grey Eagle, Truckee, Goodyear's Bar, Sierra City, and Downieville.

"We just don't like to publish bad news if we can help it," said Hal. "This is a 'good news' newspaper. Of course, people die and we have to run obituaries." How about scandals, he was asked. "Oh, we don't have scandals," the old editor replied. Sweetie Pie chimed in, "Of course we have scandals, Hal, but we never print them." The paper is filled with items such as: "Molly Magee became grandma for the 6th time" or "The Evening Sewing Circle met in Sierraville last Monday." Hal Wright's greatest claim to fame for years has been his aerial delivery service in his 1949 4-place sedan Aeronica, flying low over isolated ranches, and tossing *The Sierra Booster* from his cockpit. He has done this remarkable feat up to the present day—at age 93!

FORTY-SEVEN

SISKIYOU COUNTY

THE SACRED MOUNTAIN

A N ELDERLY WOMAN lost four days in a blizzard near the summit of 14,162-foot Mt. Shasta, wept hysterically when a rescue party carried her down the mountain. "Let me go! Let me go!" she cried. "I must get to the top. I must get to the top." The woman was gripped by the mysterious magnetism of eternally white Mt. Shasta that attracts thousands from all over the world.

At the base of the mountain, the village of Mt. Shasta, population 2,500, is headquarters for more sects and cults than are found in any other small town in America. All because of the mountain: Many think the mountain is honeycombed with secret cities populated by super humans called Lemurians, survivors of the lost continent of Mu. Others believe the mountain to be the final gathering place on earth of the souls of the departed.

The poet Joaquin Miller described Mt. Shasta: "Lonely as God. White as a winter moon." John Muir, who climbed the mountain in 1874, wrote: "A fire mountain built up in the blue deep of the sky by successive eruptions."

Mt. Shasta, north of Dunsmuir, is the singularly most striking mountain in California, visible from all directions as far away as 100 miles.

For 11 years a woman known around town as "Yellow Bird" sat on a bench across from the Mt. Shasta City Hall staring at the mountain for hours each day. The woman, a 75-year-old widow, was drawn to the mountain from Rhode Island. She climbed to the top of the mountain regularly. Sometimes, she said, she remained on the mountain several days to meditate.

A headline in the weekly Mt. Shasta Herald read: "Soul Fails To Return To Body In Trance" In most small towns what had happened would have been an incredible event. In Mt. Shasta it was another in a long series of strange goings on. One of the community's better known citizens, Mother Mary Maier, 75-year-old proprietor of The Inn, a downtown Mt. Shasta hotel, had died. But the death of Mother Mary, who wore flowing orange robes and sandals and was known as the Angel of the West, Guardian of The Mountain, was kept secret for a month by members of the Sree Sree Pravoo Sect. During that time a 16-year-old boy and two older men stood around-the-clock guard beside her body waiting for her soul to return. After a month passed and her soul failed to return, the body was removed from the hotel to a mortuary.

Bob Gray, a U.S. Forest Service ranger on the mountain 26 years when we met him, said he had seen thousands of people on the slopes of Mt. Shasta, many drawn there because they believe it to be a sacred place. "They're here all the time - all seasons of the year," he noted. Gray showed us a marble slab found on the mountain. It was inscribed: "Babaji Yoga. Founder Yogi S.A. Ramiah of Tamil Nad. Mt. Shasta Shrine." "We found it anchored in cement," said Gray. "Markers like this are found all the time on the mountain. So are wooden crosses. Mysterious symbols are constantly being carved in the trees."

Gray said during the 1960s and 1970s hippies flocked to Mt. Shasta. "Sometimes the hippies howled at the moon like a bunch of coyotes. Sometimes they cavorted in the nude on the mountain slopes,"

222   SISKIYOU COUNTY

recalled Gray. But the ranger insisted that in all his years on the mountain he had never seen signs of anything supernatural. "I've never had my horses or my dogs spook on me and I've spent night after night up there."

Harold Barnun, long time Mt. Shasta police chief, said he heard stories about super beings on the mountain all his life. "The police department like everybody else in town gets letters from all over the country and many places in the world asking if there's any truth to stories about a race of pygmies living on Mt. Shasta," he related. "They ask about the Lemurians, so-called super people seven feet tall with walnut-sized third eyes on their foreheads, living inside the mountain."

"We have to respect the beliefs of everyone living here regardless of how far out they may seem," said Or Apperson, editor of the Mt. Shasta Herald. "There are just too many people living in this small town sensitive about these things. They've got a right to believe what they want. We don't make jokes in the pages of the paper, at City Hall, Chamber of Commerce or service club meetings about the Lemurians, the Yaktayvians or any of the other legends of the mountain." The Yaktayvians are another race said to dwell inside the mountain. Legend has it the Yaktayvians are the greatest bell makers on earth—that they hollowed out the mountain with sounds of their bells and chimes.

Members of the I Am Movement, largest sect in town, are vegetarians. They neither drink or smoke. The women in the group wear dresses of pastel colors. They never wear red, which they believe represents danger or anger, nor black, a color representing death. The I Am Sanctuary at 525 Pine, next to the Catholic Church, is a half-block-long white structure with all walls inside painted pink. Pink, the members say, is the color of love. I Am members believe Mt. Shasta is the gathering place on earth for "souls of higher intelligence, the ascended masters of mankind."

The late Guy W. Ballard, a Chicago paperhanger, founded the Great I Am in 1930 after several visits to the mountain. In his book, *Unveiled Mysteries* Ballard described meeting high on Mt. Shasta, St. Germain, "a majestic figure, God-like in appearance, clad in jeweled robes, eyes sparkling with light and love." I Am sanctuaries sprang into existence across the country and around the world with the publication of Ballard's book. Headquartered in Mt. Shasta, the I Am group has extensive holdings in this Northern California town including the famous old Shasta Springs Resort.

The Mt. Shasta Public Library has a special section of books about legends and mysteries of the mountain beginning with Frederick S. Oliver's *A Dweller On Two Planets* published in 1894. Other books include *Lemuria, The Lost Continent of the Pacific*, published by the Rosicrucians; the I Am books *Unveiled Mysteries* and *The Magic Presence*.

Barbara Graves, the librarian, maintained files on the various cults and sects based in town. "At last count there were 13 difference occult groups here," she noted. They include the I Am, Rosicrucians, Knights of White Rose, Sananda and Sanat Kumara, League of Voluntary Effort (LOVE), Brotherhood of the White Temple, Radiant School of Seekers and Servers, Blue Flammers, Understanding Inc., and Sree Sree Pravo.

There's also a Zen Buddhist Abbey on the slopes of the mountain headed by an English woman who spent 10 years in a Japanese monastery.

At Number One Vista near the Mt. Shasta High School set in a forest of pine is the Gate House of the Sananda and Sanat Kumara Sect. A sign on the door of the large redwood headquarters cautioned: "In this house no gossiping, no flesh eaten, no dogs." Thedra, high priestess of the group during our visit, was a 71-year-old widow. "I spent five years in training in the Andes of Peru before coming here," said Thedra, who also mentioned space ships from other planets regularly visiting "the masters on the mountain." She displayed photo albums filled with photographs in black and white and in color of "space ships enveloped in protective cloud cover."

"The U.S. Weather Bureau maintains a station here in Mt. Shasta primarily because of the flying-saucer shaped clouds," reported Wade English, who had been in charge of the station 20 years. He described the clouds as lenticular and said they "occur only in a few places in this country. Lenticular clouds just happen to look exactly like what people envision flying saucers to look like. When lenticular clouds appear in the vicinity of Mt. Shasta, people who do not understand the phenomenon are convinced flying saucers are hovering about, landing or taking off from the mountain." English said the phenomenon occurs several times a year and is caused by strong winds buffeting the high mountain.

"Sometimes we can look out and see a whole train of saucer-like clouds hovering around the mountain. They may be hanging in there all day, the shapes changing all the time as air is funneling in and funneling out of clouds continuously." English filed reports throughout the day about winds around the mountain and presence or possibility of lenticular clouds. These reports were included on daily pilot weather briefings, important to both private pilots as well as commercial airlines flying in the area.

Rosie and Ed Stuhl, lifelong mountain climbers and both natives of the Austrian Alps, admitted they, too, were drawn to Mt. Shasta by the magic of the mountain. "We grew up in the Alps," said Stuhl who was then 84. "Yet, Mt. Shasta was the most beautiful sight we had ever seen, the way it stands all by itself. The first time we saw it, we walked from Redding 80 miles to the summit." That was 48 years earlier. The Stuhls had been climbing the mountain ever since. "Everything about it fascinated us when we first saw it. We have been passionately in love with the mountain from that day on."

Stuhl was custodian of the Sierra Club Lodge for mountain climbers at the 8,000 foot level for years. "I have hiked and skied practically every inch of Mt. Shasta including the five living glaciers on the mountain," he said. "The strangest part about all the legends of the mountain is that people actually believe the stories. I have met people from all over the world, from Australia, New Zealand, Europe, South America, all over the United States, climbing the mountain to find Lemurians, to find the little people and the giants that are supposed to live here. They honestly believe those fairy tales."

SPIRIT OF THE OLD WEST—FREE BURIAL

COST OF DYING, EXPENSIVE? Sure it is in most places, but not in Siskiyou County. When someone dies here, relatives and friends dig the grave. And cemetery lots are free.

In places like Scott Bar, Hamburg, Etna, Callahan, Horse Creek, Sawyers Bar, Seiad Valley, Fort Jones, Forks of Salmon, Cecilville and other hamlets, cemeteries are community property. "Most graveyards have been in these little towns 100 to 150 years," Dan H. Girdner, one of three morticians in the county, said. "Nobody has title to the cemeteries. They're just there. Always have been since the first person died in those places."

Betty Hegler, former Scott Bar postmaster, Bob Turner, a U.S. Forest Service ranger and his wife, Dolores, told of the latest burial in the community at that time, that of Mrs. Adaline Krause, 84, a blind woman. "Burying our dead has a much closer meaning for all of us - not only the relatives, but everyone in town," said Hegler. Turner told us, "The day Adaline died, her niece stopped by our place and asked if I would help dig the grave. That's an honor in itself to be asked."

The deceased woman's brother, Percy Weeks, and a couple dozen men of the community went up to the cemetery at 10 in the morning. Townspeople put up lunches for the gravediggers and brought them beer. "First we had to blast the gravesite with caps and powder," said the ranger. "This is rough country. Then we took turns digging." He said the gravediggers really worked up a sweat. "The beer is most always part of the ritual," he added. It took a day and a half to dig the grave in the rocky ground.

Services for Mrs. Krause were held the following day in the old Scott Bar community center, formerly the community's one-room school. "After other graveside services, the men changed into old clothes while the women prepared a community luncheon," said Mrs. Hegler. The men covered the grave.

Scott Bar Cemetery has been in existence since 1857. Many headstones date back to the 1850s, 60s and 70s. There are a number of family plots with wooden or iron fences surrounding them. But there also is much more empty space than marked graves. "It's tricky," said ranger Bob Turner. "You never know when you start digging whether you're going to run into an old grave."

What if a stranger were to die on a visit to Scott Bar? "No problem," said Mrs. Hegler. "There's plenty of room up there on the hill. We'd be glad to give him or her a decent burial, no charge for gravediggers or cemetery lot."

FORTY-EIGHT

SOLANO COUNTY

BENICIA, THE FORGOTTEN CAPITAL

T HEY CALL BENICIA CALIFORNIA'S LOST CAPITAL. That's because few have ever heard of it, or know that the small town was once the metropolis of the West, California's number one city. It was also the second oldest chartered city in the state (Monterey being the first), founded by Gen. Mariano G. Vallejo, and named for the general's wife.

Benicia has a long history of being "forgotten": As California's third capital, Benicia lasted only 13 months, from February 1853 through February 1854. The stately Greek Revival two-story brick capitol still stands. It became the Solano County Courthouse. Then true to form Benicia lost the county seat after five years. Three colleges were here in the 1850s and 1860s. Now there are none. California's first law school was here. But it shut down. Mills College, the prestigious girls school, was first established here in 1852. The school moved to Oakland in 1871. For years Benicia was the nation's military headquarters on the Pacific Coast supporting an Army arsenal and barracks. The military is long gone.

Benicia was the biggest port in the West when California became a state. Located 23 miles northeast of San Francisco, on the shores of Carquinez Strait at the north end of San Pablo and San Francisco Bays, the town was founded in 1847 as a major seaport. Today Benicia, which means "blessed" in Spanish, has 25,000 people and has numerous well preserved homes dating back to when it was California's capital.

This was the home of America's first heavyweight boxing champion, John "Benicia Boy" Heenan. Charles Dickens wrote a tale about the championship fight between Heenan and British fighter Tom Sayres. Dickens and Sayres were close personal friends. The title match, fought in London, lasted 37 rounds and continued for 2 hours and 6 minutes with the Benicia Boy finally victorious. A later heavyweight match between James J. Corbett and Joseph Choynski took place in Benicia in 1889. This was the home of poet Stephen Vincent Benet. Jack London lived here for a few years. President Ulysses S. Grant served time in Benicia's brig as a young officer for a minor infraction of military regulations. The state's first Masonic Hall is still in use here. St. Paul's Episcopal Church, the first Episcopal cathedral in Northern California, was built by Scandinavians who created a ceiling that resembles an inverted ship's hull, typical of ceilings found in old Norwegian stave churches

Across from the Capitol is Fischer-Hanlon House, a restored gold rush hotel. Benicia's biggest disappointment is the impressive capitol in Benicia Capitol State Historic Park, that looms large over the historic business district. Town founders were so sure Benicia would become the state capital that they built the two-story structure in 1852. Then they invited the governor and legislators to abandon the capital in Vallejo 10 miles to the west, which the state fathers did. But the bubble burst 13 months later when the capital was moved to Sacramento.

Many landmark pieces of legislation were adopted here, including California's first labor law establishing a 10-hour work day and the state's first woman's suffrage act permitting women to own property.

The old capitol has been restored as it was during that historic 13-month period, the 27-seat Senate on the first floor, the 60-seat Assembly upstairs. Interior columns were fashioned from masts of gold-rush ships abandoned in San Francisco Bay. Floors are pine with square nails. Windows were crafted by Pennsylvania Dutch glaziers.

Most people in California never heard of Benicia, nor have any idea what transpired here, of the importance of this place in the early history of the state.

SCHOOLCHILDREN MAKE FIELD TRIPS TO A SALOON

SCHOOLCHILDREN from miles around make field trips to a saloon in Rio Vista, a small Central California river town. While regulars belly up to the 60-foot-long bar at Foster's Big Horn, teachers and students parade through the saloon "oohing" and "ahing" —not at the drinkers, but at the 252 mounted animal heads hanging from the walls.

Foster's Big Horn Bar is famous to big game hunters the world over. Since 1945, it has housed one of the largest private collections in existence of wild game trophies from throughout the globe. One of the few mounted heads of a full-grown African elephant, complete with tusks is here, as well as one of less than a dozen giraffe heads on display anywhere. There are rhinos, gazelles, dik-diks, tigers, leopards, kudus, sassabies, hartebeests, big horn sheep, buffalo, you name it. Some of the trophies are of entire animals, like the stuffed platypus that hangs beneath the walrus. There are no doubles of any one species.

The late big game hunter, Bill Foster, shot all these animals while on several safaris in the 1920s and 1930s. Foster spent a fortune mounting the best for display. He paid a taxidermist $4,000 just to mount the elephant head.

When Foster died in 1962, his widow sold the bar and collection to a big game hunter. The new owner went broke five years later and the mounted heads and the saloon were taken over by the Internal Revenue Service. In 1969, Tony Brown, a lifelong resident of Rio Vista, 50 miles southwest of Sacramento, bought Foster's Big Horn and has operated it ever since with his wife, Dorothie.

"Townspeople were afraid an outsider would buy the collection and move it away. A lot of hunters from various parts of the country submitted bids but I submitted the highest and got it," Brown explained. "We continue to operate the Big Horn as a bar with restaurant in the back, but it's more than that. The place is really a museum. "How many saloons have you ever heard of that are regularly visited by schoolchildren on field trips?" Brown asked.

FORTY-NINE

SONOMA COUNTY

LUTHER BURBANK'S WIDOW

I N 1968 I INTERVIEWED BETTY BURBANK, widow of Luther Burbank, the most famous plant breeder of all time. It was a rare visit with Elizabeth Waters Burbank, then in her 78th year, at her home in Santa Rosa. The fact that she agreed to talk to a newsman came as a great surprise to her close circle of friends. She lived in a tiny cottage on the grounds adjacent to gardens filled with the Burbank creations that enriched all mankind.

Thousands came to Santa Rosa each year to honor the memory of Luther Burbank and visit his gardens. Few who came were aware Burbank's widow lived right there. That was in keeping with her desire for privacy, eagerly sought by the remarkable, but modest and shy lady. But Mrs. Burbank, it must be explained, did not seek the interview, on the contrary, she tried to discourage it. But she finally relented, and welcomed photographer Ben Olender and me into her home, the same homestead built by the great naturalist himself in 1888, 11 years after he migrated to the West from his birthplace, Lancaster, Massachusetts.

"Mr. Burbank told me to live my own life, not his," explained the widow of the man whose name is known and respected throughout the world. They were married in 1916, when he was 67 and his secretary, Betty Waters, was 25. Her husband died in this very cottage in 1926. And from that time until June 1977 when she died, at age 89, Mrs. Burbank lived a quiet life, shunning the attention of the curious public. Even here in Santa Rosa, 60 miles north of San Francisco, little was generally known about her, and yet, her generosity, her compassion for all living creatures, touched the lives of many over the years.

Presidents, premiers, royalty, people from all walks of life made pilgrimages to Luther Burbank's gardens while Mrs. Burbank was alive and since her death, as they did when the famed horticulturist was alive and conducting his magical experiments. When Nikita Khrushchev visited California in 1959 the one person he asked to see —and the wish was granted—was the widow of "the wizard of plants and trees."

The cottage is a museum of Luther Burbank memorabilia in the middle of The Luther Burbank Home and Gardens, a city park and national historical monument. Inside the home are Burbank's personal papers, letters, books, field notes, scrapbooks, with photographs and paintings of the naturalist and flowers he developed.

"If I opened my doors, I would never have a minute's rest," said Mrs. Burbank, "as it is, the house and everything in it in due time will belong to the people. Until then they belong to me." She deeded the house and its contents to the city of Santa Rosa. Childless, she held a life tenancy in the homestead.

The cottage was shaded by a 120-foot-high Cedar of Lebanon tree planted by Burbank in 1888. He was buried beside the tree as he requested. The tree stood as a tombstone to his unmarked grave, also in keeping with his wish: "When I go, don't raise a monument to me—plant a tree." When Mrs. Burbank died, she was buried next to her husband.

The great tree was dying of a root disease and had to be removed in 1989. A bench was installed in its place, next to the unmarked graves of Luther Burbank and his wife.

When he was alive the famous and humble met with Burbank under the Cedar of Lebanon, which served as his lanai. Those who often visited him beneath the Cedar's spreading boughs, included: Thomas Edison, Henry Ford, Jan Paderewski, Theodore Roosevelt, John Burrough, John Muir, Helen Keller, Jack London and many other of the best known of his contemporaries. In one of Burbank's scrapbooks treasured by his widow, author-neighbor Jack London wrote: "I'd rather do what you're doing than be Roosevelt, Rockefeller, King Edward and the Kaiser rolled into one."

What Burbank did was revolutionize the fruit, vegetable and flower industries in his experimental gardens. By a conservative estimate he introduced 800 new plants. He developed more than 250 varieties of fruits alone: 112 different plums, 55 kinds of berries, numerous varieties of cherries, apples, grapes, nectarines, pears, prunes, cactus, quinces, almonds, chestnuts, walnuts, grains, grasses, forage plants, beans, corn, sorghums, potatoes, peas, peppers, rhubarb, squashes, tomatoes. He had as many as 3,000 experiments going at the same time in his Santa Rosa gardens and greenhouses. His objective was to improve the quality of plants and thereby increase the world's food supply.

Mrs. Burbank walked among her husband's creations in her backyard, watering giant flowered agapanthus, "red hot poker" tritomas and Shasta daisies. Passing a tomato patch, she remarked: "People used to argue more about tomatoes. They'd write Mr. Burbank demanding to know, 'Settle it for once and for all. Is a tomato a vegetable or a fruit?'"

Her home was furnished as it was when Burbank was alive. Although old fashioned in manner, dress and in the furnishing of the cottage-museum, Mrs. Burbank was hardly old fashioned in her thinking. She ground coffee each day in a coffee grinder that dated back prior to the turn of the century. No TV cluttered her living room. But a well-thumbed morning paper rested on a coffee table. And a just finished book on the life of Robert Kennedy was close by. "Betty is a person who cherishes the past, but is extremely flexible and keeps up with everything of the day," said a good friend, Margaret Dixon.

Mrs. Burbank founded the Sonoma County Humane Society in 1931. Through the years she had been a director and one of the society's most active members. "I'm not a botanist, but Mr. Burbank and I shared a common love for animals," said Mrs. Burbank as she reached for her cat, Sally, up in a greenhouse rafter. "Betty loves nature and animals," explained Mrs. Margaret Richardson, executive director of the humane society at the time. "She has always worked hard for state and national humane legislation. She personally goes out to pick up animals and work cases."

Betty Burbank made a public appearance each year in May when she was guest of honor at the annual Luther Burbank Rose Festival Parade in Santa Rosa. She continued to plant trees and flowers at schools named after her husband on his birthday, March 7, set aside in California since 1909 as Arbor Day. And each year Mrs. Burbank attended a commencement breakfast at Santa Rosa Junior College, where, since the 1930s, she had presented an annual Luther Burbank scholarship to a student of botany. She personally awarded the scholarship in her home, where the student was shown personal items of Luther Burbank seen then only by a handful of people through the years.

From her cottage windows, the widow of one of California's most revered citizens looked out each day onto one of the most famous gardens on Earth. And since she died in 1977, the home has been opened for visitation April through October. The gardens, with many of Burbank's original plantings, are open year round.

RUSSIAN OUTPOST IN CALIFORNIA

A TELEVISION DOCUMENTARY about a relatively little-known episode in California history has been shown throughout Russia. The "Story of Fort Ross" tells the story of the settlement of soldiers, farmers and fur hunters on a lonely stretch of the rugged Sonoma County coast 100 miles northwest of San Francisco. It was Russia's most remote outpost from 1812 to 1841. A Russian TV crew filmed the documentary at Fort Ross State Park.

"The story of Fort Ross is widely recounted in my country where it is part of the school curriculum. The California outpost was Imperial Russia's deepest penetration eastward," said Svetlana Fedorova, a Russian ethnologist, visiting Fort Ross for her fourth time when we encountered her.

"In Moscow, I have had numerous letters and phone calls from friends from all over Russia, telling me they have seen the documentary about Fort Ross on TV," she related. Russia's leading authority on the period when Russia owned Alaska and Fort Ross, Fedorova is based at the Academy of Sciences' Institute of Ethnography in Moscow. She has written four books and numerous scientific papers on the subject.

Fort Ross, a large, square enclosure within 20-foot-high redwood plank walls, contains several rough-hewn timber structures overlooking the Pacific Ocean. It was established as a state historic park in 1906.

The Russians came to California to hunt seals and sea otters, to grow vegetables and fruit and raise livestock to support their outpost in Alaska. Fort Ross was the first shipyard of any size in California. Nineteenth-century Russian scientists came to Fort Ross to study the Indians, the plants and animals. Kashaya Pomo Indian bows, arrows, baskets, feathered capes, ornaments and crafts collected by the Russian scientists are on display in museums in Moscow, St. Petersburg and Siberia. Port Rumiantsev, now known as Bodega Bay, 20 miles south of Fort Ross, was the Russian's principal port in California.

Among the 25 to 75 Russians stationed at the fort at any given time, fewer than half a dozen were women, wives of ranking officials. Aleut and Eskimo hunters of sea otters and sea mammals who were brought here from Alaska by the Russians were all men, although many of the Alaskan and Russians paired off with Kashaya Pomo Indian women.

In the 1820 census at the fort, 42 local Indian women were listed as married or cohabiting with Russians. When the Russians sold the fort to John Sutter in 1841, many took their Indian wives and children back to Russia with them. Russian descendants of those American Indians live in Russia and some Kashaya Pomos living near Fort Ross have Russian ancestors. There are several Russian words in the Kashaya Pomo language. "We are working with the local Kashaya Pomo people to collect information from their oral tradition pertaining to the Russian colony," noted Professor Kent Lightfoot of UC Berkeley.

On the Russian side, documents provide some idea of what life was like. "What an enchanting land California is," wrote Alexander Rotchez, reflecting on his five years as the last Russian commandant at Fort Ross. "Everything is so fragrant, the iridescent hummingbird flutters, vibrates and shimmers over a flower. The virgin soil of California yields marvelous fruit. I spent the best years of my life there."

Otto Von Kotzebue, a Russian navigator, described the Kashaya Pomo Indians in his 1824 journal, noting:

"The inhabitants of Ross live in the greatest concord with the Indians who work as day laborers for wages. The Indians willingly give their daughters in marriage to Russians and Aleutians; and from these unions ties of relationship have arisen which strengthen the good understanding between them."

The Russians eventually gave up their colony in California because of the depletion of the local sea otter population, failure of farming and the clash of international political interests. The United States, Spain, France and Great Britain objected to the Russian presence in California, so in 1841, Czar Nicholas I ordered his colonists home.

Visitors see memorabilia of the Russian period on display, walk through the old Russian buildings, the barracks, a jail, workshops, the Russian commandant's house, fur barn, seven-sided watchtowers, the community kitchen and the first Russian Orthodox chapel built in North America outside Russia.

Since the turn of the century, members of the Protection of the Holy Virgin Russian Orthodox Congregation of Palo Alto have made a pilgrimage each year on Memorial Day to hold services in the Russian Orthodox Chapel at Fort Ross. The Orthodox Church of America in San Francisco holds services in the chapel each Fourth of July. Constructed in 1824, the redwood chapel inside the stockade burned to the ground in 1970 and was rebuilt.

"Fort Ross chapel has great meaning for us," said Father Vladimir Derugin, pastor of the Palo Alto church. "It is the nexus of the coming together of the East and West, spiritually and culturally, our mother church in the Lower 48 states. Two of our saints were at the church when Fort Ross was a Russian colony, St. Innocence the Apostle, who was there in 1836, and St. Peter the Aleut, a hunter and gatherer at the fort in 1816."

The leading expert on the history of Fort Ross in America is Nicholas Rokitiansky, a teacher of Russian and history at De Anza College in the San Jose suburb of Cupertino. Rokitiansky first heard of Fort Ross as a student in Manchuria in 1929. He came to the United States in the early 1930s and spent eight years as a librarian in the Russian section of the Library of Congress. Then he moved to California.

Rokitiansky, known as Fort Ross' "Russian Connection" made a dozen trips to Russia visiting historians who are experts on the Russian colonies in Alaska, California and Hawaii, and gathering data about Fort Ross from Russian archives. In 1976, he delivered the U.S. Bicentennial lectures at Moscow Academy of Sciences on "Fort Ross and the Russian Settlement in California."

The gift shop has more books on the Russian episode in California history than any bookstore, including two by Svetlana Fedorova translated into English. Russian cookbooks, needlework books, traditional folk tale books (all in English) as well as Matreshka dolls (the Russian stacking dolls) are sold, along with descendants of apple trees planted by the Russians.

Archeological digs are ongoing at Fort Ross, as much is still being learned from buried artifacts. A cemetery with 50 Russian remains has been exhumed by the University of Wisconsin Archeology Department. Students led by Professor Lightfoot of UC Berkeley have recorded 24 sites surrounding Fort Ross. These sites were used by Russians, Aleuts and Eskimos sea animal hunters from Kodiak Island, and by Kashaya Pomo Indians. "These are exciting times at Fort Ross," said Lyn Kalani of the Fort Ross Interpretive Association. "In addition to all the archeological activity, we are getting more visitors from Russia than ever before. We were told by a group of Russian visitors that a rock opera about Fort Ross is being performed in Moscow."

FIFTY

STANISLAUS COUNTY

OLD ORDER OF DUNKERS

T HEY ARE KNOWN AS THE OLD ORDER OF DUNKERS. There are about 5,000 of them in the United States, about 700 in California, not counting children. Their official name is the Old German Baptist Brethren. They are a small "plain people" religious sect. They don't listen to the radio, record or cd player, watch television, vote or take part in civic affairs. They consider dancing, card playing, drinking, smoking, gambling, attending carnivals, and other worldly and frivolous entertainment the works of Satan. Here in California the sect is centered around Modesto in Stanislaus County.

Women of the sect wear no makeup or jewelry and do not go to beauty shops. They wear 19th-century style, homemade dark blue cape dresses with buttons up the front. They keep their hair long and covered with nylon netting. The bearded men dress in work clothes or black suits with black vests and black hats. "God made man to have a masculine appearance and a beard is part of that appearance. Our men look like men," said Ed Gish, a minister in the faith. "Our women look like women. They never wear slacks. They always wear dresses."

The Old German Baptist Brethren Church is one of the most conservative remnants of the Brethren movement, begun in 1708 by a handful of people in the riverside town of Schwarzenau, Germany. The largest of the U.S. Brethren churches today is the relatively contemporary Church of the Brethren. The Old German Baptist Brethren Church split from the movement in 1881 because of what they regarded as liberalizing tendencies. The 5,000 members in the United States, again, not counting children, attend 57 churches, four of them in California. All of the members in the Modesto area are descendants of those who came to California by oxcart in the 1860s.

The Brethren have been dubbed the "Dunkers" in this country because of their baptismal practice of being immersed in a river three times—in the names of the Father, Son and Holy Ghost.

Unlike some of the other "plain people" religious groups, the Brethren are not adverse to owning modern automobiles, the latest farm equipment and using modern appliances in their homes. They are a hard-working, industrious group. "Traditionally our people had always been farmers," said Durand Overholzer, one of the leaders of the California group. "But with the disappearance of the small family farm and the rising cost of agricultural land, many of our families have been forced to move into rural towns. We try to keep to ourselves. That is why most of our men who no longer farm now work in the trades with their own businesses as carpenters, plumbers, painters."

Most social activities for adherents are centered around the meeting houses, plain white frame churches with old-fashioned wooden pews and no pictures, statues, crosses, altar or other furnishings. "All the social needs of our people involve interaction within the group," Overholzer explained. "When we're not in the meeting house, we have gatherings at farms or grange halls where we have pot-luck dinners and do a lot of singing. We follow a strict and disciplined lifestyle," Overholzer said. "Divorce and swearing, for example, are not tolerated. A person cannot be divorced and remain a member, nor can a person who swears."

The liveliest issue in the church for some time has been the survival of the group's simple life-style. "What really worries us is that our young people are getting involved with the world. We are losing our young people," noted Overholzer. "Our children are becoming easy prey for sinful, vain and worldly things," Ed Gish lamented.

To separate their youth from the mainstream the sect established its own schools. Parochial schools are common with many religious denominations. But Brethren children historically were enrolled in rural public schools until the late 1970s. In 1978 Overholzer and Michael Wray, both ministers in the faith, established the First German Baptist Brethren school in California. Enrollment that first year was 20. By 1995 enrollment had increased to 140. The school is located on member Robert Rossel's farm near Modesto.

"Our religion discourages higher education, but our teachers in this school are doing their best to give these youngsters a good basic education," said Frances Rodrian, one of the group's high school teachers. "We call our school the Brethren Heritage School because it is here we are hoping to save our heritage," explained Overholzer, the school's principal.

Overholzer is also chairman of the board of the Overholzer Church Furniture Company in Modesto. It was his father, Elvan Overholzer, also a leader in the sect, who founded the church furniture factory in 1952, a firm that does an $8 million annual business. A mile of church pews is turned out every week by the company that employs more than 100 workers.

Overholzer Church Furniture produces altars, communion rails, communion tables, kneelers, lecterns, pulpits, choir screens, clergy chairs, crosses, baptismal fonts, hymn boards and dozens of other specialty items for churches and synagogues. "We furnish religious edifices in all 50 states, throughout Canada and overseas," said Durand Overholzer. "There are about 100 companies in the United States manufacturing church furniture but only about 20 make church furniture exclusively," said Michael Shuck, general manager of the company and Overholzer's son-in-law.

Overholzer is one of the largest church furniture manufacturers in America. "Our company is the only one aggressively marketing the entire U.S." said Overholzer. The firm has 30 representatives scattered across the nation and operates a fleet of trucks delivering church furniture coast to coast. And they sell furniture to every major religious group in America. "Our biggest market is the fundamental evangelical churches, the fastest growing segment of the religious community," said Overholzer.

The Overholzer family got into the church furniture business by chance. "Dad ran a cabinet shop in Modesto. One day the pastor of a local church stopped by to ask him if he could custom make some church furniture," Durand Overholzer recalled. "It wasn't any time at all that Dad quit making cabinets and began spending all his time furnishing churches."

FIFTY-ONE

SUTTER COUNTY

LITTLE INDIA OF THE VALLEY

YUBA CITY, a small Central California town in Sutter County, is known by many as "Little India." Women dressed in saris and bearded men in turbans are a familiar sight on the streets here. A dozen shops, "bazaars," feature bolts of fabric from Bombay, along with spices, beans, pickles, incense, jewelry, wood carvings and other products imported from India.

An estimated 10,000 Sikhs, originally from the Indian state of Punjab, make their home on farms around Yuba City. Many are descendants of Sikhs who came to the United States shortly after the turn of the century to work on railroad construction in California, as the Chinese had done two and three decades earlier.

"The valley around Yuba City reminded them of home; the weather and terrain is much like Punjab," said Dr. Gulzar Singh Johl, a local ophthalmologist. "When the Punjabi pioneers finished working on the railroad, they stayed on in Yuba City and became farmers as they had been in India."

The Punjabis are a close-knit community. But assimilation into the mainstream of American culture has been accelerated with the younger generations. Many of the young men and women of the community graduate from universities and leave the farms to become professionals in larger cities. For the most part, however, the Sikhs have been content to devote themselves to their peach and prune orchards, rice farms, walnut and almond groves that range in size from a few acres to 12,000 acres.

As recently as the mid-1970s the Gurdwara or Sikh Temple on the outskirts of Yuba City was one of only eight Sikh temples in the United States. By the mid-1990s there were four Sikh temples in the Yuba City area and more than 50 of the temples across the nation. The Sikh religion, founded in 1469 by Punjabi Guru Nanak, has 15 million followers, the vast majority in Punjab.

In India, as here, Sikh men are readily recognized by their turbans and beards. In the Yuba City area about half the Sikh men have shed their turbans, shaved their beards and adopted Western-style dress. Also, Sikhs in India have the same surname—Singh, meaning lion. They are named after Guru Gobind Singh, 10th and last of the Sikh gurus, the greatest poet, scholar and warrior of the Sikhs. In California, to avoid confusion, all but a few of the Sikhs use Singh as a middle name and have adopted the name of their home village, town or city as their last name.

The Sikhs of Yuba City are bilingual, speaking English and Punjabi (Gurmukhi). For many years Yuba High School was the only one in America offering classes in Punjabi. Now many high schools in the area offer the language course.

"America for us has truly been a land of opportunity," said Didar Singh Bains, 54, most successful of the Indian farmers. Bains harvested 20,000 tons of peaches and 2,000 tons of prunes on his 12,000 acres in 1995, where he also grows rice, grapes and almonds. In recent years he also has been growing cranberries on his farm in British Columbia.

"We love America. We also respect our age-old traditions from the old country," he said, adding, "For years we held our church services in a barn. One cold day in 1968 we decided we should be ashamed of ourselves because we did not have a Sikh temple in Yuba City. We passed the hat and within 10 minutes the Sikh farmers pledged $22,000 to start building a temple." The next year, the farmers dedicated their spectacular onion-domed Sikh Temple.

THE ERB OF YUBA CITY

THEY CALL THEMSELVES **ERBS.** There are several thousand ERBs scattered around the world—all over the Americas, in France, Germany, Italy, England, Africa, Japan, Russia, Australia. I caught up with one in a fast food cafe in Yuba City—Bill Dutcher, then 34, a hamburger-slinging bachelor, and an ERB since he was 13.

An ERB is a surperfan of the life and works of the author and creator of Tarzan, the late Edgar Rice Burroughs. ERBS come in many varieties: circus acrobats, company presidents, writers (like Ray Bradbury), accountants, electricians, college professors, priests, the young, middle-aged, elderly. President John Kennedy was an ERB. He had excellent credentials. His father produced one of the 43 Tarzan movies.

When Bill Dutcher wasn't tossing hamburgers onto the grill, he was busy publishing an ERB magazine called Josoomian. During an interview in his apartment, crammed with an incredible assortment of Tarzan and Burroughs memorabilia, Dutcher nibbled Tarzan vinegar-flavored potato chips made in Quebec and explained the name of his publication, "Burroughs' first novel *Princess of Mars* was one of 10 science-fiction books he wrote about Mars. He wrote 90 novels in all, 26 in the Tarzan series. In his books appear 18 languages invented by Burroughs including the language of Martians. Jasoomian is one of Burroughs' Martian words. It means earthman."

Dutcher's 32-page illustrated slick magazine had a circulation at the time of 2,000, with ERBs in Europe, Africa, South America, Asia and Australia among regular subscribers. "I like to think of Jasoomian kind of like a Time Magazine of Tarzan buffs," said the 5-foot, 1-

inch, 210-pound surperfan. The magazine is filled with photos, special features, and news items about Tarzan and ERB activities.

Before going into the hamburger business, Dutcher worked for seven years as a printer for the St. Petersburg (Florida.) Times. His Tarzan-Burroughs collection included first editions of all Burroughs' novels; 10,000 Tarzan still photos, and early-day Tarzan comic books. Dutcher had tapes of Tarzan radio episodes aired in the 1930s, a series in which Jane was played by Burroughs' daughter, Joan, and Tarzan by Joan's husband, Jim Pierce. He had silent and sound Tarzan movies, old movie window cards and original Tarzan movie scripts. Dutcher's apartment was cluttered with file cabinets brimming with Tarzan bubble gum, cigarettes, potato chips, T-shirts, games, records, trading cards, posters, paintings, wrappers from Tarzan bread and ice cream bars.

His magazine, issued quarterly, contained Tarzan and Burroughs related features such as stories about Tarzana, California, and Tarzan, Texas. One issue reproduced a copy of the Rand McNally rejection slip for "Tarzan of the Apes" written by Burroughs in 1912. The rejection read: "We have given the work careful consideration and while interesting we find it does not fit in with our plans." More than 35 million copies of Tarzan books have been published in 36 different languages.

Dutcher had endless Tarzan statistics, "Tarzan films started in 1918 and are still being made today, the longest running motion pictures series ever made. 'Tarzan of the Apes,' starring Elmo Lincoln, the first Tarzan, was the first film to gross over $1 million. Burroughs was born in Chicago, September 1, 1875. He died March 19, 1950 at his home in Tarzana. He never set foot in Africa. He was the oldest American war correspondent during World War II."

Dutcher had been a member of the Burroughs Bibliophiles for years. The group had a membership of over 2,500 and held annual convention in several cities in the U.S., England and Germany. "You'd be surprised at the widespread interest in Tarzan and Edgar Rice Burroughs after all these years," insisted Dutcher, the hamburger-slinging ERB of Yuba City.

FIFTY-TWO

TEHAMA COUNTY

ISHI, THE LAST YAHI

I SHI WILDERNESS is a remote cliff country, crisscrossed by roaring canyon streams, swollen by melting mountain snow, and choked with dense brush and tall timber. It was set aside as a wilderness area by Congress in October, 1984, to protect the natural and archeological resources from as much human intrusion as possible. The area, in Tehama County, is a seldom visited, difficult-to-penetrate section inside Lassen National Forest in Northern California, called Ishi in honor of America's last Indian living in the wild.

For 45 years, from 1866-1911, this was the last home and hide-out for the lost tribe of Yahi Indians, a tiny band that managed to avoid contact with anyone else for all those years of concealment, numbering just 16 members, at most, in 1866.

Anthropologists and archeologists had voiced concern about setting the area aside as a protected wilderness because it calls attention to an area with more than 100 ancient Indian village sites, many yet to be scientifically excavated. Until the establishment of the wilderness area, no more than 200 people a year had visited the area. One anthropologist said he was here for five weeks and saw only two people.

Black Rock, a spectacular pyramidal hill looming 250 feet above Mill Creek, is the gateway to the wilderness. It is reached by a 20-mile, single-lane, twisting, pot-holed dirt road perched on the shoulders of a perpendicular cliff. From Black Rock, the historic center of the world for the Yahi, the way into the wilderness is by foot. Vehicles are prohibited.

Ishi became the last of his people, living alone in the wild for three years without a single encounter with another human being. He emerged on August 29, 1911, on the outskirts of Oroville, emaciated and starving, a bewildered and frightened man of about 50, convinced that he would be shot and killed by the white man, as had happened to many of his people. A Stone Age survivor confronting the 20th century, he spoke a language no one could understand.

There had been an estimated 300 to 400 Yahis living in what is now Ishi Wilderness in the early 1850s, at the time of the first settlement of Tehama County in the Sacramento Valley. Within 15 years, the Yahi were virtually annihilated in a series of massacres described by anthropologists as the "fiercest and most uncompromising resistance met by Indians on the West Coast." During their long concealment, said anthropologist Alfred L. Kroeber, the Yahi made up "the smallest free nation in the world, a nation that succeeded in holding out against the tide of civilization."

The wilderness covers 40,670 acres (13 miles long, eight miles wide) of the forest, about 50 miles southeast of Redding. As a wilderness area, it is protected from development. There can be no roads, no structures, not even an outhouse. Visitors need a permit to enter and are required to leave no trace of having been there.

For Lassen National Forest archeologist Jim Johnston, the creation of the wilderness area and naming it after Ishi makes him both happy and sad. Johnston has spent 14 years on and off doing archeological research here. "There could not be a better name for the wilderness,"

Johnston said. "However, I fear the name may be counterproductive, as it will attract more pot hunters." Despite the fact that the wilderness is a difficult place to get to, vandalism and theft at many of the more than 100 village sites have already been serious problems.

At the village site on Mill Creek where Ishi is believed to have spent his early years, there was fresh evidence of digging in house pits when we were there. The Indians dug holes in the ground and around them erected homes with conical-shaped roofs constructed of branches and hides. Scattered on the ground were metates (grinding stones), scrapers, cutting tools and obsidian flakes, not prime objects of value to pot hunters.

"People come in here and dig for baskets, beads, arrowheads and other Indian artifacts. It is a crime to remove anything from a national forest, punishable by fines up $20,000 and two years in jail," Johnston explained. He said rangers have increased patrols since the area was given the special designation. "I would love to place interpretive signs in here pointing out caves and the bear den where Ishi, his mother, his sister and an old man lived for several years in hiding, and note other historically significant Yahi sites," he said. "But we cannot risk the chance of people coming in and destroying these important areas."

Johnston followed Mill Creek until he came to a cave he had explored in the mid-1970s. A dozen years ago he had discovered the skeleton of an adult female, which he reburied and left intact. "Look at this," he said dejectedly on entering the cave. "Someone has come in here and removed the remains of the Indian woman." All that was left was a single human rib.

When Ishi stumbled out of the wilds, he was taken into custody and held by Sheriff J. B. Webber in the Butte County Jail at Oroville. Kroeber, head of the University of California's Anthropology Museum, then in San Francisco, read an account of Ishi in a newspaper. He immediately sent a telegram to Sheriff Webber: "Hold Indian till arrival. Will take charge."

For the next four years and seven months, until Ishi succumbed to tuberculosis on March 25, 1916, he lived at the museum in San Francisco. No one ever knew his name, as it was a Yahi tradition never to say one's own name. So Kroeber called him Ishi, Yahi for man. While living at the museum, Ishi mastered a vocabulary of about 600 English words, and Kroeber compiled a dictionary of the Yahi language. The museum was jammed each weekend by people who came to watch Ishi chip arrowheads, shape bows and answer questions with Kroeber's help.

Ishi developed a close friendship with physician Sexton Pope, his doctor, who became fascinated with the Indian's skill with the bow and arrow. That friendship triggered a renaissance in archery in America and throughout the world. Pope, who became known as the father of modern archery, wrote articles and books about archery and about Ishi and his knowledge of the bow and arrow.

In 1914, Pope, Kroeber and anthropologist Thomas T. Waterman spent the summer with Ishi in Yahi country. Ishi took them on a tour of his Stone Age world. He stalked and hunted deer with bow and arrow. He speared salmon. He gathered and ate acorns, brodiaea bulbs and green clover.

Ishi was interested in everything about modern man. He adapted rapidly, proving, according to Kroeber's wife, Theodora, that "Stone Age man and modern man are essentially alike." She chronicled the last years of the Yahi and Ishi in her book, *Ishi: A Biography of the Last Wild Indian in North America*, published in 1961 by the University of California Press.

When Ishi died, his body was cremated, as was the Yahi custom, with one of his bows, five arrows, acorn meal, beads, tobacco and obsidian flakes. His remains were placed in a small, black Pueblo jar in the Mount Olivet Cemetery south of San Francisco.

Each summer, June 1 through August 31, the University of California's Lowie Museum of Anthropology at Berkeley has a small exhibit of its Ishi material and photographs of America's last wild Indian. "Ishi's spirit is still here," mused Frank Norick, assistant director of the museum and curator of the Ishi collection.

THE PRESIDENT OF THE REPUBLIC OF CALIFORNIA

THE GREAT-GREAT GRANDDAUGHTER of the Republic of California's first and only president thought it was a shame her illustrious ancestor has been all but forgotten by history. "In

Texas," declared Mrs. Thelma Smith, "everywhere you turn there's something named after Sam Houston. But in California hardly anyone's ever heard of William B. Ide. Houston was the first president of the Republic of Texas and Texans regard him almost as a saint. Few Californians know that Ide led the Bear Flag Revolt." Mrs. Smith talked of her great-great grandfather at Red Bluff as she stood on the porch of his adobe home in the Tehama County seat 200 miles north of San Francisco.

Ide was a 51-year-old school teacher who led a small band of Americans into Sonoma on June 14, 1846, captured the Mexican garrison there and proclaimed the establishment of the independent Republic of California. But the republic was short lived—the bold move by Ide and his men proved so effective that 25 days later the Bear flag was lowered and the Stars and Stripes run up in its place. Then on September 9, 1850, California entered the union as the 31st state.

"If it wasn't for the bravery of William B. Ide and several other early-day citizens of Tehama County," said the county's superior judge Curtis E. Wetter, "We would all be citizens of Mexico today."

"William B. Ide is truly a forgotten man," said his great-great granddaughter. "There isn't a village, town, city or county named in his honor. Sam Houston's birthday is a state holiday in Texas. You would think California would at least have a William B. Ide day at the state fair."

A native of Rutland, Massachusetts, Ide settled in Independence, Missouri, then migrated west in a wagon train with his wife and nine children. He built a home on the Sacramento River in Red Bluff. In the spring of 1846 rumors spread that Mexican authorities were going to drive all Americans out of California. Ide and a number of ranchers planned a revolt with Ide selected by the group to serve as president.

They fashioned a flag with a star and bear in its field, then rode by horseback to Sonoma, principal town north of San Francisco where they captured Gen. M.G. Vallejo and the Sonoma fort. In his first official declaration as president of the California Republic, Ide proclaimed: "We were invited to this country by a promise of lands on which to settle and a promise of a republican government. Having arrived in California we were denied even the privilege of buying or renting lands, were oppressed by a military depotism. We invite all peaceable and good citizens of California to assist us in establishing and perpetuating a republican government."

The Bear flag, the official flag of California today, featured the emblem of the grizzly because "the grizzly attacks no man when left alone but fights to death when molested."

After his brief reign as president of the Republic of California, Ide remained active in public life. He served as judge of Colusa County and mayor of Monroeville. He also made a small fortune mining gold and operated a cattle ranch. Ide died in December 1852, at the age of 56.

However, he hasn't been entirely forgotten. In 1959 his adobe home on the banks of the Sacramento River in Red Bluff was set aside as a state historical monument. "We are indebted to the state for restoring the adobe and setting aside a small park surrounding it," said Thelma Smith. "But the fact still remains, few people in California know the state was once a republic with a president named William B. Ide."

FIFTY-THREE

TRINITY COUNTY

HIDDEN TREASURES

W HEN WE CAUGHT UP WITH JOANN BAXTER, she had spent the last four years exploring 500,000 acres of densely forested, mountainous wilderness in Northern California's Trinity County. "I'm finding and cataloguing hidden treasures," the 31-year-old U.S. Forest Service archeologist said as we accompanied her into Shasta-Trinity National Forest. Her treasures at that time included a 50-mile-long, narrow-gauge railroad abandoned in 1917, a long-forgotten mining town, old homesteads, two 1850s cemeteries of Chinese miners, Indian village sites dating back to 1200 AD and much more. Similar inventories of cultural resources were under way in several other of the nation's 155 national forests.

For four months Baxter and two assistants, Anne Carlson and

Donna Kerrigan backpacked into the wilderness following the roadbed of the La Moine Logging Railroad. "We stayed in the forest three and four day stretches at a time, came out for a few days and went back in again. We walked the 50-mile length of the old railroad," the archeologist related. "We recorded everything we encountered—16 logging campsites, three mill sites, 97 wooden trestles. At one point deep in the forest we came upon five 19th-Century railroad cars." The railroad operated from 1898 until it was abandoned at the beginning of World War I.

"There are laws prohibiting artifact collecting in the national forests, yet, until recently, not much attention was paid to people who walked off with relics of the past," Baxter noted. "Now, we're trying to get a handle on all of the cultural resources and preserve and protect anything of value in the forest."

When timber sales were scheduled for sections of the Shasta-Trinity Forest, she visited the area where logging would take place to record historical sites and items. Those areas with historical material are set aside and not logged.

Baxter had recorded prehistoric Indian villages and camping sites where she discovered ancient stone tools carbon-dated as early as 1200 AD. She also accompanied an old cowboy on horseback to a long-forgotten mining town miles back in the Trinity Alps. The town consisted of cabins, a general store and postoffice, all weathered and in various degrees of deterioration but still standing. Nearby was a huge stamp mill, rusting shovels and other mining equipment.

One Chinese cemetery of the 1850s located by the archeologist was intact with bottles, pottery and porcelain objects in place on the graves. Another Chinese cemetery out of the 1850s and 1860s, close to an inhabited area, had been vandalized. Coffin boards and broken artifacts were strewn about. Scattered homesteads, abandoned cabins and barns dating as early as the 1830s were noted by Baxter in her records. She recommended a classic century-old hay and cow barn to be included in the National Registry of Historical Places. It was the last remaining building left in the woods on the pioneer Jacob Bowerman homestead. The homestead is now part of a national recreation area in the Shasta-Trinity forest.

A stark reminder of terrible times in the forest is a number of towering pines at Preacher Meadow Campgrounds. The trees are permanently scarred with deep elliptical gouges near the base of the trunks. "Ethnographers have documented that a band of Wintu Indians forced from their traditional village sites by early settlers in the 1850s took refuge in this part of the forest," explained Baxter. "Trapped here during a severe winter, they were without food and ate the soft inner bark to ward off starvation." She suggested the Forest Service erect a sign in Preacher Meadow informing visitors of the meaning of scarred pine trees. "I think it's important for campers in this area frying their bacon to realize what happened here because of man's inhumanity to man," she declared.

FIFTY-FOUR

TULARE COUNTY

SEQUOIA—FOREST OF GIANTS

"HAD A LITTLE DOG, skinny as a rail, He had fleas all over his tail. Every time his tail went flop, The fleas on the bottom all jumped on top." Ranger Mora Brown waved her arms. "Now let's sing it again. This time with more zip," she pleaded. Everybody sang louder. The youngsters loved it.

The sun had set. Flames dance from the burning log. Brown was leading a campfire sing behind Giant Forest Lodge. Campfire programs are nightly affairs at National and state parks. They're part of the tremendous fun of camping vacations, are informative as well as entertaining, and free of charge. Slides and films are shown under the stars and in the midst of the giant trees at Sequoia National Park. The illustrated lectures presented by rangers tell stories of the forest animals, flowers, trees, birds, trails, and other highlights of the park.

My wife, Arliene and I were on a camping vacation with our son, Brad, who was then 9, and our niece, Arliene, who was 5. Both have children older than that now. Arliene and Brad learned at one campfire program that the National Park and towering trees in it were named after Cherokee Indian Chief Sequoyah, who devised an alphabet of 85 characters for his tribe. They learned a great deal about the animals of Sequoia, about the bears, the eight different kinds of squirrels that live there; learned that the ever present California mule deer gets its name from its big ears.

A ranger explained that the General Sherman tree is the largest living thing on Earth, 275 feet high, as high as a 20-story building, and with a base circumference of 103 feet, consists of enough timber to build 100 5-room homes. The seed that started the tree 3,500 to 4,000 years ago was no bigger than the period at the end of this sentence.

In 6,412-foot-elevation Giant Forest we pitched our tent at Sunset Rock Campgrounds, heavily wooded with Sequoias and pine, with gorgeous buckeye and dogwood in full bloom. Every time we sat down to eat, chipmunks, golden-mantled squirrels and a mule deer or two would poke their noses over the rocks, around the trees, up from the logs that bordered our campsite.

In the air, same story. Stellar jays lighted on every available limb in the vicinity of our table. Let the butter dish be in the open and that real charmer of the forest, the brightly colored red-headed, yellow-breasted, black-winged Western tanager would drop down on the table oblivious of who sat there, and nibble on the golden spread. Our pound of peanuts in the shell provided many happy hours feeding the friendly furry critters.

At Giant Forest we hiked the 482 steps to the top of glistening Moro Rock for the breath-taking view of the valley 4,000 feet straight down, the 12,000-foot high Sierra peaks that stretch magnificently across the horizon to the east. Picture a polished granite mountain dome, one that you look at hanging from the sky in the distance. That's the way it is with Moro. It's an easy climb for the entire family, well worth the effort. Other short hikes at Giant Forest include across Crescent Meadow, said by John Muir to be the Gem of the Sierra, to Hale Tharp's cabin, a fallen Sequoia lived in by the colorful pioneer from 1861 to 1890. Along Alta Trail, a steep two-mile round trip hike leads to the President and Congress group of Sequoias, the mighty McKinley, Lincoln, General Lee, Window and Room trees. Toppled giants amaze the youngsters, especially those you can hike or drive through.

LIVING MEMORIAL TO A GREAT NATIVE AMERICAN

S EQUOYAH, whose name is spelled various ways, is perhaps America's most honored Indian. He was never a chief. But he did something, so far as is known, no other person in history had ever done before or since. He conceived and perfected an 85-letter alphabet or syllabary for his nation that transformed his people from an illiterate to a literate group.

But what makes the story of Sequoyah even more amazing is that he was illiterate at the time, unable to read or write English or any other language. For that remarkable accomplishment Sequoyah's memory is honored in many ways: Sequoia National Park and Sequoia National Forest in California; Mt. Sequoyah in the Cherokee National Forest on the Tennessee-North Carolina border. Sequoiadendron *Giganteum* or giant Sequoia, the world's largest living things, are named after Sequoyah. So are the world's tallest living things, Sequoia *sempervirens,* the giant redwoods of the Pacific Coast. There are schools, streets and buildings named after Sequoyah.

In 1905, a convention was held in Muskogee and a constitution was written to form a new state to be called Sequoyah. But the attempt for statehood was premature. Two years later it did happen but the new state was not called Sequoyah, but Oklahoma, a Choctaw Indian word meaning Red People.

Sequoyah was born in the early 1770s (his birth date is unknown) and died in 1843. The county where he lived in Oklahoma from 1828 to the time of his death carries his name, Sequoyah County. In Washington D.C., in the Hall of Statuary where each state is entitled to honor its two most outstanding personalities, Oklahoma salutes Sequoyah and Will Rogers both Cherokee Indians.

Hanging in the Rotunda of Oklahoma's Capitol is Charles Banks Wilson's bigger-than-life painting of Sequoyah wearing a red turban (trademark of the Cherokees of his day), a long-stemmed pipe hanging from his mouth. He is dressed in a long coat, long shirt, buckskin pants and moccasins and carries a walking stick. He is shown holding a scroll with the 85 letters of the Cherokee alphabet. Behind him in the painting is his log cabin at Skin Bayou on the outskirts of Sallisaw. There are also statues to Sequoyah in Tulsa, Anadarko and Sallisaw, Oklahoma, and at Calhoun, Georgia.

In the Cherokee National Capital at Tahlequah, Oklahoma, Durbin Feeling conducts regular classes in reading and writing the Cherokee language in Sequoyah's script. "We Cherokees have the only Indian alphabet in America," noted Feeling.

During the 12 years Sequoyah spent creating his alphabet, from 1809 to 1821, he came up with a particular letter for each sound in the Cherokee language. Although he neither spoke nor read English, he borrowed many of his letters right side up and upside down from the English alphabet without regard to pronunciation. In Cherokee, the letters DHA are pronounced like the Spanish word amigo, D sounding like *A*, H like *me* and A sounding like *go*.

Even though he had no schooling, Sequoyah realized reading and writing was the magic that would turn the tide for his people. He was scorned and ridiculed by his family, friends and fellow tribesmen who could not understand his motive. They thought he was practicing black magic or another evil activity that would bring the wrath of the gods upon the Cherokees. His wife destroyed his bark carvings; a log cabin in which he lived and worked in North Carolina was burned. But Sequoyah persisted. And, because of his alphabet, the Cherokees became the most advanced Indians in America in the 19th-Century.

Newspapers and books were published on printing presses using the 85 Cherokee letters. The Constitution, laws of the Cherokee Nation and resolutions of its national council were all printed in Cherokee and circulated among its people. At their capital at Tahlequah, the Cherokees formed a government modeled after the U.S. government. They erected a capitol for tribal officers and offices, a Supreme Court building, and a prison. A national public school system was established by the Cherokees as well in 1841 and, by the time of statehood, consisted of 130 primary and secondary schools.

The first school for girls west of the Mississippi was the Cherokee Female Seminary at Tahlequah opened in 1851 with instructions for

Indian girls in Latin, algebra, botany, music, geography, grammar. A similar school was operated for boys. Cherokees became governors, U.S. senators, members of Oklahoma's Legislature and Supreme Court and business leaders.

Sequoyah was half white, half Cherokee. He used both his Cherokee name, Sequoyah (also spelled Sequoya, Sequoia or Sikwayi) and the English named George Gist (sometimes spelled Giss, Gust or Guess). It is generally accepted that his father was Nathanial Gist, a friend of George Washington, who spent many years among the Cherokees as a soldier. Gist, a colonel in the Continental Army, was sent by Washington to the Cherokees to secure the best warriors to fight the British in the Revolutionary War. It was during one of his visits that Gist is believed to have had an affair with an Indian woman and fathered Sequoyah.

In 1842, Sequoyah left his log cabin at Skin Bayou to lead a small party including his son and half a dozen of his tribesmen in search of a lost band of Cherokees in northern Mexico. A year later he died of natural causes in the village of the Mexican Cherokees and was buried by his son and companions in a nearby cave. The Cherokee Tribal Council has sponsored several unsuccessful expeditions in search of Sequoyah's remains in recent years. They would like to have the remains of their most famous tribal member reintered in Tahlequah. But his grave has never been found.

THE KARL MARX TREE

THE LARGEST LIVING THING ON EARTH was once known as the Karl Marx Tree. Another Sequoia tree, only slightly smaller and nearby was known as the Friedrich Engels. The trees were named by the 19th-century Kaweah Cooperative Colony, after the two men whose philosophy had inspired the colonists to venture into the fog-haunted wilderness now known as Sequoia National Park. They were communists, and their 1886 Cooperative was intended as a working model of the Marxist paradise that they believed would so appeal to the mass of American workers that the entire United States would forthwith embrace their political and economic system.

"Nothing is left of Kaweah today, of course," U.S. Magistrate Richard Combs said. "It's a part of history that is downplayed; isn't mentioned in any of the literature at the park's visitors center." For years Combs had been magistrate for Tulare County, holding forth in a courtroom at the park headquarters. And for nearly twice that long, he had been tracking down memorabilia and information, while working on a book about Kaweah.

There were 400 colonists, Combs said, followers of San Francisco orator and labor leader Burnett Haskell, who settled on the land amid the big trees, filed homestead claims and built a school, library, general store and blacksmith shop. They dug irrigation canals; planted crops, vineyards and orchards; organized their own orchestra; printed their own money, literature, and a monthly journal called the Commonwealth, and made a little (U.S. legal tender) money selling post card pictures of the big Karl Marx Tree.

"With shovels, crowbars and dynamite," Combs related, "they constructed one of the finest roads of that day, an 18-mile wagon road leading to the forests of giant Sequoias which they intended to harvest." The road, no longer used, but easily discernible, led to a sawmill built by the colonists. "But they decided against felling the giant trees," Combs continued. "They cut smaller trees instead."

Of course the colony attracted attention. "Great streams of visitors came," said Combs, "to see the idealists and their experiment, leading socialists, philosophers, many journeying from as far away as the capitals of Europe." But the experiment was doomed—by the trees themselves. In 1890, Congress passed a bill establishing Sequoia National Park, and the colonists, who had already fallen to squabbling among themselves, found their homestead claims invalidated. By 1892, the last of them were gone.

But tourists still come to see the Karl Marx Tree. It has a new name now, of course. The people who took over from the colonists had their own pantheon of heroes, and the largest living thing on earth, with its base circumference of 105 feet and lower limbs bigger than any tree growing east of the Mississippi, was named for one of them, a towering leader in a long-ago war. That big Sequoia is now known as the General Sherman Tree.

FIFTY-FIVE

TUOLUMNE COUNTY

HISTORICAL TOWN IN THE MOTHER LODE

COLUMBIA, a tiny Mother Lode hamlet in Tuolumne County is the Williamsburg of the West, the best preserved of California's old gold rush towns. Founded in 1850, with a population of 500, it has been a state historical monument since 1954. Half the townspeople live in homes built between the 1850s and the 1870s; homes now owned by the state and rented to their occupants. Even those living in old houses still in private ownership are not permitted to alter the exterior of their homes without the approval of everybody else in town.

The town's sidewalks are made of boards, brick and marble, the latter from a nearby quarry. Landmarks in Columbia include St. Anne's Catholic Church, the first brick church in the state; the 49ers Presbyterian Church, oldest Presbyterian congregation in California; the old two-story Columbia schoolhouse, and two 19th-century firehouses.

John Baker was a longtime smithy in Columbia. "I'm a throwback like everybody else around here," said Baker as he sprayed water on a red hot "tire", actually, an iron band that he was fitting snugly around the wheel of an 1860 firehose cart. Seconds earlier he had heated the tire in a circle of burning logs, the way it was done in the 1850s

Down the street from the smithy was the oldest continuously operated barbershop in the state. It opened in 1854. First time we met Bill Davis, the town barber, was in 1976. He had been the barber since l964. His predecessor, Frank Dondero, was the barber for 66 years at the Columbia Barber Shop, from 1898 to 1964 when he fell over dead on the job at the age of 94.

On that visit to Columbia when we first met Bill Davis, we met Mabel Draper, who was born in Columbia in 1896 and lived here all her life in her 1886 white frame house. Mabel was the postmaster from 1942 to 1966. One of her grandfathers was a 49er who came to California from Chile to seek his fortune in the Mother Lode. Another walked across the Isthmus of Panama in 1852 enroute here. Both her parents were born in Columbia. "When I was young," said Mabel, as she chit-chatted across her white picket fence, "none of us girls walked in front of a saloon. We were constantly going back and forth across the streets. You see, there were a bunch of saloons in Columbia."

Genuine 1880 stagecoaches roll through town just as they did before the turn of the century, taking visitors on an old stage trail through rocks and rills on the outskirts of Columbia.

Another Columbia old timer is Merl "Fuzzy" Hughes, 74 at the time I spoke with him. Fuzzy been fighting fires with the Columbia Volunteer Fire Department for 60 years. When the fire alarm sounded he was the first volunteer to swing into action. The town's fire phone was in Fuzzy's home, and the unmanned fire station was across the street. He would run across the street and turn on the siren that roused the rest of the volunteers. After sounding the alarm and picking up his crew Fuzzy climbed behind the wheel of Columbia's 1931 Dodge fire engine and was on his way to the blaze. Fuzzy had fought nearly every fire in Columbia since 1920, the year flames wiped out three blocks of downtown Columbia and Fuzzy, at 14, helped save what was left.

"Fuzzy's toothless grin, his old fire truck, and his devotion to duty represent the spirit and old time flavor of our little town," Mabel Draper confided to us. "That guy just loves that Fire Department."

For the first 11 years that Fuzzy fought fires, the Fire Department's equipment consisted of two ancient hand pumpers, the Papeete, a small truck decorated with a painting of a bare breasted woman eating grapes, and the Monumental, a much larger rig. The Papeete, built in Boston in 1852, was shipped around Cape Horn to San Francisco for delivery to Tahiti, but somehow it wound up here instead. Both old hand pumpers are on display in town. "In 1931 my dad kicked in his own money and went around town collecting gold dust from the miners to buy Columbia's first motorized fire truck, this old baby here," Fuzzy said with an affectionate pat on the hood of the old rig.

Columbia had two modern, up-to-date fire trucks but Fuzzy wouldn't have anything to do with them. "Too modern. Different style pumps than what I'm used to," he said, thumbing a wad of Sir Walter Raleigh tobacco into his pipe. Fire fighting in the old days was more to Fuzzy's liking. "Hell, today you have to stop and read the manual before answering the fire bell," he said. "We're not supposed to go to a fire unless we have our turn-out clothes on. In the old days you got there as quick as you could and cared less what clothes you was wearin'. If somebody has a couple of snorts nowadays they're not allowed to answer the fire call. Hell, in the old days you would turn out drunk or sober. You would darn right sober up fast fighting the fire."

Fuzzy was chief for 12 years before he stepped down in 1978 to make room for a younger man. His whole life was centered around the Columbia Volunteer Fire Department. "Being able to save lives and property has made it all worthwhile," he said, adding, "Hell, I know what fire can do. I got third-degree burns on my leg from boiling water spilled from a water heater in 1932. The pain was so bad I told my dad to tell the Doc to cut the leg off. My dad said to wait as long as I could before having my leg chopped off. I did. The fever broke, the infection went down and I still have both my legs." But he didn't have any teeth. He lost them all in 1954, but not in the line of duty. "They was rotten. I had 'em yanked out. The false teeth didn't work. So the hell with it. I've been gum beatin' ever since. I can eat anything except nuts. I get hungry for them, too. But what the hell—you can't have everything."

TIOGA PASS ROAD—SCENIC SPLENDOR FOR 100 YEARS

TIOGA PASS ROAD in Yosemite National Park in Tuolumne County, California's highest highway, traversing one of the most spectacular stretches of mountain terrain in America, was 100 years old in 1983. A century earlier, from April through September 1883, a silver mining company employed 160 Chinese laborers to construct the 56-mile Great Sierra Wagon Trail through the heart of Yosemite's high country.

The one-lane, twisting dirt road followed a footpath that had been an Indian trade route as early as 2000 BC. The road remained like that until 1937 when 11.6 miles were paved and widened to two lanes. And the last visages of the old dirt Great Sierra Wagon Road continued to be used until 1961, when the final 21-mile middle section was paved. Today the Indian footpath that became the Great Sierra Wagon Road is a paved two-lane highway slicing through breathtaking landscape of alpine meadows, sparkling lakes, waterfalls and tall timber, a wildlife sanctuary embraced by huge granite domes in a chain of 9,000 to 13,053-foot peaks ringed with glistening year-round snowfields.

"They come from every state, from all over the world, hiking along the road, pedaling their bikes, in cars and campers to drive this remarkable highway," said Ranger Ferdinand Castillo, 67, spending his 30th summer in 1983 as keeper of the eastern gate of Yosemite National Park at the 9,941-foot summit of the Tioga Pass Road. A car with two gray-haired couples pulls up to the kiosk manned by Castillo. "Anybody in the car American and 62 or over, or disabled?" asked the gatekeeper. "You don't have to pay if any one of you qualifies, otherwise there's a $3 fee per car," he explains to the motorists. The charge is 50 cents for hikers, bikers or passengers on buses.

An elderly man leading 25 hikers walked by. "Carl, how are you?" said Castillo, leaving his kiosk to greet his long-time friend. "Fine.

Just fine," replied Carl Sharsmith, 80, a renowned botanist and Yosemite's most experienced ranger-naturalist. He had spent 53 summers at Tuolumne Meadows and in the high country introducing visitors to California's alpine heights. Sharsmith also gave campfire talks and led parties into the towering wilderness all summer. The rest of the year he taught at San Jose State University. Five of the alpine flowers found on the peaks flanking the Tioga Pass Road were first discovered and identified by Sharsmith. One, a blue species similar to the forget-me-not, carries his name, *Hackelia sharsmithii*. On this outing he was leading a day-long hike to the upper shoulders of 13,053-foot-high Mt. Dana to see the flora and fauna as well as the finest example of tundra in the High Sierra, an isolated remnant of a landscape that existed here 60 million years ago.

Tioga is an Indian word, but not from a local tribe. It is Iroquois and means "where it forks." Stephen T. Mather, director of the National Park Service, personally put up $7,500 in 1915 to buy the road from its private owners. The Sierra Club came up with another $6,000 and two friends of Mather each contributed $1,000. The road was then presented as a gift to the federal government. In 1915 the first year cars were permitted on the Great Sierra Wagon Road; 190 made the adventurous journey.

Any one who has ever driven Tioga Pass Road will never forget the 14 miles between the 6,400-foot-high Lee Vining on the east and the 9,941-foot summit. The Pass is normally open Memorial Day through the first heavy snowfall, usually in early November. But some years when the snowfall along the road gets to be as deep as 18 feet it is not open until as late as June 30.

FIFTY-SIX

VENTURA COUNTY

CEMETERY PARK

I T'S ONE OF THE MOST POPULAR PARKS IN VENTURA for walking, jogging, throwing Frisbees, relaxing, enjoying a spectacular panorama of the Pacific Ocean and the Channel Islands—seven acres in the heart of Ventura, an oasis of manicured lush green lawns, stately pine and pepper trees. But this is not your typical green space in an urban setting. Beneath the park's surface are the remains of 3,322 Ventura County residents who died between 1842 and 1944. Cemetery Park is a cemetery that became a city park.

All the tombstones were removed in 1968 and 1969 when the transformation occurred. But the bodies were left undisturbed. No signs proclaim: "Cemetery Park." It's just there. Out-of-towners and most residents who moved here during the last 25 years are unaware the park was a cemetery for more than a century.

Trevor Rumsey and Melanie Allred, both 16 and Ventura High School juniors were at the park on a lunch break. They sat on the grass near two small, flat bronze markers at two burial sites. They know the park is also a cemetery. "I think it's great. You really can't tell it's a cemetery. There are a few of these markers scattered around. But most people I've talked to in the park are unaware people are buried here," said Rumsey.

Bob Romero of the Ventura Parks and Recreation Department is one of the groundskeepers at Cemetery Park. "This is a very unusual situation," said Romero, with the department 34 years. "The cemetery had been an eyesore for a long time. It was full of weeds. Headstones were toppled. There hadn't been any burials here since World War II. Finally the city removed the headstones, cleaned up the place and made a park out of the cemetery. My wife's sister, Eleanor Garcia, who died when she was 15, is buried here."

When the park was created, headstones were presented to relatives who requested them. Those not claimed were destroyed. At first the city planned to erect a bronze plaque listing in alphabetical order the names of everyone buried in the cemetery. But that was not done. In 1985 the city decided to place a small, flat bronze marker without charge at the request of relatives over burial sites. Only 33 of the markers have been requested and installed so far. "Every now and then someone from out of town comes into City Hall asking what happened to the old cemetery. They're usually looking for the grave of a long-deceased relative," said City Clerk Barbara Kam.

A dozen men dressed in Civil War uniforms came to the park and fired 21-gun salutes at the dedication of two of the markers, one to the memory of Medal of Honor winner James Sumner, the other to Brig. Gen. William Vandever. Sumner was awarded the Medal of Honor for heroism as an Army private, when he was wounded fighting Indians in Arizona in 1869. He died in the Ventura County Poorhouse in 1912. Vandever was a Union general in the Civil War and a congressman from Ventura from 1887 to 1891. He died in 1893.

PARK HOST IN HIS OWN "LITLE BIT OF HEAVEN"

THEY CALLED HIM "RANGER RAY" and the 84-year-old man with flowing mustache and long scraggly snow-white beard had been a fixture at Point Mugu State Park for 12 years. But Ray

Miller wasn't really a ranger. He was a volunteer, the "Grand Old Man" of the California park campground host program. Campground caretakers are permitted to live year-round without charge in state parks in return for assisting the real rangers by acting as liaison with campers.

There are volunteer camp hosts, as they are called in 69 California state parks. "Camp hosts are our eyes and ears. They're special people. As staffing levels have gone down due to budgetary constraints, camp hosts have kept our parks running at the level people expect of state parks," said Bonnie Morse ranger in charge of the campground host program at Point Mugu and Leo Carrillo Beach State Parks, in Ventura County. "They are dedicated people who agree to spend at least 20 hours a week working in a park without pay and almost always put in a great deal more time than that. They are in the campgrounds at night when we're not," Morse added.

Camp hosts perform a wide variety of tasks. They are a source of information about a state park and surrounding area. They help keep the park clean and help with maintenance. They have radios in the trailers where they live and can alert rangers in other parts of the park when problems occur. The state park campground hosts program was launched in 1980. Before that a few volunteer campground caretakers were granted special permission to live year-round in state parks. Since then, the state and camp hosts have signed one-year contracts that can be broken at any time by each party. In half the parks, the program is in effect only during summer and the contract is for that period.

Miller was camp host at La Jolla Canyon, site of a trail head for a network of 72 miles of pathways in the Santa Monica Mountains towering above the Pacific Ocean in Ventura County. Thousands of hikers have come to know "Ranger Ray" and his constant companion, Dyno, his white shaggy mutt. Miller greeted them, provided them with a trail map and watched over their vehicles while they hiked. "I'd been long gone if I hadn't lived here at the trail head in the open so many years," said Miller, who lived as a cowboy, prospector, railroader and truck driver all over the West before arriving at Point Mugu State Park.

"I got a little bit of heaven here," he said with twinkles in his eyes and a big grin that emphasized his missing teeth. "Where could you find a more beautiful spot?" he asked, waving his arms outward at the verdant mountain embracing his camp. His neighbors were deer, coyote, mountain lion, bob cat, fox, raccoon, opossum, and an abundance of rattlesnakes, which he respects but doesn't fear. Miller was a bachelor.

On November 15, 1986, the State Department of Recreation and Parks officially dedicated and named the campsite, cared for so diligently by "Ranger Ray", as the Ray Miller Trail Head.

FIFTY-SEVEN

YOLO COUNTY

WOODLAND OPERA HOUSE

F OR 76 YEARS, only the ghosts of vaudevillians and Shakespeare-an actors trod the boards of the town's old opera house, then the curtain rose again in 1989 to reveal flesh-and-blood performers. The people of Woodland through fund raising efforts and the help of the state, spent more than $2 million restoring the Woodland Opera House to the glory days that flourished from 1896 to 1913.

It was during that 17 year period at the turn of the century that over 300 touring acting companies, traveling evangelists, visiting politicians and high school graduation drew farmers and their families from miles around to this classic American theater. John Philip Sousa and his renowned band played two concerts here. Those were the days when hundreds of small towns and big cities across America had opera houses.

But when the curtain went down for the final time in 1913 the Woodland Opera House stood vacant, cold and silent, waiting. It became home to bats and rats. Inside traces of the past were everywhere gathering dust and spider webs, even graffiti from a more innocent era. One such scribbled notation reads: "Regards to Young Brothers. Will see you in Frisco on Oct. 31, 1911—Constantino Maggioni." A playbill pasted to a wall reads: "Frank Kirk, Musical Acrobat with Richard & Pringles Minstrels," and a photo shows Kirk sitting on a stack of chairs when he appeared at the theater in September, 1898. Another notice referring to Kirk declares: "The novelty of novelties. You have never seen an act like this." A cryptic scrawl says, "Carl Missionni is a SOB and a bad Elk."

From June 1896 to May 1913, the Opera House on 2nd Street at Dead Cat Alley was an important center for theatrical arts. It served a vast rural audience, which usually arrived by horse and buggy to be entertained by hundreds of touring companies. A wealthy farmer, David Newcomer Hershey, built the place, which closed in 1913, a victim of competition from a new medium, silent films.

Hershey's five daughters and a son, none of whom married, boarded up the building, and there it stood in the center of the Yolo County seat, 25 miles northwest of Sacramento, a ghost of the past, a time capsule waiting to be opened. It sat there and sat there and sat there, never used for 76 long years. Through World War I, the Great Depressions, World War II, until 1971, it stood vacant. From time to time, Hershey's heirs talked about reopening the opera house, but they never did. The last of David Hershey's direct heirs, his daughter, Florence, died in 1970. A year later, the Yolo County Historical Society purchased the opera house from the conservators of the estate for $12,000.

From 1971 to 1981 city, state, federal funds and private contributions were spent putting a new roof on the building, restoring the stages, installing air conditioning and electrical wiring. In 1980, the historical society, unable to raise any more funds to complete the project, presented the opera house to the state. Four years later the state turned it over to Woodland, which formed a nonprofit corporation to run it.

The old opera house was finally restored to its grandeur of old. The original balcony benches are still there. The interior walls were back to their original colors. The same type wallpaper was reproduced as were the seats. Electrical light fixtures resemble the old gas lamps. All the old messages and graffiti scribbled on the walls are preserved with plexi glass covers.

"To go along with the ambiance of the old opera house we're presenting a little bit of everything as happened here in bygone days, a Shakespearean play, comedy, musicals and melodramas," explained Nadine Salonites, singer, actress, voice teacher and president of the Woodland Opera Guild. After 76 years, dedicated people of Woodland, like Nadine, who refused to give up, swept out the ghosts and once again in 1989 pulled up the curtain to usher in a glorious new era at the town's beloved old opera house.

PLEASE DON'T SQUEEZE THE BEES

A BEE LANDED ON PROFESSOR NORMAN E. GARY'S NOSE. Soon, a swarm was crawling on his face and head. Not to worry, Gary trains bees to act on cue. An internationally known bee researcher, Gary doubles as a special-effects man and an actor in films and TV. When Hollywood needs bees the call goes out to the professor. Gary has been on television and movie sets with 200,000 bees buzzing around. He did the special effects for the film "Savage Bees," a story about the invasion of New Orleans by killer bees. When Leonard Nimoy did "In Search of Killer Bees," Gary and his bees were featured.

One of five Ph.D.s on the staff of the Bee Biology Facility at the University of California, Davis, Gary is a member of the Screen Actors Guild. "I do special effects, but I'm often drafted as an actor because the regular actors aren't keen about having bees alight on their hands and face," Gary explained.

How does he get one bee or thousands of the buzzers to land on him on command? He dabs his face and body with essence of queen bees. The perfume attracts bees. He knows how to avoid getting stung: "First I treat the bees with smoke to disorient them. Bees aren't mean. Stinging is a defensive mechanism. I know how to avoid getting stung. For one thing, I don't exhale on them. That really sets them off," he related. "Sure I've been stung thousands of times in my

272

years working with bees. But I know how to flick the stinger and venom off my skin right away so as not to get hurt."

He calls himself a bee behaviorist and a bee psychologist. "Bees have super-sensory systems. They see in colors as well as black and white. They have a fantastic sense of smell and sense of taste," the professor said. In studying foraging behavior he anesthetizes individual bees and affixes tiny metal numbered disks to the bee's body to learn what crops the insects prefer and what distances they fly.

He was a member of the national research council team of scientists sent to Brazil to study the killer bee. He also conducted research on honeybees for the Department of Energy's proposed solar power satellite system that someday may provide most of the nation's electrical energy.

The Bee Biology Facility at UC Davis, largest facility of its kind in the country, was started in 1908 because of the importance of bees to agriculture. "We have more than 16,000 scientific papers published on bees on file in our lab," Gary said. "Yet, man knows less than 1% of what there is to know about bees. And, bees are very important to man. One-third of all the food we eat is the result of honeybee pollination."

FIFTY-EIGHT

YUBA COUNTY

BOK EYE, GOD OF THE DARK NORTH

EIGHTY-ONE-YEAR-OLD JOE LUNG KIM banged the century-old gong, beat on the ancient drum and intoned age-old Chinese prayers. The venerable prayer director of the only temple in the Western Hemisphere dedicated to Bok Eye, God of the Dark North, located in Marysville, was praying for President Reagan.

Joe Lung Kim knelt and bowed to the statues of nine Chinese deities on the altar of the 1880 temple. He lit candles, burned incense. Then he vigorously shook a round box with an open top containing 50 oracles or prayer sticks. Up popped one of the numbered sticks. "No. 35," said Kim. "Thirty-five good number. President Reagan lucky." Kim reached over to the oracle board, plucked a prayer card marked 35 and read: "Oracle says one chicken crows early in the morning waking up rest of chickens for miles around.

Chickens wake up the people. The first chicken has something to crow about." Kim interpreted the message to mean "Mr. Reagan is like the first chicken. He stands up and does his job. It looks like the President is going to have something to crow about."

Kim had been prayer director at the Chinese temple since the 1950s. He had been shaking the box of oracle sticks at least once a year for each President since Eisenhower. Lung Kim beat the gong, banged the drum and prayed for Ronald Reagan the day I was in the temple in 1982. In 1970 when I was there he did the same for Richard Nixon.

When Kim prayed he shook the box with the 50 numbered oracle sticks. He shook the box vigorously, praying with gusto at the same time. It looks like he is jiggling pickup sticks. When he prayed for Nixon, one of the sticks flew out of the oracle box. "Aha!" exclaimed Kim. "No. 17." "No. 17!" shouted wizened old temple caretaker Ong Hong Lung from the back of the temple. Lung tore a pink slip of paper with Chinese characters from the oracle board. The slip of paper contained an ancient Chinese fable about a cow with two tails. "Interpreted to events of day, answer from Bok Eye is—it is not entirely safe yet for President and country. But not entirely hopeless. If President meet some people with wisdom, like 1,000-year-old tree, country will blossom again."

Kim called on Bok Eye to answer some pretty tough questions in the past. In the big floods of December, 1955, for example, Kim beat the gong, banged the drum and shook the oracle box vigorously. "That day Joe Lung Kim got answer No. 2," recalled Ong Hong Lung. "Bok Eye say everything be OK in Marysville and it was."

"Marysville in all recorded history have floods," said Kim, whose grandparents were born in Marysville in the 1850s. "Chinese naturally build temple to Bok Eye. You see in China whenever there is danger of flooding you find temple to Bok Eye, God of Dark North, Chinese Water God." In Marysville the temple dedicated to Bok Eye— Bok Kai Mui (North Stream Temple)—is located on the north banks of the Yuba River. "First temple to Bok Eye dedicated 1854 in Marysville. Unfortunately temple washed away by floods," Kim sighed, not going into details as to how such a calamity could happen to the home of such a god.

But in the great Northern California floods of 1955 it was a different story. As waters of the Feather, Yuba and Bear rivers reached flood stage near Marysville, Kim and other Chinese went to the temple. "I led prayer," said Kim. "I never ask Bok Eye for protection that night. I just talk to Bok Eye. Well, how about it? Think we going to have flood or not?" Kim asked the god. Then he shook the oracle sticks in the box. Out popped the stick marked No. 2. "It was story about tiger coming to village. Villagers saw tiger. They begin to worry, get skeptical. It was same as big scare Marysville having with high water. Then story ends with villagers catching tiger in cage." Kim interpreted that to mean the Marysville dikes would hold. And hold they did. In the Christmas floods of that year, Yuba City, across the river from Marysville, was almost wiped off the map when the dikes broke. There were 37 lives lost in the flood, but none in Marysville.

Joe Lung Kim prayed for visitors who came to the temple same way he prayed for Presidents, banging the gong, beating on the ancient drum and reading the oracle stick. Chinese from throughout the United States and many parts of the world make pilgrimages to the temple to pay their respects to Bok Eye. "My job is to pray to Bok Eye and to the other gods represented on the altar and get their messages through the oracles," explained Joe Lung Kim. "Temple is like post office. You come here to get your messages."

Beside Bok Eye, the other deities in the old temple are the goddesses of Mercy, Seafarers, and Childbirth, the Great Holy Father, and the gods of War, Medicine, Time and Money. God of Money? "Oh yes," said Kim. "We have money god. It is OK to pray to him provided you not too selfish or greedy."

On the temple altar were oranges, tangerines, wine, and barbecued pork. "We Chinese pay respect to our dead in temple and in cemetery. Part of our belief is to bring food and drink for our departed relatives and friends," said the old prayer director. "One man once asked me, did I really think my relatives will come up and eat that stuff. I asked him did he think his relatives would come up and smell the flowers?"

The temple has several rooms filled with antiques brought to the

United States by Chinese pioneers before the turn of the century—teak parade sedan chairs, parade dragons, gongs, drums, statues, paintings, scrolls, all draped with cobwebs. One huge scroll lists 700 donors and the amount of money they contributed to build the temple in 1880, donations ranging from $2 to $150.

In 1981 the government of Taiwan sent two $17,000 marble lion statues to be placed outside the temple. Kim said the Taiwan officials sent the statues "hoping that the gods in the temple will root for them." For some unexplained reason Kim didn't fancy the marble lions. He used a parable to describe the gifts: "Did you ever see a man wear tuxedo without wearing any underwear?" This inscrutable parable Kim did not explain.

Joe Lung Kim has died since my last visit to the temple of Bok Eye. The God of the Dark North must surely miss Joe Lung Kim banging the old gong, beating on the ancient drum and shaking the hell out of the oracle box. I would like to think Bok Eye and Joe Lung Kim are both in the great beyond, chatting and having a marvelous time together.

Also related to Bok Eye in Marysville is the Bok Kai Parade (named after the temple), which has taken place every Spring since 1880, and is said to be the oldest parade in California. When it was first held, 5,000 Chinese lived in Marysville, one of the largest Chinese populations in the state. In those early years, everyone in the parade was of Chinese ancestry. Today, with less than 100 Chinese living here, only a few participate. But every year there's a convertible carrying the parade's princess, a Chinese girl from Marysville, often accompanied by princesses from San Francisco's Chinatown Festival.

The Bok Kai Parade and Festival are steeped in Chinese traditions. A bomb signals the start of the parade, then thousands of firecrackers are set off to scare away evil spirits. Boy Scouts bang the Bok Kai Temple gong as it rolls down Main Street on a cart. The parade's dragon, Lung Huang, was imported from China especially for the Parade in 1991, and is 152 feet long and requires 35 dancers to animate. The dancers inside the dragon are, however, not Chinese. There are many bands and floats with Chinese themes, but, also, few of the participants are Chinese. "For those of us Chinese living in Marysville, we are honored and pleased that it is the non-Chinese in our community who have kept the Bok Kai Parade and Festival going all these years and we are truly indebted to them," said Katie Lim, at 74 in 1997, the oldest Chinese person born and raised in Marysville. A wonderful Chinese tradition continues in this small Northern California town.

THE PEOPLE OF TIMBUCTOO AVOID EACH OTHER

LAVINA RAY hated to fill out forms that asked for her birthplace. "They never believe me," explained Mrs. Ray, who was born in Timbuctoo—California, that is, not Timbuktu, Africa.

When I visited Timbuctoo in 1970 only three people were left in the old mining camp on the banks of the Yuba River, 20 miles east of Marysville in Yuba County. There was Lavina Ray, a 73-year-old widow, who had spent her entire life in Timbuctoo, and two miners, Bill Gruber, 70, and Dave Chambers, 72.

"There's nothing here," conceded Mrs. Ray. "Never has been as far back as I can remember. Mind you, I'm not complaining," added Mrs. Ray who lived in the same house in which she was born in 1897. "We don't have any riots. We all get along pretty good. Mind our own business. Do what we want."

Three people in a town that burst on the scene as a roaring Mother Lode gold mining camp in 1850. Timbuctoo got its name from the first miner in the area—a Black man who said he came to California from Timbuktu, the fabled ancient city in Africa. "Historians have been trying for years to run down some definite information on that miner who came from Africa," noted Thelma Neaville, Marysville librarian. "As far as I know, no one has ever come up with his name, whether he struck it rich in Timbuctoo and whatever happened to him." Mrs. Ray said she heard the story about the Black miner all her life."I don't think he died here," said Mrs. Ray. "His headstone isn't in the old Timbuctoo Cemetery."

During its heyday, Timbuctoo had hotels, eight saloons, churches and theaters. Miners' shacks and homes dotted the Timbuctoo hills. At one time 2,000 Chinese miners were here. But miners deserted Timbuctoo for other diggings by the early 1860s. A fire in June 1878 destroyed all but a few buildings. Remaining were the crumbling brick ruins of the old Wells Fargo Building, Mrs. Ray's comfortable century-old home and two miners shacks lived in by Gruber and Chambers. Chambers was paying $15 a month rent for his place, Gruber, $25. Timbuctoo was two miles from Smartville by dirt road. The people of Timbuctoo called for their mail at Smartville.

Although living a few feet apart the Timbuctoo trio saw one another as infrequently as possible. "We can't afford to get too chummy," said Gruber. "You know the deal with three old loners like us. It doesn't pay to be too close." When Mrs. Ray was asked about the two men, she referred to Gruber as "Old Whiskers next door." She wasn't aware her neighbor shaved off his beard several months ago.

Chambers said he never saw much of the other two because "I'm seldom home." Gruber spent his time "sniping" for gold in the old Timbuctoo crevices. Mrs. Ray took in ironing from families in nearby Nevada City and Grass Valley. "She doesn't have to. She does it to pass the time," said Gruber, who said he last spoke to Mrs. Ray a year ago.

Mrs. Ray turned down an invitation to come out of her home to be in a photograph showing the entire population of Timbuctoo, all three of them. As far as their relationships went, the three Timbuctooers might just as well have lived as far away from one another as to that other Timbuktu—in Africa.

PHOTO CAPTIONS

All photos by the author unless otherwise indicated

1. ALAMEDA COUNTY: Heinold's First & Last Chance Saloon on the Oakland waterfront. (Photo by Skip Sahlin.)
2. ALPINE COUNTY: High school students from Alpine enroute to school in Nevada.
3. AMADOR COUNTY: The grinding rock at Chawíse Indian Grinding Rock State Park. (Photo by Ranger Curt Kraft.)
4. BUTTE COUNTY: Sketch of the historic Inskip Inn, by Dana Farrington.
5. CALAVERAS COUNTY: John Cilenti at Courthouse Museum diplaying wooden gold pan in front of large photo of early miners.
6. COLUSA COUNTY: Ostriches on the Flying S Ranch at Stonyford.
7. CONTRA COSTA COUNTY: Ken Dothee, president of U.S. Bocce Federation, rolling ball on one of many bocce courts in Martinez.
8. DEL NORTE COUNTY: Easter lilies in bloom in Smith River, Easter lily capital of the world.
9. EL DORADO COUNTY: Vikingsholm, the viking castle at water's edge of Lake Tahoe. (Photo courtesy of Helen Henry Smith.)
10. FRESNO COUNTY: Karla and Tom Hurley operate the Sierra Queen to ferry hikers across 7,327-foot Florence Lake.
11. GLENN COUNTY: Snow geese flock from distances as far away as Russia to the National Wildlife Refuge.
12. HUMBOLDT COUNTY: Sculptor Dick Crane with his 25-foot copper statue of a fisherman, later placed on the shores of Humboldt Bay in Eureka.
13. IMPERIAL COUNTY: Ranger Bill Cardinal on patrol at Picacho State Park on the Colorado River.
14. INYO COUNTY: California Highway Patrolman Dave Flegel wipes away the sweat on another blistering day on the job in Death Valley.
15. KERN COUNTY: While planting flowers outside Ridgecrest City Hall, The Desert Planters Garden Club get an unexpected drenching from the sprinklers.

16. KINGS COUNTY: Richard Wing (left), who saved China Alley in Hanford, with mayor Stan Ham, in front of Wing's Imperial Dynasty Restaurant. (Photo by Art Rogers.)

17. LAKE COUNTY: 1920s postcard photo of Clear Lake off the shore of the town of Nice.

18. LASSEN COUNTY: Atsugewi Indian and park ranger Lillian Snooks displays 100-year-old Atsugewi baskets at Lassen National Park.

19. LOS ANGELES COUNTY: (Left to right) Angeles Forest Supervisor Bill Dresser, Charles Hillinger, and Alfred Boysen, surveyor for Los Angeles, at the highest point in the city. (Photo by John Malmin.)

20. MADERA COUNTY: Charles Hillinger at Devils Postpile National Monument.

21. MARIN COUNTY: Biologist Gordon Chan gazing down on Duxbury Reef. Through his efforts the reef was set aside as a Reserve.

22. MARIPOSA COUNTY: Mariposa County Courthouse, erected in 1854, oldest still in use west of the Mississippi.

23. MENDOCINO COUNTY: Picturesque view of the Mendocino County coastline.

24. MERCED COUNTY: Sweet potato expert Bob Scheuerman, on a farm in Livingston, the sweet potato capital of California.

25. MODOC COUNTY: Charles Hillinger at Capt. Jack's Stronghold, where 52 Modoc warriors held off 1000 soldiers for six months in 1872-1873. (Photo by John Malmin.)

26. MONO COUNTY: Bodie ghost town.

27. MONTEREY COUNTY: State park rangers placing *luminarias* at Robert Louis Stevenson House, as part of "Christmas in the adobes."

28. NAPA COUNTY; Charles Hillinger at ease in a mud bath in Calistoga. (Photo by Fitzgerald Whitney.)

29. NEVADA COUNTY: Jim West, the "Covered Wagon Man" of Rough and Ready, a Mother-Lode town that once declared itself an independent nation.

30. ORANGE COUNTY: Walter and Cordelia Knott at their original Berry Stand. (Photo courtesy of Knott's Berry Farm.)

31. PLACER COUNTY: Auburn's old fire house, built in 1891. (Photo courtesy Placer County Museum.)

32. PLUMAS COUNTY: The Taylorsville quilters.

33. RIVERSIDE COUNTY: One of the restored streetcars at Perris, the valhalla of trolleys.

34. SACRAMENTO COUNTY: California State Capitol in Sacramento.

35. SAN BENITO COUNTY: Pinnacles National Monument. (Photo courtesy National Park Service.)

36. SAN BERNARDINO COUNTY: Charles Hillinger (on right), with photographer John Malmin and railcar operator Charley "Roadrunner" Mendez, patrolling the track in the Mojave Desert.

37. SAN DIEGO COUNTY: 1863 windjammer "Star of India" under sail off San Diego. (Photo by Karl Rosenquist, San Diego Maritime Museum.)

38. SAN FRANCISCO COUNTY: Wayne "Mr. Lighthouse" Wheeler, founder of the U.S. Lighthouse Society, at the Yerba Buena Lighthouse in San Francisco.

39. SAN JOAQUIN COUNTY: Floating cops lend security to life on the Delta. Here a Sheriff's boat is dwarfed by a freighter.

40. SAN LUIS OBISPO COUNTY: Pismo Beach at low tide, with the dunes in the background.

41. SAN MATEO COUNTY: Handsome sea elephant lounging on the beach.

42. SANTA BARBARA COUNTY: Beth Fulsom, the lone ranger of Santa Barbara Island.

43. SANTA CLARA COUNTY: Replica of an ancient tomb at the Rosicrucian Egyptian Museum.

44. SANTA CRUZ COUNTY: Santa Cruz Beach Boardwalk, oldest amusement park in the state.

45. SHASTA COUNTY: Park ranger enforces no-alcohol policy in Whiskeytown National Recreation Area.

46. SIERRA COUNTY: Historic gallows in Downieville, seat of Sierra County.

47. SISKIYOU COUNTY: 14,162-foot Mt. Shasta, believed by many to be a sacred mountain.

48. SOLANO COUNTY: California's Capitol from Feb. 1853 to Feb.

1854 in Benicia. (Photo courtesy of Benicia Camel Barn Museum.)

49. SONOMA COUNTY: Lyn Kalani holds two books on the Russian presence in America at Fort Ross.

50. STANISLAUS COUNTY: Old German Baptist Brethren leader Durand Overholzer and family.

51. SUTTER COUNTY: Punjabis doing a traditional folk dance. (Photo by Janmeja Singh Johl.)

52. TEHAMA COUNTY: Ishi, the last of his tribe. (Photo courtesy U.C. Berkeley Archives.)

53. TRINITY COUNTY: Carol Norris raises her own meat and vegetables in Post Mountain, a small Trinity town without electricity.

54. TULARE COUNTY: Charles Hillinger (left) snowshoeing through Sequoia. (Photo by Cal Montney.)

55. TUOLUMNE COUNTY: The Columbia school was saved by children who contributed dimes and nickels to restore the old building. Teacher Ralph Hilbert assists Nicolette Perry and Hayley Kenny.

56. VENTURA COUNTY: The Lopez family enjoy a picnic in Cemetery Park in Ventura.

57. YOLO COUNTY: The Woodland Opera House.

58. YUBA COUNTY: 1997 Bok Kai parade in Marysville. (Photo by Linda Plummer.)